PENGUIN BOOKS

UNCOMMON GENIUS

A former trial attorney, Denise Shekerjian is also the author of *Competent Counsel*. She lives with her husband and son in New Providence, New Jersey.

UNCOMMON
GENIUS

HOW GREAT IDEAS ARE BORN

DENISE SHEKERJIAN

PENGUIN BOOKS

PENGUIN BOOKS
Published by the Penguin Group
Penguin Books USA Inc.,
375 Hudson Street, New York, New York 10014, U.S.A.
Penguin Books Ltd, 27 Wrights Lane,
London W8 5TZ, England
Penguin Books Australia Ltd, Ringwood,
Victoria, Australia
Penguin Books Canada Ltd, 10 Alcorn Avenue,
Toronto, Ontario, Canada M4V 3B2
Penguin Books (N.Z.) Ltd, 182–190 Wairau Road,
Auckland 10, New Zealand

Penguin Books Ltd, Registered Offices:
Harmondsworth, Middlesex, England

First published in the United States of America by Viking Penguin,
a division of Penguin Books USA Inc., 1990
Published in Penguin Books 1991

10

Grateful acknowledgment is made for permission to reprint excerpts
from *The Moral Life of Children*, by Robert Coles. Copyright © 1986
by Robert Coles. By permission of The Atlantic Monthly Press.

LIBRARY OF CONGRESS CATALOGING IN PUBLICATION DATA
Shekerjian, Denise G.
Uncommon genius: how great ideas are born/Denise Shekerjian.
p. cm.
Includes bibliographical references.
ISBN 0 14 01.0986 2 (pbk.)
1. Creative thinking. 2. Creative thinking—Case studies.
3. MacArthur Fellows Program. I. Title.
[BF408.S448 1991]
153.3'5—dc20 90-43620

Printed in the United States of America

For my Mother and Father

In every field, things get so specialized. The generalist—and artists are often, by necessity, generalists—winds up feeling a sense of futility. At the moment I'm trying, for example, to write about Kobo Abe, the Japanese novelist. I'm reading him, as I have to, in English. There are Japanese souls who have spent the last few *decades* pondering him. Am I going to come up with anything new or special? Well, my hope is yes. I cling to the optimistic belief that the haphazard and the hopscotch, the creature that sips among many flowers, may actually come up with something. It's finally an irrational belief, in most cases, an unrealistic goal. But one holds to the sense that just sipping broadly enough, from enough flowers, strange and fruitful pollinations will arise.

> Brad Leithauser, MacArthur Fellow
> *In conversation,*
> *March 4, 1988, Amherst College*

CONTENTS

IN THE BEGINNING

▪ 1 ▪

THIS PROJECT WAS BORN from a line in the newspaper. "Think of it," was the tease. "You're at home minding your own business when the phone rings. 'You don't know me,' a voice says, 'but I'm calling to congratulate you. In recognition and encouragement of your creative capabilities, you have just been awarded a prize in the six-figure range to be paid out over the next five years with absolutely no strings attached.' "

I read on. The facts were staggering. Anywhere from thirty to seventy thousand dollars a year for five years, with a few lucky people supported for the remainder of their lives. No applications allowed. No follow-up or accountability of any kind. Top-drawer prestige. A steady stream of checks in the mailbox. Cash them, or bank them, or rip them up in a sorry moment of madness—the decision entirely yours, no explanations sought nor owed.

In the beginning it was the fairy-tale freedom that attracted me to the MacArthur Award. Win a MacArthur and enjoy the ease of financial strain, the gift of time, and the star-making machinery that goes along with it all. Win a MacArthur and those long and frustrating years, the suffering of fools, are behind you now. Win a MacArthur and your phone rings with well-wishers and opportunity.

Freedom, money, time, choice, validation—initially, these were the things I found seductive. But beneath it all lay something far more interesting, far more enduring, and important, and explosive: the idea of creativity itself, the spark of the creative impulse. Through man's finest creative moments giving rise to inventions like the wheel, the thread screw, the sewing machine, the Brandenburg Concertos, our culture progresses. Through creative achievement we find a new measure of human dignity. What exactly is creativity? How does it work? Is it possible to fan the embers of our own uncommon genius? I wanted to find out.

But that gets ahead of the story.

◾ **2** ◾

TO TELL IT RIGHT, the story starts with a man named John D. MacArthur, to some a hero with a brilliant flair for making money, to others a contentious, coarse-grained miser, graceless in all aspects.

Those who thought him evil had something in common with his Bible-thumping father, who saw the smoke of hellfire everywhere, especially in John, the youngest of his seven children. A hot-blooded evangelist, he committed his family to a wandering, penniless life. Lectures on how their bodies would blacken in satanic flames were driven home with the aid of a vinegar-soaked leather strap. Food and what little money he earned were given away; the disciples, he said, would provide.

In fact it was John's mother who did the providing, scrimping and stretching the few resources she managed to keep from her husband. She died when John was fourteen. Even before then, though, what little spare time and affection she had for mothering her brood were spent on one of his older brothers, who she believed shared her love of the cultured, literate, artistic life.

According to the stories, certainly the chances that John D. MacArthur would amount to anything were slim: an eighth-grade dropout, a failed reporter, a pilot in training who recklessly crashed three planes in the first two months with the Royal Canadian Air Force, AWOL from the armed services, a ne'er-do-well who caused three businesses to fail, a scrappy fellow relentlessly pursued by a half-dozen governmental agencies, a man who claimed litigation as his favorite sport and who boasted about having as many as thirty-five hundred lawsuits going on at the same time, a father embroiled in a long-running, emotionally charged, and deeply personal feud with his only son, Roderick. . . . The stories about him had the markings of legend.

At the age of thirty-eight and destitute, his biographer reports, he borrowed twenty-five hundred dollars and bought the then ailing Bankers Life & Casualty Company of Chicago. Hitting upon a scheme to sell one-dollar-per-month insurance policies through the mail at the tail end of the Depression, he had his first million eight years later.

At his death in 1978 at the age of eighty, he was the second richest man in America—and possibly the cheapest. It's been said that he consistently flew coach, pocketed half-eaten sandwiches left behind by fellow passengers, scraped salad into a plastic bag for later consumption, saved half-smoked cigarettes, and kept a frozen birthday cake that he sliced away at year after year. A shrewd and brazen businessman, he ran his deals from a table in a grimy coffee shop of a Palm Beach Gardens hotel. That he owned the hotel (and some 42,000 acres of neighboring real estate) might lead you to believe that he occupied the penthouse suite. Not so. He and his second wife, Catherine, and two poodles lived in a modest apartment overlooking the parking lot.

Whether or not these stories are exaggerated, certainly they have been repeated often enough to have become clichés in the biography of the man. What is given less emphasis, however, is his extraordinary entrepreneurial talent. At his death his holdings included all the stock of Bankers Life & Casualty, at the time the second-largest accident and health insurance company in the world. He was also the largest landowner in Florida and counted among his assets the ritzy PGA golf courses and clubhouse. In addition, at various points in his long life, he had huge holdings in Chicago and Cincinnati, farm- and ranchland in Arizona, Illinois, Georgia, Colorado, and Michigan, a salvage operation in Alaska, a record company in New York, oil wells in New Mexico, resort land in Wisconsin, real estate in West Germany and Argentina, restaurants, airplanes, and limousines.

To escape the tax man at his death, in a strategy which was in keeping with his general disdain for government bureaucracy, he left the bulk of his two-and-a-half-billion-dollar empire to establish a foundation named after himself and his wife. At the time it was the second-largest foundation in America, trailing Ford. Along with his fortune he left the following instruction to his board of trustees: I figured out how to make the money, you boys figure out how to spend it. It was a flamboyant gesture that perfectly fit a man well schooled in making money but completely at odds with how to give it away. Still, onlookers had to linger a moment on the irony of a notoriously tightfisted man leaving in his wake a powerful philanthropy, the irony of a strong-willed tyrant leaving behind a fortune with absolutely no instruction as to its management. It was a true-story denouement to MacArthur's life that even Hollywood couldn't have invented.

The MacArthur Prize (variously called an award and a fellowship, which illustrates both its congratulatory and generative, sponsoring nature) is just one of the many projects the Foundation took on and amounts to a distribution of roughly nine million dollars per year—less than ten percent of the total annual disbursements.

Though accounts vary, the idea for the MacArthur Prize began with an observation by Dr. George Burch of Tulane University, who noted the difficulties of writing a grant proposal for truly remarkable advances in knowledge. William T. Kirby, John D. MacArthur's attorney for the last twenty-five years of his life, refined and suggested the idea to the foundation. From the start, it caught the enthusiasm of J. Roderick MacArthur, himself a self-made millionaire, and as eccentric and individualistic as his father. But unlike John, Roderick possessed a romantic, artistic, visionary streak. He believed that the role of philanthropy in American society should be marked by risk-taking and forward thinking. He talked passionately about a social consciousness having nothing to do with politics. He believed ardently in "the maverick geniuses" of America and worked diligently to get his program launched. In the end, the program was unanimously endorsed by the board, and in June 1981, with the announcement of the first set of awards, the MacArthur Fellowship was born. But Roderick died a few years later, before he could appreciate the full effect of the ideas he championed.

The way the award works is that they come to you, you can't go to them. The only way to become eligible is to be recommended by a specially designated group of nominators scattered throughout the country. There are roughly one hundred to one hundred and twenty men and women who serve in this scouting capacity at a given time, all experts of a sort in one thing or another. Working anonymously, the nominators secretly gather information about a candidate and submit it to the small foundation staff for further development. The award is not limited to a specific field—rare-book binding, crafts, climatology, crystallography, international security and arms control, genetics . . . even a clown has received one. Apart from competence and creative potential, the only requirement is that the person be a citizen or residing in America and not hold elective or appointed office.

Once a candidate's file has been suitably fattened with various assessments of potential, it is passed on to the Selection Committee chosen by the Board of Directors. The monthly private gatherings of the Selection Committee are something like attending a graduate seminar on everything. The debates are reported to be lively, intense, and amiably querulous. When at last agreement is reached on a fresh crop of fellows, one or two times a year, by no particular timetable, the awards are announced.

Almost immediately, in the service of headlines, the press began to call it "the genius award," a gilded label that irritates the Foundation and most Fellows. In fact, the purpose of the award is more subtle than that: it is to promote those leaps of creative thinking that may occur when gifted people are left to their own devices. For many, the award is an opportunity to refocus work, or to pursue projects that might appear wildly speculative, or even to change fields completely. "Could Einstein have written a grant application to discover his theory of relativity?" the late Roderick MacArthur was fond of saying. "Like the Medicis, we'll fund Michelangelo. If even one of them produces a great work of art, it will have been worth the risk."

▪ **3** ▪

INTRIGUED WITH THIS QUIRKY and idiosyncratic award that was designed to foster man's noble instincts and highest urges, I began to formulate my idea for this project. It started innocently (ignorantly and immoderately) enough: I wanted to learn all I could about the creative impulse. Where does it come from? How does it work? Why are some people more creative than others? Can it be encouraged?

These questions have been asked at least as early as Aristotle's time and probably earlier still. They are, in a sense, loaded questions: to pose them opens up a whole range of considerations that fly like buckshot from a double barrel.

For starters, there is the matter of turf. Where does one look to find answers about creativity? It's the kind of search that leads deep into science, art, and philosophy—a net so widely cast that, lacking direction, it may come up empty.

There is also the matter of definition. Can you search for the beginnings of creativity without knowing how it is defined? The dictionaries proved unsatisfactory, leaning on words like "originality," "invention," and "imagination." In fact, according to *The Oxford English Dictionary*, the word "creativity" didn't appear in print until 1875.

I looked elsewhere for definitions and came up with a file full: A creative genius is one who is smarter in his art than he is in his life. Creativity is the ability to look sideways at problems. A creative person is one who enjoys, above all else, the company of his own mind. A creative enterprise is one that produces an effective surprise. Anything done well, from baking a soufflé to putting together a winning stock portfolio, receives the honorific "creative." The creative person is one who can look at the same thing as everybody else but see something different. A creative act takes unremarkable parts to create an unforgettable whole. . . . In short, "creativity" is one of those overstretched concepts made to stand for too much and therefore hardly stands for anything at all.

And how do we identify creative output? The oldest approach among those interested in creativity is to take a look at the works and ideas of people widely considered creative and see how they function. But who is creative? In the eighteenth century, Shakespeare was thought coarse, almost unfit as a writer. The nineteenth century considered Bach stiff and lacking in soul. Edison was laughed at, James Joyce sneered at, the Impressionists spat at and their paintings attacked. Tastes change, the objects of veneration come and go.

My search for explanations to the mystery of creativity was aided considerably by using the confines of the MacArthur Fellowship. With respect to turf, the award is not particular and has been given out to all kinds of scientists, artists, scholars, and businessmen. With respect to definitions, the Foundation understandably adheres to none in particular. And with respect to the identification of creative talent—the sifting of the greeting-card verse from the poetry, the breakthrough from the repackaging—the Selection Committee has done the work for me, applying standards that are neither bizarre nor highly personal.

■ **4** ■

SLOWLY, THE PROJECT took shape. Wouldn't it be interesting to pick an assortment of these MacArthur Fellows and talk to them about how their best and most creative work gets done? Are the same things involved for the astrophysicist as for the actor? Is the process of a filmmaker the same or similar to that of a poet, or a research scientist, or an environmentalist? Would it be possible to isolate what was central and prevalent in the interests and methods of these people and connect the pieces in such a way as to create a coherent picture of how creative work gets done? Do common themes shore up highly idiosyncratic lives? And if we study those common denominators, can we learn something about how to improve our own creative capacities?

Digging in, I set about designing pages of interview questions that I thought might lead me closer to an understanding of the creative impulse. Like a billy goat finding everything tasty, I worked my way through shelfloads of research. So armed, I then whittled down the list of the now more than two hundred MacArthur Fellows to a manageable forty—the highest number feasible given the constraints of the project.

This was harder than it sounds. For example, I wanted to meet Michael Malin, a planetary scientist living in Arizona who is as capable of investigating the Antarctic as he is of designing the camera system for the upcoming NASA Mars mission. And John Horner from Montana, a self-taught paleobiologist captivated by dinosaurs. And Beaumont Newhall in New Mexico, who has been highly influential in the development of photography as art. And James Randi, the magician who travels around claiming to debunk, among other things, the assertions of faith healers.

The philosophers, the architecture critics, the country doctor, the lady who investigates sorcery, the novelists from whom I have derived much nourishment, the seismologist who monitors underground nuclear explosions . . . I wanted to talk with all of the MacArthur Fellows not simply because their biographies were so intriguing but also because I understood that creativity is a subject that, if approached at all, is done so only occasionally and accidentally. To grasp the essence of it, one had to look at many images. How to choose?

In part the choice was made for me: there were only so many dollars and even less time. In addition, I wanted at least a rough balance of interests and geography—not all East Coast writers, say, or all scientists. I wanted a mix of well-known and lesser-established talents. I also wanted a spread of ages and, as luck would have it, managed to converse with both the youngest and the oldest of the MacArthur Fellows to date.

All of these considerations helped to pare the list down. On top of that, I sought the advice of the MacArthur Foundation itself, specifically Dr. Kenneth Hope, Director of the MacArthur Fellows Program, who steered me away from people he guessed might be unresponsive. In time, I had my forty, as diverse in personality and perspective as they are in achievement. They are listed at the end of the book, should you wish to view them as a group.

■ 5 ■

EVENTUALLY, ARMED with my questions, I began to make my calls. Again, this was much less straightforward than it sounds. In the course of an interview there is far more going on than a single person can keep track of, with every interview following its own peculiar trajectory. Nonetheless, to give you an idea of how they went, stand for a moment in my stead.

You ring the bell, confirm who you are, shake hands, and in the next two to three minutes—literally—either establish rapport or not. And if not, you're in trouble. But no matter what, you get right down to work trying to find out what you came to learn, feeling something like a juggler with twenty balls in the air.

There's the question you asked that is not, curiously, the

question he is trying to answer. There's the spoken answer and the unspoken answer. There's a split-second decision as to whether to pursue a follow-up question or shift the line of inquiry altogether. There's the question that worked well for the last guy but you couldn't possibly ask it of this guy, or maybe he thinks he's answered it already. There's the problem of trying to get him to elucidate what he thinks, indeed *knows*, is incredibly self-evident. There's the problem of the themes to develop and the assumptions you've grown to really like and, therefore, hate like the dickens to hear they're not true.

The "what" questions are easy: What do you do? What caused you to be interested in this? What influenced that decision? The "how" questions are another matter altogether: How did you get that idea? How did you know you were right? The direct question almost never works. The indirect question can't be too cagey or he'll think you're shifty and lose confidence in the enterprise.

From time to time you ask just the right question in just the right way, which sets the person off on a long, windy discourse on the nature of Art and God, Being and Nothingness. He sails on, embarked upon a solitary voyage, talking out loud but to himself, mostly. What he says sounds useful but you don't interrupt, making notes instead on the points that need clarification. As he continues, distancing himself even further from the here and now, you begin to feel increasingly like an eavesdropper who catches the vague drift, the occasional phrase, but can't quite make out the whole of what he's saying. Still you remain attentive, listening for the imminent disclosure of something vital, something revelatory.

All the while you've an eye on the tape recorder, watching that the batteries are still strong and the tape still spinning. As long as the person is willing to talk, you'll keep the tape rolling, putting in the fresh one as swiftly and as unobtrusively as possible. In your pocket are eight hours of tape—generally two hours was sufficient but one time you ran out.

You're listening—hard—fighting the urge to fit what you're

hearing into what you already know. A fixed idea should never prevent you from listening to something with fresh ears; it's too easy to miss a lot that way. Along these lines, in preparing for the interview, you took pains to strike the delicate balance between knowing too much, which can deaden the exchange, and walking in a damn ignorant fool.

The complications multiply. There's the thing he just said that's brilliantly lucid and fantastically revealing and utterly wonderful which he then tells you not to use because he's thinking of putting it into an essay himself. There's the problem of how to skirt (ever so gently) his question about how other Fellows have answered—it's irrelevant and besides, you can't afford the shift in roles: *you're* supposed to do the asking, *he's* supposed to do the answering. There's the problem of choosing the right words and speaking the right language—a poet doesn't talk like a medical researcher, and the dancer hardly talks at all. There's the problem that just by asking the question, you've interjected bias and influenced the answer—a variant of the Heisenberg Uncertainty Principle.

At times, it seems like two wholly separate agendas—yours and his—which brings to mind the split screen of the Andy Warhol movie, *The Chelsea Girls*, where on one side a boy babbles incoherently about sex and drugs, while on the other half is a girl, equally incoherent. It is a dialogue of sorts but without the two communicating, as sometimes happens when people talk.

And then you see him sneak a glance at his watch and the lights in his eyes switch off. The end is near and you try to condense the remaining list of twenty or thirty critical questions into the next seven minutes. You have to establish priority but there's no time to reflect on how to do it. Besides, you've been working from memory, so to shuffle now through the notes in hand would be awkward and, worse, hasten an abrupt end.

But the end is inevitable and there's the pull of the coffeehouse you spotted earlier where you'll go to recuperate, and make sure all the tapes are labeled properly. It's the kind of place that has Christmas tree lights twinkling in July, and plywood showing through the linoleum. It's the best kind of place to catch your breath, take stock, and take notes because they keep your coffee cup filled and leave you alone there.

▪ 6 ▪

FORTY PEOPLE, forty humors generating a titanic mass of notes and transcripts. The struggle now was to make sense of it, to see what could be said in answer to the question: How can a person improve his or her creative capabilities?

The paradox is neatly presented: the question doesn't appear to be unreasonable yet reasonable terms don't begin to answer it. There are a lot of things worth knowing that resist being made familiar, but still we are sure the answers must exist in the same way that astronomers of long ago were sure of the existence of the planet Neptune. They couldn't see it, but were certain it was there from the uneven orbit of things around it.

In the end, the common themes linking these creative people separated and floated to the surface like cream. Some of what I discovered I expected: they were all driven, remarkably resilient, adept at creating an environment that suited their needs, skilled at honoring their own peculiar talents instead of lusting after an illusion of self, capable of knowing when to follow their instincts, and above all, magnificent risk-takers, unafraid to run ahead of the great popular tide.

But some of what I learned was a surprise, like the discoveries about cultivating a widely flung mission, trying to encourage luck, and allowing for the tastes of the culture. And in certain circumstances, it's better to loosen up, throw away the instruction manuals, and get your hands dirty.

With these conclusions in hand, the problem then was to devise an artful structure for telling the story, keeping in mind that creativity is a nonlinear phenomenon, which is to say that "a" does not lead to "b," "c" may well be followed by "q." Considerations fold into each other the way egg whites are folded into a cake batter.

Somehow, I had to allow for the untidiness and inconsistencies of it all. And, too, there were the subtleties of reducing an interview to the written page: people should sound the way they really talk. A casual statement, isolated from the whole, shouldn't be made to stand for an entire formal dogma. Live people need to be protected: we can't—any of us—afford to go around telling all. Embarrassing passages and whatever is patently dull, self-serving, repetitive, trivial, foolish, clumsy, or cruel should be cut. And despite the strong temptation to overseason the paragraphs with pungent, spicy detail, in deciding what to include, remember the advice of Elias Canetti: "One should fear words more."

Accordingly, as the pages of this book progress, some of you will wonder if I verified the written statements with the Fellows themselves. The answer is that I have done so where there was doubt as to what was meant, or as to the proper shading of a remark, or where as a condition to the interview the Fellow requested that I call upon him again to confirm quotes. Beyond these three circumstances, I did not retrace the path because I think people editing their words get far too much of a taste of themselves and the tendency is strong to adjust one's remarks to be either entirely bland or clever by adding a quip you might have said at the dinner party if only you'd thought of it then instead of later, preparing for bed.

Which brings me to the matter of authenticity, best addressed before we proceed any further. I come to this work as a curious outsider, which I like to think is justified because what I hope to do is engage the curiosity of outsiders. I am not a reserach scientist, anthropologist, sociologist, psychiatrist, or statistician, and my methods reflect the absence of this classical training. And while I believe that there is a decided value to striving for "objective" information—that is, research based on careful surveys, batteries of tests, fair samplings, cross sections, control pools, and all of that—this work holds nothing of the kind. Fast, breathless, intuitive, this work is not meant to qualify as a systematic study: it has, if I have succeeded, an intentionally different quality to it.

If this project had culminated in a painting instead of a book, it would no doubt have been done in the soft, loose style of Impressionism and have many vanishing points and no harsh right angles to trip up the eye. It would hold lots of images to look at and to store away for later private reflection. It would be full of suggestion, a hint here, a dash there, a splash of paint, no more, to depict the full majesty of a face. There is ample room for interpretation, and the viewer fills in the gaps with what he knows and has already decided is true. The effect, on the whole, would be pleasing and coherent from a distance, but perishable and incomprehensible close up or if taken apart piece by piece. That, it seems to me, is the nature of creativity.

In this loose fashion, it comes as no surprise, then, to learn that I am not trying to provide a formula or a recipe that, if slavishly followed, would turn a pedestrian imagination into a Michelangelo, a James Joyce, or a Mozart. The phenomenon of the creative spark is larger than any of my findings can suggest. But I do *firmly* believe that if we cultivate a consciousness about the way we think and work and behave, improvement in our creative abilities is possible—and improvement is not something to be taken lightly.

■ 7 ■

"I'M HERE BECAUSE I'm interested in creativity," I said, thinking it was a suitable introduction yet at the same time knowing that any opener would fall flat.

"Oh, well," he answered with a weary shrug, "that."

Joseph Brodsky had been pacing warily near his cluttered desk, fingering unopened mail, dropping it again. Reluctantly, he sank into the couch, a puff of dust glittering in the sunlight.

He had the view of the ivy-hemmed patio. I faced a bunch of tattered photographs tacked up as if according to a wild game of darts. In the corner, a shelf sagged under the weight of books. Bach was on the turntable. Between us, I readied my tape recorder.

"Will never do," he said in the thick solemn speech of a Russian claiming English. Mississippi, the cat, had sent the recorder flying with a swat of her tail.

I reached to draw her into my lap while righting the machine. She purred contentedly; he focused only on her, his eyes gazing steadily from behind steel-rimmed spectacles.

In a moment of broken concentration, I wondered if he purred cat noises to her the way he used to meow to his mother in a boyhood game back in Leningrad some forty years ago. The cat calls were an expression of endearment, the prerogative of an only child. He confesses this intimacy in *Less Than One*, the essays for which he was awarded the 1987 Nobel Prize in Literature. His MacArthur came a few years earlier. It seemed unjust that his mother lived only long enough to experience the sorrows in her son's life: the tribunal, the Siberian exile, and the long periods of grief.

Mississippi was curled peacefully in my lap.

For his part, Brodsky flicked the cigarette he was smoking toward the fireplace already littered with a half dozen butts. In silence, he groped for another from his shirt pocket. Cigarette pinched between thumb and forefinger, he tore the filter out with his teeth, shot it toward the hearth, and lit up. It was a manner of smoking which by comparison made the American habit look breezy and inconsequential, as if suited merely for cocktail parties.

"What's your interest in all of this?" he asked, exhaling.

"It's a long-standing question with me and I've an idea or two about it," I told him.

"Grand ideas?"

Grand ideas? Certainly not. To the contrary, the point was to take some of the mystery *out* of creativity, to explain as clearly and as fully as possible where good ideas come from, how the creative impulse works, and how one's own uncommon genius can be cultivated.

"Probably very simple, very obvious ideas, but it'd be nice to settle the matter and get on with it," I answered.

He didn't respond, but something about his posture—relaxed now—told me it was okay to begin. Mississippi eyed the red light on the tape recorder, stiffened for an attack, but changed her mind.

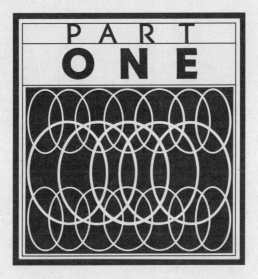

PART
ONE

TALENT AND THE LONG HAUL

THERE'S NO USE in trying to deny it: a conscious application of raw talent, far more than luck or accident, is at the core of every creative moment.

No, no, that will never do. Even if it's true, it's not the kind of thing a reader wants to hear. It comes across as brutal and heartless. Most decent people are modest and tentative in their efforts. They suspect they have no special talent for anything. They fear they are ordinary. Better start over.

I tell you, there's no use in trying to deny it: the cultivation of aptitude, far more than coincidence or inspiration, is responsible for most creative breakthroughs.

Hardly better. You're going to discourage readers with a line like that. What everyone wants is magic, a prescription a druggist can fill, the key to the secret rose garden where the flowers bloom forever. What they want is The Trick to creativity so that they will be assured of a richer, more satisfying life. Try again.

The trick to creativity, if there is a single useful thing to say about it, is to identify your own peculiar talent and then settle down to work with it for a good long time. Everyone has an aptitude for something. The trick is to recognize it, to honor it, to work with it. This is where creativity starts.

Well, a little blunt maybe, but it has the advantage of being direct. Let it stand and go on.

■ **2** ■

THE WAITING ROOM of Harvard's Museum of Comparative Zoology was little more than a large exchange point between hallways, the hub with spokes trailing off. There were no windows, the air was musty. Off one corridor were mounds of fossilized animal parts, a veritable boneyard of skeletons and jaws, the teeth coated with dust. Lining another corridor were floor-to-ceiling showcases of petrified bits of shells, ferns, and insects, each numbered according to some grand classification scheme. In still another direction was a lecture hall.

"You're waiting for me, I suppose?"

Dr. Stephen Jay Gould emerged from yet another doorway. I had heard that he was ill and was not prepared for the robust, even portly figure who stormed by. I jumped up and trailed after him down the hall of the endless fossil cases. Every few feet our progress was halted by people soliciting his attention. Someone wanted a petition signed. Another wanted to confirm a conclusion. His secretary waved the afternoon mail at him. A fourth flitted about, a moth to his flame, and pressed him for an autograph. At length, we arrived at his office door.

It was dark inside and spooky. Through the deep gloom, the room felt huge with high-vaulted ceilings. It served once as the main exhibition hall for the museum. Now it was filled with file cabinets, boxes, and stacks of queer things piled so high that it would take tiptoes to see over the top.

Gould, with his rounded shoulders, kept his eyes on the floor. I followed suit, staying close to his heels as we made our way though the labyrinth to his desk in the back.

He was prickly this morning, slightly acidic, feeling pressed. It was a predictable condition for a driven and overworked researcher hot on the trail of the question of questions: the mystery of evolution. Stephen Jay Gould is a man who understands the game at its highest level. He has been described by some as the most important person in the field since Darwin; to others, the comparison falls short.

Dr. Gould settled at his desk, first sweeping away a carton loaded with copies of his new book. Wasting no time, I started in with my standard warm-up questions: work habits, interests, how he felt about success, how he handled failures. He swatted them aside: "Rubbish." After all, what was the search for creativity to a man involved in penetrating Creation itself?

I moved on to questions of aptitude, and here, finally, broke ground.

Look, he explained, there's so much nonsense circulating about the creative process. People are all caught up in these notions of the *Sturm und Drang* of it, the so-called magic of inspiration, this utterly ridiculous fantasy of a muse:

"Twaddle. Absolute twaddle and one of the worst heritages of romanticism."

If I have any insight at all to contribute, he continued, it is this: find out what you're really good at and stick to it.

"Look at some of the *real* creative geniuses. Look at Bach. He wrote a cantata every week. Some weeks he was tired and others he was sick. But every week he wrote a cantata. Sometimes he didn't have much time so he copied stuff he wrote before. And they're not all as good as the others, but the point is this: he put it out."

It was a message others would repeat, in their own way: "Listen for the special music," a MacArthur Fellow affirmed, "the song that nobody else can sing but you. Your own karma badly lived is better than someone else's karma lived well." "What we poets can do," concurred another, "in terms of what we know and our own honesty about that, is to write well within the articulation of our own experience. That is, to write within the immediate perimeter of not more than twenty miles from home."

Gould elaborated: "Any human being is *really* good at certain things. The problem is that the things you're good at come naturally. And since most people are pretty modest instead of an arrogant s.o.b. like me, what comes naturally, you *don't see* as a special skill. It's just you. It's what you've always done."

He was warmed up now, leaning forward to weight the point.

"Take the person whose body works really well without a great deal of training, or the person with perfect pitch or a musical skill—I mean, they don't give it a second thought because they've *always* done it. They're good at it.

"On the other hand, you really can get very unhappy or jealous or angry or woeful about the things you *don't* do well. I always wished I was better in math, for example. I realized, early in my career, that there were certain things in the sciences that I couldn't do well because of that, which I guess I've regretted, but what I did do well I never realized was a skill."

I wondered what he thought he did do well. Certainly there were no shortage of possibilities. For starters, he was a riveting lecturer with many a class at standing room only. Zoology, geology, evolutionary biology, invertebrate paleontology, natural history, the history of science—he was at home in all these subjects, ranging through them the way a lion stalks a plain.

He was also a first-rate field researcher, retiring to the Caribbean most winters to scramble about the rocks and grasses on his hands and knees, a plastic specimen sack clenched between his teeth, his keen eyes examining the evolving rings on snail shells, oblivious to the clouds of flies and the blazing heat. The snails make a perfect subject for a man interested in evolutionary theory, a man whose favorite motto of all time derives from Mies van der Rohe: "God dwells in the details."

Further, Gould is an essayist, a writer in an exacting art form all but lost in modern times. For years he's been writing a monthly column in *Natural History* called "This View of Life." Blending wit and wisdom with a graceful elegant style, Gould's award-winning essays continue to ring months, even years, after you've read them. Marrying the humanist's perspective to the rigors of science, he exemplifies a return to the tradition of the philosopher-scientist, a tradition that begins with the dialogues of Galileo.

Though he could have easily spoken about any of these things as his special talent, the arena for his creative effort, he chooses instead to comment on something more subtle:

"My talent is making connections. That's why I'm an essayist. It's also why my technical work is structured the way it is. How do the parts of the snail shell interact? What are the rates of growth? Can you see a pattern? I'm always trying to see a pattern in this forest and I'm tickled that I can do that.

"My talent concerns connectivity. I can sit down on just about any subject and think of about twenty things that relate to it and they're not hokey connections. They're real connections that you can forge into essays or scientific papers. When I wrote *Ontogeny and Phylogeny* I had no trouble reading eight hundred articles and bringing them together into a single thread. That's how it went together. There's only one way it goes together, one best taxonomy, and I knew what it was.

"It took me *years* to realize that was a skill. I could never understand why everybody just didn't *do* that. People kept telling me these essays were good and I thought, All right, I can write, but surely what I'm doing is not special. And then I found out that it's not true. Most people *don't* do it. They just don't see the connections."

He was loose now, at his edifying best, the momentary gruffness having given way to the sparkling personality that glints between the paragraphs of his essays.

"And another funny thing: A lot of people think I'm very well read because I quote all these sources and they're reasonable quotations. They're not hokey. They're not pulled out. And I keep telling them, 'I'm not particularly well read. I just don't forget anything.'

"I'm not *badly* read—I'm just sort of an average intellectual in that respect—but the thing is, I can *use* everything I've ever read. Most people cannot do that. They'll probably access just a couple of percent of what they have. So, therefore, when they see me citing so much they assume I have fifty times more but I don't. I'm using a hundred percent of what I have.

They're using two percent of what they have. I can just *do* that. I've never had any trouble with it. But I never knew it was a skill until a few years ago. I bet that's true of everyone. I hardly even recognize what I do well. I just do it."

Gould's special talent, that rare gift for seeing the connections between seemingly unrelated things, zinged to the heart of the matter. Without meaning to, he had zeroed in on the most popular of the manifold definitions of creativity: the idea of connecting two unrelated things in an effective way. The surprise we experience at such a linkage brings us up short and causes us to think, Now that's creative.

The highly controversial journalist, science writer, and philosopher Arthur Koestler spun an entire theory around this idea of connectivity in his weighty tome *The Act of Creation*. Koestler maintained that usual, normal thought proceeds from a single frame of reference (or matrix), and that while a person may be familiar with many points of view, most of us operate from only one frame of reference at a time. Creativity occurs, he continued, when a person can relate what are normally independent matrices or frames of mind. This phenomenon he called "bisociation."

Even the most casual look around the home at the objects that populate our everyday lives illustrates the connectivity idea of creativity. The Ziploc food-storage bag, which takes a cue from the zipper used on fabric, the Teflon-coated face of an iron, an idea borrowed from the stick-free frying pan, adding honey to nuts, cheese to popcorn—these are all illustrations of combining two different frames of reference to come up with the kind of effective, pleasing surprise we call creative.

But there's an even easier way to observe the phenomenon of connectivity: a good joke operates on the same principle. When a joke is funny it's because the punch line produces an unexpected surprise. It connects things in a way we never suspected. For instance:

One day the husband of a woman who was sitting for a portrait by Picasso dropped in on the artist at his studio. "What do you think?" Picasso asked, revealing the nearly finished canvas. The husband cleared his throat, stalling for time in which to think of a polite response. "Well," he said at last, "it's not how she really looks." "And how does she really look?" the painter countered. Refusing to be bullied by this fierce artist, the husband reached into his wallet and produced a snapshot. "Like this," he said. Picasso studied the photograph. "I see," he concluded. "Small, isn't she."

Koestler, among others, saw the parallel between the broad sweep of creativity and a good joke, citing humor as one of the most basic forms of bisociative thinking. In his often-quoted essay "The Three Domains of Creativity" he noted the similarity between various kinds of creative expression: artistic originality giving rise to the ah! reaction, scientific discovery leading to the aha! reaction, and comic inspiration resulting in the haha! reaction. With all three reactions, two different frames of reference collide to produce the surprising result.

Stephen Jay Gould's talent for forging vital connections happens to go to the heart of creativity, but, even so, it's a talent that wouldn't amount to much if he didn't work at it. Endurance counts for a lot in cultivating talent to the point of being able to do creative things with it—endurance *and* a concentration of effort to a specific sphere of activity. As D. N. Perkins, another researcher in the field of creativity, put it: Be creative in a context, for to try to be original everywhere, all at once, all the time, is an exhausting proposition.

■ **3** ■

"A SINGLE DISCOVERY within a lifetime is a very remarkable thing," said Alar Toomre, in his words, an astrophysicist disguised as a mathematician. "Two over the course of a career—why you'd be lucky indeed."

He was fiddling with a projector of 16mm vintage hardly seen anymore in this age of the slick cousin, the videocassette player. A great big burly man full of good humor, he nonetheless showed remarkable agility as he bounded about his office moving furniture and books until at last, below the blackboard, he found a freshly painted piece of wall to serve as a screen.

The projector rattled to life. It was hard to know what would appear: majestic galaxies, heavenly orbs, exploding suns— these were the kinds of mysteries that made up the currency of his best ideas, the context for his most creative thought.

He had been talking all morning about such things and the progression of his interest in them. The story began with his emigration from Estonia as a young boy, a journey he undertook to escape the Russian bombing of his homeland and the American shelling of Germany. Educated in both the United States and England, he settled down at the Massachusetts Institute of Technology, where he has enjoyed a long and comfortable tenure.

Love of airplanes, flying machines, and the vast, uncharted territory of space attracts most young boys, he explained; he just took it a bit further, narrowing his arcing interest in the cosmos to a single question, a mere pinpoint of inquiry: What happens when two galaxies spin near each other? It seemed incredible that such a strange and solitary question could occupy his attention off and on for over two decades.

"It sounds so awfully dull, so technical, when you say it," he chuckled, "but when you plot it on the computer it makes very beautiful, very inspiring pictures." A stack of them were on his desk. To the untrained eye, they looked like New Age tantric drawings, or the designs of a child who has just discovered geometry.

"Here, look!" he said as images began to dance on the scrubbed wall. On this makeshift screen swirled two separate forms. They were galaxies depicted as computer-printed *xxx*'s and *ooo*'s, each a separate mass spinning around a core.

"Now watch what happens as they get close to each other."

He was completely absorbed, even though he had not only made the film but had probably seen it hundreds of times, most recently in a class he taught earlier that morning.

He watched as the galaxies spun closer and closer together. They didn't collide but merely brushed near each other. The result was the creation of long tails of *xxx*'s and *ooo*'s, wisps that spiraled off and eventually broke free from the mass, dissipating into space. "Beautiful," Toomre pronounced, "just beautiful."

I had no doubt that his discovery was technically astonishing, though certainly beyond the comprehension of one unschooled in the intricacies of physics. But while the nitty-gritty of galactic tidal interactions would be lost on the novice, the aesthetics were easy enough to appreciate. The elegance of it—Toomre's big discovery—was sublime.

"I've been fiddling with this old friend for more than twenty years. I suspected some twenty years ago that a single orbiting lump in a galaxy, such as a Saturn disc or a solar system, would have this zone of influence resulting in these spiral streaks, but I couldn't do anything about it. Partly it's because twenty years ago I couldn't deal with these questions as comfortably or as easily as I can now. There were no graphic displays of the quality available now and sheer observation—telescopes—was much more limited. Of course I published and bragged a bit and continued to work on it, but now I can compute it much more convincingly. You can never make anything certain in this business, but you can make it very plausible or implausible. And I kept working in this context until I could demonstrate it at least to my satisfaction."

We watched as more spinning galaxies wheeled near each other, forming long, elegant tails before they moved off to the edges of infinity. Toomre was engrossed. He talked about all the projects he had brewing which are related to this one and how one project sustains or gives insight into another.

This interrelationship of projects seems to be typical of creative activity. The exploration of an interlocking network of enterprises revolving around one specific activity allows the researcher to look at the problem from lots of different angles. The advantage is that a big question can be broken up into discrete portions, each variation of the theme affording a slightly different emphasis, a more sharply focused outlook. What is useful can be isolated, redefined, and pursued further. What is ambiguous can be examined again and again from varying perspectives. What is frivolous, or desperately embryonic, or implausible can be closed down or maybe just set aside for the time being.

Toomre has been working on various aspects of galaxy dynamics for a couple of decades, and to show for it he has more projects than he knows what to do with, more ideas and theories to pursue than he can complete in a lifetime. It's a rich feeling, a store of creative wealth, the by-product of a long engagement in a given field.

But how do people find a context worthy of a lifetime of intense and prolonged concentration?

In Toomre's case, it had to do with temperament. He's a physicist by disposition and physicists are always looking around for things to gnaw on. They are collectors of odd but remarkable facts, very few of which are understood. But you try, Toomre says, to make headway on the little issues, not the big ones, nothing grand. What is important is to focus your interests on one or two discrete, localized, particularized questions pulled out from a universe of one's interests. Work on the small matters utterly, he explains, and the large necessities can be left to take care of themselves and of those who trusted accordingly.

But how does a person know which issues to pull out? How does he decide what is worth a lifetime of energy? How does he know what will be productive and useful to pursue?

"Utility?" Toomre stopped short, baffled for a moment. "That's dangerous ground when you're talking to an astronomer."

He was joking, of course, but it was a point well taken. The hope of discovering something useful is only one of the many possible impulses that might cause a person to seize upon a set of issues intriguing enough to occupy his or her attention for a sustained period of time. The challenge of an unexplained mystery, the drive to be the first, the lust for power or respect or love, a religious or political belief, a deep and abiding social consciousness—any of these things could serve as the catalyst for defining one's primary lifelong focus. It almost doesn't matter what the impetus is as long as the context one chooses gives wings to one's particular talent. Even accident can be a sufficient catalyst to launch a long involvement in a given field.

▪ 4 ▪

"I DON'T KNOW," said Andy McGuire, resting his head between his hands. "How *do* people settle on a single ambition, a context for their efforts? I suppose it is partly a question of temperament and partly a matter of recognizing your own talents."

But in McGuire's case it seemed to me that there was yet another element at work. As he related the twists of his life— he is an easy-going, soft-spoken Californian—I began to get the idea that accident had a lot to do with it. Or, if you prefer, call it destiny, kismet, fate. Any way you put it, it's a shapeless, hard-to-hang-on-to idea, something like trying to grab hold of mercury with bare fingers.

We were in his office on the second floor of San Francisco General Hospital, an institution renowned for the handling of trauma cases. The office had the makeshift look of one occupied by a man who just moved in, though McGuire's been inhabiting this space for several years. In the corner is a video camera on a tripod. A long line of certificates and awards marches across the wall. There is paper spilling off every counter and windowsill, towers of transcripts from government hearings, stacks of mail and clippings, and a week-old package he hasn't had the time to open.

The offices are officially closed today, so it's quiet and he's feeling unrushed. He opens the package: an ingenious anti-scald shower-head device that operates on the principle of "metal memory." Now that's creative: applying the principle of metal expansion under heat to prevent hot-water burns. McGuire is intrigued and sets it aside with a bunch of other inventions he wants to take a closer look at.

"I come from—how should I put it—blue-collar roots," he explains. His speech is gentle, measured, patient; he never uses a fifty-cent word when a nickel one will do just fine. He has the rough-around-the-edges look of plain folks; I couldn't picture him in a suit and tie.

"My father was a factory worker, the kind of guy who sees things very simply. Something is either black or it's white, right or wrong. No middle ground. No special words with which to duel. No frills. I grew up with the idea that problems should be viewed in very basic terms."

Growing up wasn't easy. He spent a lot of years on an assembly line. College was a struggle both academically and financially. When he finally made it out, he traveled east to apprentice himself to a harpsichord maker in Waltham, Massachusetts. As an illustration of his naïveté, he mentions that he didn't think to write or call the man to say he was coming. He just showed up one day, on the doorstep, ready to go to work. Naturally, the master craftsman couldn't use him but promised to consider him in eight or nine months when the next opening came up. In the meantime, McGuire took a job as a machinist in a manufacturing shop.

Then one day, quite by chance, the story continues, his wife noticed an announcement in *The Boston Globe* about a group that was being formed at the nearby Shriners Burn Institute to lobby for legislation requiring flame-resistant sleepwear.

"The article hit something pretty deep. When I was seven I was severely burned. My bathrobe caught fire on the kitchen stove. It was early in the morning, the morning of my seventh birthday actually, and somebody must have left the stove on all night. My sister was the one who found me. She was four at the time and ran to tell my parents. They had to call an aunt and uncle who lived nearby to take me to the hospital; we didn't own a car. I was placed on the couch until they came. In all, I spent three and a half months in the hospital and had four different skin grafts. Later, much later in life, I re-created the scene together with my sister. I can't begin to tell you how helpful that was. It's incredible how much of it I could recall—the contortion of my limbs, the changing of dressings, the mental games I devised to cope with the pain."

In his first act of public service, McGuire went to the organizational meeting and to all the meetings that followed. It was the start of his lifelong involvement with issues of public health and safety. From there he tackled the ominously powerful tobacco industry and won the fight for fire-safe self-extinguishing cigarettes. At the same time, he expanded his concern to include mandatory seatbelt laws, handgun laws, and the rights of the disabled. He's remarkably effective in his efforts, working harder and harder against increasingly stiff opposition to improve the way we live.

Later, at his favorite hamburger joint in a working-class neighborhood overlooking the shipyard—"a stone's throw from where O.J. played ball"—he detailed some of the intricacies of his astonishing ability to leverage power and mobilize public sentiment. It's important to link up with similarly minded people who might have become involved with an issue through a personal tragedy but are incapable of responding with anything more than a wringing of hands. He finds them and teaches them that if they can get past the anger and grief, there are ways to effect permanent change.

Step-by-step, person-by-person, McGuire forms armies of concerned citizens—one hundred, eight hundred, thousands strong. He steps aside and lets them shine in the spotlight of press conferences and public hearings. Andy likes to stay in the background, to remain completely anonymous if he can get away with it. In this way, he builds a groundswell and fans out the power base, not incidentally depriving the opposition of a single, focused target for attack: "some kook out on the West Coast."

A waitress with a crystal dangling from her ear and a Grateful Dead T-shirt finally got around to serving us a pair of Corona Extras. All this talk about the various accidents in life that shaped the context for his best and most creative work has left him parched.

"And then there are my films," he says after a long pull of *La Cerveza Más Fina*, "which have to happen in the cracks of my other work."

The first feature-length documentary Andy McGuire ever made was about a seven-year-old boy named Rob who sustained a seventy-five-percent full-thickness burn in a house fire some years ago. McGuire had absolutely no experience with filmmaking, but he didn't let that bother him ("I mean, hell, everything's an obstacle if you look at it that way"). The important fact, the only one that mattered, was that an artistic, medically accurate, socially sensitive film about burn injuries would be a useful tool in his fight to enact legislation to prevent such tragedies.

Working on and off for three and a half years with a local filmmaker and drawing on the home movies Rob's mother had taken before the accident, he produced *Here's Looking at You, Kid*, which was shown to families at the Shriners Burn Institute as part of the orientation services they offer. But, much to McGuire's amazement, it also won an Emmy that year in New York and was aired on public television.

"You're on your third film," I said, "you talk with doctors, and fire chiefs, you tour burn wards, you attend grand rounds in hospitals all over the world, you organize people, you advise numerous boards, you put on a tie and speak at universities, you're deeply concerned about fire, and handguns, and Ford Pintos that blow up, and air bags in cars, and accidental drownings in unfenced swimming pools, you're worried about the

handicapped, you've dedicated your life to trauma preven-
tion—what's next?"

He considered the question seriously. Certainly I didn't
expect him to stray far from the primary node of his activities—
the health, safety, and welfare of people—but at the same time
it seems he already had a hand in all the major issues, ex-
pending the energy of five men. What was left? He thought
about it carefully.

"War, I guess. It's the ultimate injury."

▪ 5 ▪

AS HE IS NEVER one to fasten on minor goals, the scope of
his mission is magnificent. But that gets ahead of the story of
creativity and we'll come to it later, in the chapter on "Investing
Your Work with a Vision." For now, the first clue lies in the
matter of talent and the long haul. The lesson here is to find
your talent by looking in all the obvious places, at the things
you do well and take for granted. After that, settle in for a
long engagement within the confines of a specific context. In
this way, your talent—that vague and indefinite word we use
for magic—has a chance to develop, you can tackle the same
set of problems over and over again using different approaches,
and your eye is given enough latitude to begin to notice the
surprising connections.

The esteemed photographer Alfred Stieglitz knew all about
this first clue. When questioned about his habit of making as
many as one hundred shots of the same brick wall, he answered, "One theme with endless variations, like life itself."

TAKING ON RISK

AT AN EARLY POINT in this project, just to see what would happen, I informally canvassed a collection of complete strangers to determine if creativity was important to them, and if so, how important. I was indiscriminate in my buttonholing: secretaries on coffee breaks, delivery boys, businessmen on the commuter train, idle waitresses and hotel clerks, librarians, mothers on park benches . . .

There are two conclusions I feel safe in reporting: First, I have the kind of face people lecture, advise, confide in—and talk to. Second, it was the rare person who didn't warm to the subject, roundly perceiving imagination to be a good thing, along with health, happiness, and money, not necessarily in that order.

But after hearing puffed-up tales of some of their best and most creative ideas, when I asked what they'd be willing to risk for even greater creativity—friends? income? security? reputation?—people dissolved into giggles, or acted skittish, or even excused themselves altogether. Risk makes people nervous—which might explain why so many of us have trouble realizing the full length of our creative potential.

An unfortunate aspect to creative work is that it requires an element of risk-taking. The risk, say, of exposing something of your own private persona. Of revealing something not quite ready for public scrutiny. Of having to go beyond the sure footing of experience and expertise. Of having to part paths with friends and mentors. Of jeopardizing resources and making mistakes. Of suffering unintended consequences and even ruin. Society shuns its heretics.

Nevertheless, without the courage to step outside accepted wisdom in order to pursue something different or strange or speculative, there is little chance for the survival of a creative idea. The MacArthur Fellowship encourages risk-taking and, appropriately, has been awarded to people willing to accept the challenges that come with the pursuit of the long shot. "Thank you," wrote one Fellow to the Director of the program, "for giving me the freedom to fail." "Thank you," wrote another, "for encouraging me to do something I didn't know I had in me." The validation and financial largesse of a MacArthur makes it a little easier to take a chance, but even without it this collection of creative people were well used to running against the prevailing winds.

▪ 2 ▪

I CHECKED THE ADDRESS again: 106th and Madison. East Harlem. And yet looking around all I saw was a vacant lot strewn with broken glass, an old man sweeping out a fruit stand, and a young boy bouncing a ball against a school named Jackie Robinson.

"Excuse me," I asked the boy. "Do you know where Central Park East Secondary School is?"

He jerked his thumb. "Third floor."

"What, you mean in here?" The idea of a school within a school was a new one on me. When you enter an office building, he reasoned, do you expect to find only one company?

Central Park East Secondary School is the fourth in a series of public schools started by MacArthur Fellow Deborah Meier. When the first one opened in 1974, nobody could have predicted that it would spawn a full twelve grades of education.

In fact, there was ample reason to doubt that the solitary seedling elementary school would survive at all.

The year of its christening was a year of educational shock in New York City, marked by library closings and the layoff of fifteen thousand teachers. There was talk of illiteracy, apathy, and absenteeism. There was concern over drugs and flashing knives. Parents and teachers alike demanded a system-wide upheaval. In particular, progressive educators suffered the most, not simply because they tended to be among the younger faculty and therefore hit hardest by the cutbacks, but also because it was widely believed that "alternative curriculums" and "openness" were dead—and a good thing too.

"With no constituency, no student body, and no real power base, it was a job between a joke and an impossibility," one insider remarked. Only a fool would have taken on the opportunity to start a new and innovative school in this adverse climate, but when public-school teacher (now principal) Debbie Meier received the offer to try she accepted the challenge, privately confirming what she had long suspected, her inability to say no.

From the start, the chances for success were slim. To begin with, the new school was to be housed in a seventy-five-year-old tumbledown building in East Harlem, already inhabited by a school whose staff naturally looked upon the newcomers as parasites who would compete for students and resources as basic as the lunchroom and playground.

Adding to the difficulties, Meier's fledgling school was to draw from two of New York's poorest neighborhoods. More than half of the families had an annual income of twelve thousand dollars or less. Forty-five percent of the neighborhood was black; thirty percent Hispanic. It's fair to say that most weren't learning: of New York's thirty-two school districts, the East Harlem students consistently scored last on standardized reading tests. Dropout rates had reached panic proportions. Those who remained enrolled switched schools as in a game of musical chairs. Seventy-five percent never made it to high-school graduation. And there was also the problem of resources. In the first years there was such an acute shortage of chairs, for example, that the youngsters had to carry them from class to class.

In time, though, word got around that something very exciting was going on in this strange new school and that tough, jaded, bored children who were never much interested in class before couldn't wait for school doors to open.

■ **3** ■

THE FIRST LOOK I had at Debbie Meier was to see her storming down a highly waxed corridor in her sensible schoolmarm shoes, swooping to pick up a piece of crumpled paper, and continuing her purposeful stride without missing a beat.

The last place you'll find Debbie is at her desk, an assistant remarked. She was right. Of the three classes visited at random that afternoon, Meier managed to appear in all three, sometimes just observing, sometimes participating, as in Laurie's seventh- and eighth-grade humanities class.

They were preparing to debate this question: Was there one nation or more than one here before the Europeans came? Meier wasn't convinced that the kids understood the principle of gathering evidence to support a point of view. While Laurie was occupied with half the class, Meier angled her sturdy frame into a pint-sized chair and sat among the other team, firing questions in a manner Socrates would have applauded. She was stern yet caring, with an unyielding, no-nonsense quality that had the effect of settling down a group of bouncy boys with the jitters in their legs. She had captured their undivided attention through the force of her presence alone.

"What is it you're trying to prove? Is it that you're trying to prove we are a nation? What's a nation? What's the difference between a nation and a country? What's a country?"

One of the sweet, bright-eyed boys sped off to get a globe and thrust it forward as if to answer her questions. Someone else reached for a battered dictionary. Meier was unimpressed. They tried harder.

"How can you know what you are debating if you don't know what a nation is, what a country is? Canada is right next to us—how would you prove to someone that we are separate nations? Do you need a government to have a nation? Do you need only one religion? Do you need only one kind of money? Do you need borders? What if I told you that I know of at least one nation without borders?"

"Don't make no sense," a youngster volunteered. "Anybody knows you get *killed* with no borders."

"*Doesn't* make *any* sense," she corrected, "and as a matter of fact, what if I tell you that they have fewer wars and deaths than other nations?"

The little one was utterly astonished and thoroughly magnetized by the thought. "Musta had luck on their side," he concluded.

She was thinking of the Bedouins, but it would be several days before the debate team would succeed in prying the information out of her. In the meantime, they had been fired into action, scattering to the library to find the answers.

▪ 4 ▪

THE FIRST STATISTICS generated from Meier's experiment were impressive: The turnover rate had dropped to five percent (less than one-tenth the city-wide average) and almost all of the first graduating class went on to finish high school, while half continued on to college. Test scores were equally encouraging. By 1979, a staggering seventy percent of the sixth-graders tested on a city-wide exam were scoring above their grade level on reading.

But that didn't stop the snipers from expressing their keen

outrage. They couldn't figure out why white kids were attracted to a ghetto neighborhood. And why the same was true for white teachers. Weren't the black and Hispanic kids being shortchanged? They wondered why all the classes had two grades in them, with first- and second-graders lumped together, for example. And why weren't there more textbooks, and traditional curriculums? Whoever heard of anything so wild as an entire year spent studying the vicissitudes of power, or the year before that, immigration? And why were elementary students calling adults by their first names, and doing volunteer work in social services around town, and leaving class for music lessons, or theater rehearsals, or discussion groups on sex, or trips to the bathroom whenever they felt the urge?

It was heresy and the proponents of it the pariahs of the neighborhood.

"Risk is everything, it's the story of my life," Debbie Meier says, taking a long drag on a cigarette she bummed from a co-worker. The spirals of smoke tangle in her unruly gray curls. "I wouldn't know where to begin to tell you about the risks we faced here in the beginning. And that we still face."

It's four o'clock, an hour after the official close of the school day. Meier is slouched in a chair in the classroom that serves as command central. There are ink and crayon stains on her blouse, but appearances are the last thing that concern her. Ideas matter. Though exhausted, she has a nervous kind of energy that will keep her humming long past midnight—reading, studying, and rethinking her reactions to events in the day.

"You saw what happened in Laurie's class today. There's the risk she'll be offended that I usurped her power, so tomorrow I'll have to find a minute to smooth that over, to get her to realize that the kids haven't grasped the concept of evidence and point of view. I have to figure out how to raise it with Laurie without making her feel inadequate, without making her feel as if I'm challenging her control.

"But I assume you want to know about another kind of risk," she continued, "the kind that relates to the survival of what we are trying to do here."

What she's trying to do is nothing short of creating a new system of public education.

"On different days I say it in different ways. Largely my ideas about teaching and learning focus on small-*d* democratic values, by which I mean a respect for diversity, a respect for the possibilities of what every person is capable of, a respect for another person's point of view, a respect for considerable intellectual rigor. . . . My concern is with how students become critical thinkers and problem solvers, which is what a democratic society needs. If we believe that our schools are failing us and that children can't or refuse to learn the basic educational skills, then what we are saying is that democracy is a utopian ideal, an impossibility, and I just don't believe that. There is nothing in the nature of being human, to my knowledge, that makes democracy an impossibility."

Meier took on the job of creating a new school from the rubble of Harlem because she wanted to try out her theories of education. As part of this effort, curriculums are arranged around "core themes" broad enough to encompass a wide variety of projects and learning possibilities.

For example, when third- and fourth-graders were studying cities, they walked neighborhoods, talked to shopkeepers, mapped, made models, and painted landscape murals. With this background, they then developed a mythical city from a blueprint they fashioned, and planned the construction of the houses, making several until they found a design they could agree on. After that, they populated their city with monsters, gods, boats, tools, and fanciful musical instruments. They molded cooking utensils out of clay and wove fabric to clothe their imaginary townsmen.

Is it a rich curriculum that inspires youngsters with wonder and a lust for knowledge new? Perhaps not in the private sector, she explains, but inner-city children haven't had the advantages of these ideas applied on a system-wide basis. There might be the idiosyncratic teacher tucked here and there, but an entire public-school system spanning kindergarten through high school, built on notions of respect and participatory democracy, is something else again. To pull it off required raw boldness and immense patience—not a combination that is politically easy to sustain.

"If you ask me, taking on risk and being more daring is a real important part of creativity. There are some wonderful teachers here who are every bit as good a teacher as I ever was and who have all kinds of ideas but who are considerably less willing than I to take a flier at things. But that's necessary. I'm willing to take on a number of risks at one time. I even put myself in situations where half the time I don't even know what the risks are likely to be."

But isn't that dangerous? Isn't she afraid?

A long silence follows. It's dark out now and a wet December chill seeps through the leaky windows. The school is quiet except for the distant sound of the janitor's radio and the irregular thunder of subway cars rumbling somewhere far beneath us.

"Do you remember that age in adolescence where you didn't believe you could ever die or that any harm would come to you so you took all kinds of risks? In a certain sense, you couldn't really call adolescents courageous because they really don't believe any harm could follow. I'm like that in a way; call it foolishness, or not knowing any better.

"I remember once there was a time when my mother was dead and my father had a stroke and was no longer accessible to me as a possible source of support and my husband and I just divorced, and right then I did something dumb that put the school into a risky situation. I was in danger. Not physical danger, but I knew I had an enemy, a person who wanted to hurt me. And I remember that unique sensation of feeling *scared*. I thought, My God, this must be what people feel more often than I even know. There was a sense of being afraid that I might not make it, that I might not be able to pick myself up, that I might look foolish, that I might have really gone further than I realized. But there's a part of me that's so *impatient* with the results of that feeling that I wall myself off from it. I ground myself and close off to the danger since I *can't stand* what feeling that way would lead to."

What it would lead to is the status quo—playing it safe, following the rules. What it would lead to is the great yawn of boredom born from doing the same old thing in the same old way. That's not Meier's style. She's brimming over with creative ideas she wants to try, changes she wants to make. She's a risk-taker who acts with the unreasoning courage of a visionary.

"I'm willing to take on risk because I'm invested in the project and because I believe in what we are doing here and want it to succeed. The drive is toward that, toward the goal, not the problems. Of course, I don't like to fail. I don't like to make mistakes. I'm afraid of looking foolish. I'm afraid of dying. But I'm not afraid of risk because risk is a part of change, and change is what new ideas are all about."

▫ **5** ▫

IF YOU ACCEPT the proposition that the ability to take on risk is a vital component of doing creative work, the next question, inevitably, is, Where do people find the courage?

The glib, easy answer is that for high achievers with a demonstrated track record, courage is no problem: surely they must assume that they will succeed again and again in each new risky situation. But while it is true that a past record of success is a comfort in uncertain times, not a single person among the forty Fellows cited a reliance on past laurels as the primary source of courage. Every new beginning—whether of a poem, or of a symphony, or of a research project—is as hard and risky as every other beginning. There is always the chance of failure, and so, in the discussion of courage, there was never any suggestion of inflated confidence, never an indication that arrogance carried them through the hard times.

Instead, a certain quiet humility and sense of gratitude prevailed. The courage to create, it seemed, often came not from looking within but from looking *outside* themselves, from relying on something perceived as distinctly larger than their own tiny vulnerable beings.

For some, like Deborah Meier, the external source of strength could be characterized as a belief in a set of values that gave her the confidence to make decisions that ran counter to the public sentiment. Meier's deep-seated belief in an educational system based on democracy and the potential of a child's mind carried her through the treacherous struggle with doubt, uncertainty, and despair.

For others—many others—what mattered was to be steeped in the thick juice of family, or warmed by the solidarity of a friend, or uplifted by the encouraging well-timed word from a mentor. Any of these things was catalyst enough to send them arrowing along an irretrievable course of rebelliousness.

Still others, like woodworker Sam Maloof, credited an even higher authority as the source of his courage. It's a difficult concept to express, but the patient Maloof struggles to get it right. "It's like this," he says, and then starts to explain, falters mid-sentence, knots his mossy eyebrows together, and starts again. All the while his hands are in motion, gesturing and molding the air. Sam's hands are magnificently expressive: compact and sturdy, strong despite seventy-two years of hard use, deeply etched and darkened to the color of walnuts, with stubby, thick fingers, his nails kept short with a trace of sawdust under them. "It's like this," he says, and starts again.

■ **6** ■

SAM MALOOF WAS thirty-two years old when he abandoned his steady job as a self-taught graphic artist to pursue an uncertain future as a woodworker. Together with his wife, Alfreda, he moved from Ontario clear across country to southern California, the land of his boyhood. Here, against the backdrop of the snowcapped, shadow-streaked San Gabriel Mountains, he settled in the nucleus of a small lemon grove. Over time he cultivated the land, adding orange, avocado, sweet plum, fig, olive, and apricot trees. He also built a thousand-square-foot workshop, and a home for his family.

The house, perhaps the best reflection of the man himself, requires an extra word. It's a hand-hewn thing, possessing the common strength and bulk of the hands that raised it. Both peculiar and dramatic, it is also *alive* in a way that inanimate things are not supposed to be.

In most people's homes it is possible for a stranger, by concentrating, to sense or construct in his mind's eye an approximation of the whole house and the relationship of its various parts. But when you are seated quietly in any one spot of Sam's magical mystical creation, it is utterly impossible to sense the whole of the place, let alone the spatial relationships, one room to the next. Rooms open up into halls, which lead to more rooms and middle sorts of spaces that are neither foyers nor passageways, with more doors and vaulted middles and spiral staircases and balconies that open up into more rooms.

It's not uncommon, even, for the first-time visitor to circle in and around the courtyard, ducking under branches heavy with brilliant yellow fruit, trying to decide which of the many doors was meant to serve as the main entrance . . . and so, in the end, you decide to knock timidly on all the doors until

Freda opens one of them and kindly invites you in, explaining that Sam is out back in his shop but you're welcome to have a seat in the living room. With that she stirs the fire in the cast-iron stove and disappears in the direction of some wonderful peppery-smelling corn chowder, leaving you to puzzle out just which space was meant to qualify as the living room and feeling something like Goldilocks trying out all the different chairs, especially Sam's graceful, long-tailed rocking chairs, silken to the touch, and shaped with a profound understanding of a body's need to rest.

Over the years, Sam built his home and every piece of furniture in it out of the scraps he could spare from his workshop. Gnarled roots for door latches, uprooted tree stumps buffed back to life, strange sticks for hinges, twisted beams in the rafters, odd slabs of sun-bleached and earth-darkened woods—every surface has grain and texture. Filled with the riotous color of a lifetime collection of art, the house *breathes* with its own power. Earthen pots and textiles, baskets and ceramics, are not "arranged" per se but artfully placed, high or low, according to his own sensibility.

The communion with wood is unmistakable. Cypress, black walnut, ebony that has been cured eight years out in the yard, eucalyptus, English yew flecked with reds and golds, Brazilian rosewood, teak, English brown oak, cherry, lemon wood that dries to look like ivory, Indian sycamore, poplar—he's been called the Hemingway of hardwood, the dean of American woodworking.

People turn up at his door to see his pieces and to place an order. Using his home as a showcase, Sam handles all his own transactions, never resorting to an agent, gallery, or brochure. The idea of a craftsman selling his own wares is almost a medieval concept in these highly commercialized times. A couple of decades ago he was offered advances and projected royalties in excess of twenty-two million dollars for the rights to mass-produce a line of his pieces. He refused. Sam likes to work with his hands. He likes the tangy smell of wood and the sensuousness of rubbing it to a gentle gleam. He revels in making every piece himself, no two alike, each one signed on the underside.

Actors, presidents of the United States, businessmen, well-known artists, museum curators—they all come to see this man who barely finished high school. They stay for lunch or for dinner or for the weekend. They chat with Freda, resting their elbows on tables that have never known the feel of a tablecloth. They look, they touch, they sigh with admiration. Sam's rocking chairs alone now sell for about ten thousand dollars apiece. One sits in the White House. When he started, he felt lucky indeed to collect an even hundred.

It took tremendous courage to strike out on his own as a woodworker, fashioning furniture out of cast-off railroad box-cars. It took tremendous conviction to adhere to the same set of simple designs for more than forty years, never changing to follow the whim of fashion, never deviating from the clean serene lines that characterize the pious beauty of his pieces. It took tremendous strength to adhere to his craft when his Lebanese relatives all clucked their tongues and shook their heads, remarking on how sad it was, how shameful, that poor Sam had to make his living with his hands.

In talking about the risks associated with a creative enterprise, one must inevitably address the issue of courage. Where did Sam Maloof find the courage?

"Well, certainly the risks were enormous," he says, fingertips pressed together, his voice as rich and deep as his wood, "but I've always believed in living a good life, aiming myself—oh, how shall I put it?—aiming myself *true*. I never worried too much about material security. I used to tell Freda that if we could just make five hundred a month, why, that was all we ever needed. It was a spiritual security that mattered. I really believed in the importance of living right and being thankful and grateful. If your mind is right, I think that all things fall into place."

Like many of the other Fellows, Maloof derives his strength

from resorting to something outside himself, from an appeal to an honorable code of conduct, an elevated sense of order, to a deep, abiding faith. He lives an ethical, right-minded life and cites integrity as the most important part of his work and of his creativity.

"I try to live right. I always try to adhere to what I think is right, and that, to me, is the most important part of creative work. Fashion comes and goes, but my pieces have to have the integrity of my vision. When I was just starting out, I made a piece once that the customer dictated and I ended up feeling so bad about the whole thing I just gave it to him. Didn't charge him anything. I just wanted to get rid of it. It wasn't right. It didn't come from the right place.

"And I tell other people about living right. I teach workshops. I have no secrets. If I can make it easier for someone than it was for me, I'm happy to do it. I share everything I know."

He pauses a moment, his grave, dark, watchful eyes moving methodically across the room, noting each of his pieces, remembering the trouble he had with that music stand, the satisfaction he felt with that baby cradle, the care he took over that chair, the delight he experienced in fashioning that rarely seen hinge.

"When people come to me and say how they are caught in jobs that they hate and how they really want to work with wood, I feel bad for them because of the courage they lack. I've never had a bad day. But I tell them, too, there are risks. I try not to paint a rosy picture. So many risks—economic, spiritual, emotional. You may sell, you might not sell. We didn't know from week to week if we'd earn anything. You have to work maybe twelve, fourteen hours a day. I see in my mind what I want to make. I risk my time and a good piece of wood to do it. There's the risk that in the transformation I won't match the vision in my mind. But I believe in aiming myself true and that frees me to accept those risks."

From the very beginning to the present day Sam believes in the unseen influences that guide and fuel him. That is the source of his risk-taking, of his courage to create. He gives a quiet thanks, he shows respect, he behaves in the most correct way he knows how, and then he sits down to make a piece of furniture.

■ 7 ■

SPEND ENOUGH TIME with Sam Maloof, falling into the rhythms of his workshop—the quiet sounds of his gentle josh-ing, the soft whispered hush of a piece of wood being sanded, oiled, caressed with his thumb—and you begin to wonder if, in order to solve the riddle of creativity, we will, after all, need to construct an entire scaffolding of theology. How *do* people assume risk? I would like to know—precisely. Where *do* people turn for the courage to run along ahead of the others or to lag behind awhile to look more closely at something while the masses skip on, blithely, contentedly?

Courage, risk, faith, trust, hope, strength—in the fullness of time these notions blend together into one seamless inquiry. Nonetheless, we try so hard to pin down these concepts as neatly as the wings of a butterfly in a sixth-grade science proj-ect. It's not that simple, not that crisp.

Courage is a difficult, serious, weighty concept. The honest man recognizes the hardships of it and is acutely aware of what he perceives as his constant deficit in this regard. Take A. K. Ramanujan. After months of trying to contact the emi-nent poet, translator, MacArthur Fellow, and all-around in-tellectual, a faintly plaintive and distant reply, which demurred on the basis of time, travel, and the terror of interviews, turned up in my mailbox. The picture on the postcard, by no means chosen casually, was a photograph of a snowbound path slicing through a section of the University of Chicago. On the path were two figures coming at each other but with heads tucked down against the cold, destined to miss even the most casual eye contact with one another.

Which is another way of saying, fear touches everyone—

even the successful people, the golden boys, the people who give the appearance of passing through life with their hands deep in their pockets, a whistle on their lips. To take on risk you need to conquer fear, at least temporarily, at least occasionally. It can be done, especially if you look outside yourself for a strong ledge to stand on, at least temporarily, at least occasionally.

■

STAYING LOOSE

ONE HEARS THE STORIES—how can you help hearing the
stories?—of how great creative discoveries are born. In all of
them, there comes a point of irresistible drama. "And just at
that moment," the narrator says, his voice at a whisper for
greater effect, "the dark storm clouds broke and a shaft of
brilliant light came down touching the rippled surface of waters
in the very instant that something lovely and magical
emerged."

From the fateful apple falling on Newton's head to Samuel
Taylor Coleridge's widely heralded epic poem "Kubla
Khan"—said to have popped into his mind whole while he
was enjoying an opium-inspired reverie one day—such tales
always build to a decisive moment of inspiration, heavily
weighted for dramatic emphasis, embellished with every telling.

The best of these vivid tales of discoveries are wonderfully
inspiring—but misleading. What they underemphasize, and
occasionally omit mention of entirely, is the long period of
uncertainty that precedes the magic moment of epiphany. It's
not simply the question of hard work that's been neglected.
More to the point is that by failing to pay proper heed to the
long dance with uncertainty that precedes most creative breakthroughs, these stories neglect the very soil from which the
creative flower blooms. Cut short the floundering and you've

cut short the possible creative outcomes. Cheat on the chaotic stumbling-about, and you've robbed yourself of the raw stuff that feeds the imagination.

For many of us, staying loose is an uncomfortable, unsettling feeling if sustained for too long. Ambiguity is confusing, even alarming. We like to frame our inquiries in sharply delineated terms and prefer clean, tidy resolutions to yes or no decisions. Fuzzy circumstances, the ragtag and bobtail of daily uncertainty, exhaust us. It's much nicer, we think, to have our options cast as either black or white, entirely excluding the hazy middle zones of gray.

Creative people, by contrast, seem to have a greater tolerance for the ambiguous circumstances that begin most projects and are more accepting, even welcoming, of this unstructured time. They aren't lusting after quick outcomes or definitive bottom lines. They are more willing to entertain a prolonged period of leisurely drifting about, curious to see where the unpredictable currents will take them. From this lightness of spirit come the fruits of imagination; there will be plenty of time for the sweat of exertion later on.

This period of uncertainty was addressed by many of the MacArthur Fellows. It's what the poet Douglas Crase was referring to when he spoke of "the dim and mushy start" of a poem. It's what the young Mayan scholar David Stuart is up to when he sifts randomly through stacks of hieroglyphics with nothing in particular on his mind. It's what neurophysiologist Robert Shapley was referring to when he commented—only partly in jest—that what distinguishes a good experimental lab from an inferior one is the large quantity of junk kept about that can be cannibalized to suit the needs of a project. It's what political scientist Robert Axelrod is doing when he routinely scans magazines having nothing whatsoever to do with his field. And it is precisely how filmmaker Frederick Wiseman, a master of uncertainty, the grandmaster of the documentary, goes about making his movies. In fact, staying loose is so great a part of Wiseman's methods that it's well worth taking a closer look at how he operates.

□ **2** □

THE FIRST FILM Fred Wiseman ever made is titled *Titicut Follies* (1967) and tells the story of inmates at the Massachusetts Hospital for the Criminally Insane. In typical Wiseman style, it opens right in the middle of action. There is no narrator, no melody, no sonorous introduction of any kind to orient the viewer.

Without warning, the audience is plunked into the intense black-and-white world of naked men, trying feebly to hide their genitals at bath time. We hear the pathetic thud of a man whacking his head against a wall. We witness the convulsive rage of frustrated patients kept captive in stark white rooms. We eavesdrop on guards who make small talk in the corridors, and in that moment we despise them for their indifference and callousness.

But, as in all Wiseman movies, it gets worse.

In a sequence one would pay dearly to forget, we see the hated guards joking around with a doctor who is force-feeding an elderly patient. The doctor is patently bored with the task. A cigarette dangles from his lips. Next we see the guards gently shaving the old man, his dried-out beak of a nose pointing straight up as if it were a sail in the wind. We see the patient's absent eyes, the fly crawling on his white forehead. But once again the camera shifts and we see the doctor's cigarette ash lengthening over the patient's feed tube.

It doesn't make sense, this cutting back and forth between the feeding and the shaving, but by this time Wiseman has us fixed pop-eyed to the screen. Back and forth the camera swings, to the doctor then the guards, to the guards then the doctor, until finally, in a moment that freezes the blood, we realize what's going on: the old-timer is dead and the guards whom we had condemned for their lack of humanity were performing the last ritual of a shave with a kind of wrenching tenderness that makes us ashamed for having so misconstrued the complexity of their emotions.

Fred Wiseman was thirty-six when he made this film, too old, some might say, to have given up his solid law career in order to take up, willy-nilly, some artsy thing like filmmaking. That he had only a peripheral idea of how to make a film didn't discourage him. He was too busy hustling up money, arranging permission to film, and renting equipment that he couldn't borrow with that low-key charm of his.

He was also assembling a crew. It consisted of a young writer (it apparently not being recognized in this first Wiseman film that a writer was unnecessary), a photographer whose only previous credit was a self-financed anthropological study of African bushmen, and Fred, who was supposed to do the even though he had never done it before.

David Eames, the writer on this reckless mission, later recalled in an article for *The New York Times Magazine* (October 2, 1977): "I don't think Fred had any notion that this project, so vaguely conceived, so loosely defined, so fuzzy and wacky and chancy, would turn out to be, a long year later, a film called *Titicut Follies*. Which is not to suggest he didn't now what he was doing. He did, after a fashion. 'There's a film there, there's a film there,' he would tell me. Part of his genius lies in his unilateral trust in his own instincts and his unswerving dedication to them. *Follies* was made on a joke budget; friends were skeptical; wives got cranky; we quarreled among ourselves far into the night on more than one occasion; we began to smell of the place we were filming—of rancid cooking oil and disinfectant. Wiseman and I began to wonder—at least I know I did—what the hell it was that we were up to. But if Fred wondered, he kept it to himself."

Titicut Follies attracted a lot of attention at the 1967 New York Film Festival, won awards in Germany and Italy, and was shown commercially for a very short time until the Commonwealth of Massachusetts sued, claiming that Wiseman violated an oral agreement to let the facility view the film before it was released. There were also allegations that he failed to get written consents from the inmates and that privacy rights were violated.

Wiseman lost the case, in part thanks to the alleged turncoat behavior of Elliot Richardson, then Lieutenant Governor, who Wiseman has said helped him to secure permission to make the film and privately praised it—until the trouble started. (An old newspaper photo of Richardson hung for years above the toilet at Zipporah Films, Wiseman's Cambridge film studio.) As a result, Wiseman was barred from showing the film to anyone but mental health personnel, law students, and professionals in related fields. The Supreme Court has twice refused to review the case, but still, more than twenty years later, he continues to file legal papers in the hope that his First Amendment rights will be restored.

"It's a dubious distinction," he explains one cold morning in New York. "To my knowledge, it is the only document of any sort—films, books, plays—in American constitutional history that has a partial ban on its use other than a matter involving national security or obscenity."

Despite the viewing restrictions *Titicut Follies* went on to become a legend among civil libertarians; Wiseman went on to make a film a year. His subject—a look at the way we live, our institutions, our stress—hasn't changed. His style remains blunt and austere. Even his titles are stark and minimalist: *High School, The Store, Hospital, Primate, Meat.* . . . And, like *Follies*, the succession of films that followed provoked the mixed reaction of disgust and applause, libel and legend.

▪ **3** ▪

"I DON'T DO MUCH advance work at all," Wiseman says. "The most I do is spend a day trying to get a sense of the geography, what the daily routine is, where the centers of power are. I do that by simply walking around talking to people, looking at the daily bulletin if that exists, asking when there are regular staff meetings, who the chiefs of the various sections are, that sort of thing. I think of the shooting of the film as the research. I don't like to be at a place not prepared to shoot what's going on. If some great event goes on and you're not there and you don't know about it, you don't know what you've missed. But if you're there and something spectacular happens, you want to be in a position to film it."

It's a method of working that illustrates his tremendous capacity for floating free in a period of uncertainty. All of his movie projects begin the same way: with only a very broadly construed feeling for the subject matter, almost no preparation or research, and as few preconceptions as possible about what he'll find in the institution he has decided to investigate.

He enters a scene quietly, casually. He leans up against walls, he wanders, he lingers, he observes. He doesn't work with a script (hence no need for writers). He doesn't stage the action. He doesn't direct the people he shoots. In these initial weeks of the project, he isn't interested in proving a point or fleshing out a theory or chasing down an angle. He rambles. He roams. He sinks into the chaotic welter of detail and doesn't worry about trying to make sense of it all.

A modestly built man with dark, soulful eyes and a shy grin that never quite breaks the surface, he is far from intimidating, which helps in his effort not to call attention to himself. He has the kind of earthy weather-creased face that Eames has called "crooked" and "Dickensian." This morning he's dressed in his usual attire: plain wrinkled clothes, the color an olive-green shirt or gray pants would become if baked in the sun. There is nothing slick about him and that includes his hairstyle, a hopelessly deranged tangle more suited to a Bowery bum than to an acclaimed master of the documentary. Everything about him is calculated to melt into the walls. He is geared to listen. Even his ears tilt forward.

When he happens upon something interesting, he signals his photographer to start filming. An old pro now, Wiseman handles the sound, microphone in hand. A third person, the last member of the on-site team, runs relays to and from the airport to get the film cans shuttled up to Zipporah Films for processing.

The approach is loose, hazy, open. Some of what he films makes no sense to him. Some of the action is cryptic, the dialogue obscured, the motivation disguised. He films it anyway. He might film a classroom or a jail cell a dozen or two dozen times, not at all sure what it is that attracts him to it. He'll think about it later. In the meantime, he stays open, available.

"I think if these films work, it's because they: (1) suggest some of the complexity of what's going on in a place; (2) illustrate a wide range of human experience and resist easy, simpleminded explanations; and (3) represent a variety of points, sometimes contradictory, sometimes complementary, and frequently ambiguous because that's the way reality is."

Four to six weeks later Wiseman stops filming, somehow knowing that he has accumulated enough material. Back in his editing studio on the top floor of the small town house occupied by Zipporah Films, a disorganized mess awaits him: fifty to ninety hours of unordered film. For the remainder of the year he'll try to edit the hundred thousand feet into the essential two or three thousand. The editing process—creating form from chaos—is at the heart of his art, but that involves the exercise of critical judgment, an aspect of creativity I'll come to later. For now, the point to notice is that in the beginning of a creative effort, a period of uncertainty is a helpful state of affairs.

■ **4** ■

THE WAY WISEMAN WORKS, open to any and all possibilities in the early stages of a production, is consistent with what the cognitive psychologists are beginning to tell us about the way all sorts of other creative people work.

Cognitive psychology is that emerging territory of science that stakes a claim to such issues as how memory works, how we perceive shapes and sounds, and how we fashion and manipulate symbols. These are the types of concerns that go to the core of what it means to be creative, what it means to construct the makeup of our daily existence purposefully. It's a field that bumps up against philosophy, stealing all the best and most enticing issues for itself: What is thought? Why do human beings create? How do we perceive reality? What are dreams? How does the mind perform the miracle of conceiving something new?

The findings coming out of such heady investigations allow us to creep ever forward toward a deeper understanding of the nature of a creative enterprise. Harvard-based D. N. Perkins, in *The Mind's Best Work*, talks about one such study, conducted by researchers Jacob Getzels and Mihaly Csikszentmihalyi, which demonstrates that a period of rambling discovery at the start of a creatively minded project is preferable to premature closure.

In the experiment, art students were asked to select and arrange objects from which they were to create a still-life drawing. Analyzing the results, the team discovered a relationship between the procedures of the students and the quality of their products and professional standing seven years later. The most creative among them (as judged by their eventual commercial success, which in a field as slippery as creativity is as valid a standard as any) played with more objects, inspected them more carefully, and chose more unusual objects for their compositions. They tended not to have a clear and precise idea of the sort of principle they wanted to capture in their drawings, but rather discovered the arrangement through the handling, positioning, and repositioning of the objects. And even as they proceeded to finalize their drawings, they continued to change and adjust the position of the objects as well as to experiment with different paper.

Whatever name you ascribe to this style of working—flexibility, open-mindedness, divergent thinking—staying loose in the early stages of a project greatly improves the chances for a more creative result.

But why?

One reason is that a loose, uncensored approach increases the amount of material you have to work with. Volume alone produces options; options permit the exercise of opinion and taste.

This is the philosophy that gave rise to the so-called fluency tests popular in the 1950s, but dusted off and enlivened by modern-day "innovation management" firms. At times the drills resemble parlor games. Morton Hunt, in his admirable work *The Universe Within*, talks about a couple of the fun ones:

How many uses can you think of for a brick? Build a house, line a path, make a chimney, a wall, a bench, a barbecue, a doorstop, a weight, an anchor. Or break up the brick and call it modern art, or freeze the pieces and use them as nonmelting ice cubes. Or use it as a murder weapon to kill a cat and then deep-six the corpse.

A professor asks a physics student to determine the height of a building with the aid of a barometer. Tie a string on it, lower it from the roof, and measure the length. Drop it from the top, time the fall, and calculate the distance by using a free-fall formula. Compare the shadow of the building to the shadow of the barometer and work out the ratio. Offer the barometer to the building's superintendent in exchange for the information.

Some cognitive psychologists criticize the fluency approach

on the grounds that quantity does not necessarily guarantee quality. The answer the professor was looking for, Hunt tells us, was to take the barometer to the roof, record the difference in air pressure between the top and the ground, and convert the difference into an altitude reading.

But apart from the sheer fluency of ideas, there is another reason to embrace a period of rambling discovery—the possibility of being exposed to influences that at first appear to be completely unrelated to the work at hand. What blocks a creative solution to a problem is often an overly narrow and single-minded concentration from a single frame of reference. The person who can combine frames of reference and draw connections between ostensibly unrelated points of view is likely to be the one who makes the creative breakthrough.

That's the moral of the story of Archimedes and the King of Syracuse. The king had received a beautiful crown of filigreed gold, the story goes, which he suspected had been adulterated with silver. Archimedes was charged with investigating the matter, and though he knew the weight of gold per volume measure, the problem was to determine the volume without melting down the crown. He meditated on the problem for days and days, but always came up against the same stumbling block: how do you measure the volume of an irregular shape? One day, tuckered out from his frustrated efforts, he drew a bath and was lowering himself into it when the solution occurred to him: a solid object displaces water of a volume equal to its own. Eureka.

It's an old story, which can be easily updated. Consider, for example, the experience of Synectics, a creative consulting firm godfathered by George Prince. (The firm takes its name, incidentally, from the Greek meaning "connections," or the bringing together of diverse elements.) Harnessing a grab bag of techniques ranging from colored pens to metaphors, Synectics seminars bring alive the notion of idea generation through connected irrelevance.

Charged, for example, with the mission of coming up with a method for reducing the vandalism of telephones, the firm considered a variety of images, including the incredibly durable mesas that dominate the Southwest. From that emerged the idea for a telephone built into the side of a building.

A similar type of consulting group, the Invention Section at the Cambridge firm Arthur D. Little, gets the credit for this one: Asked by a client to discover a new kind of can opener, the leader of the think team presented the problem simply as one of "opening." This led to a discussion of all kinds of mechanical devices, until finally someone mentioned the soft seam of Mother Nature's pea pod. This, in turn, inspired the group to consider the possibilities of nonmechanical devices—such as today's plastic strips on juice cans and cookie-batter rolls that pop open with a whack on the edge of a counter. It was a creative leap in reasoning made possible by defining the problem very broadly from the outset.

The idea of breaking out of a single frame of reference is not an unfamiliar one to many of the MacArthur recipients. Poet and essayist Joseph Brodsky reported that he listened to music often, especially Haydn, as a student of literature can pick up a lot of pointers on composition from composers. Vision scientist Robert Shapley, a man who spends a lot of time trying to figure out how the eye perceives shading and color, was very much moved by a show he saw of Caravaggio's work. Fred Wiseman reads poetry and looks at art to see how others have solved some of the same problems he faces. So does theater director Peter Sellars. Environmentalist Lester Brown makes it a point not to hire impressively educated specialists to staff Worldwatch, his Washington, D.C., think tank, so that he can avoid "hardening of the categories."

Staying loose, allowing yourself the freedom to ramble, opening yourself up to outside influences, keeping a flexible mind willing to entertain all sorts of notions and avenues—this is the attitude that is most appropriate for the start of any project where the aim is to generate something new.

▪ 5 ▪

THE MESSAGE LIGHT on my answering machine was blinking. "Hi, it's Dan Starer [my research assistant]. Three o'clock
on Thursday. Listen, I ran that computer search you asked
for. Are you ready for this? Six thousand eight hundred
twenty-one hits on creativity in print from 1967 to date—and
those are just the ones in English. Maybe you better call.
Thanks. Bye."

SETTING UP THE CONDITIONS

▪ 1 ▪

THE LIGHT BULB, the compass, the ceiling panel of the Sistine Chapel, which shows a life-giving God fingering a poorly prepared Adam—how perfectly contained and self-sufficient all of these creative accomplishments must have appeared when the world first took notice.

The printed circuit board, the calculator, the compact disc, the muon (the latest in the Greek alphabet soup that describes the inner life of an atom)—unless one had been intimately involved with the research or at least following the developments from the bleachers, it looks as if these things simply burst on the scene without warning or foreshadow.

What an incredibly brilliant discovery, we say, lingering over the newspaper at the breakfast table. How creative. Such potential. What a moneymaker. And why didn't I think of it first?

To our eyes, these striking moments of creativity stand as magnificent monuments that appear so suddenly and with such impact, we assume a genius has been at work. The appeal of such an assumption is strong. It's far nicer to think in terms of a mighty hand stretching down from the heavens sowing genius in the land than it is to believe in the kind of tedious plodding that goes into the cultivation of a creative idea. It's far preferable to believe in thunderbolts than it is to have to face up to the mundane, trivial workaday world. It might come as a disappointment, then, to realize that behind any creative piece of work is a lot of earthbound effort, part of which is concerned with the conscious arrangement of the conditions suitable for encouraging one's creative impulses.

What conditions?

It's a question everyone must decide for him- or herself. Taste and instinct serve in this effort. So do trial and error, superstition, and accident. Certain conditions we might require—lots of time, say, or money, a comfortable room, a sturdy, nurturing friend, a housekeeper, the right kinds of stimulation—are more or less things we can influence. But other conditions, prime among them being the receptiveness of the culture, matter dearly to the creative process but resist manipulation.

The solution: you do what you can to form a harmonious marriage of the enabling conditions and hope that the rest falls into place of its own accord.

◻ **2** ◻

DOUGLAS CRASE, a MacArthur Fellow and poet, sets out a dish of freshly iced sweet rolls and two sea-blue earthenware mugs filled with very strong, pitch-black coffee. He stands back to inspect the offering, his blade-thin frame casting a long, arcing shadow across the room. Something is missing. The napkins. He fishes two out of his blue-jean pocket and then settles lightly on the couch, satisfied that he has created the conditions suitable for a conversation about poetry and the creative impulse.

If he had been writing this afternoon instead of talking, he would have set up different conditions for himself. He would have been seated at his desk away from the windows, he probably would have done without the pastry, and he wouldn't, presumably, be wearing that tie.

It seems like a modest list of needs: a familiar desk, a room without distraction, comfortable clothes. "The conditions suitable to inspiring a poem," I mutter half aloud, but in the presence of a poet, words must be meted out very carefully. A good poet is on intimate terms with language and listens with finely tuned ears.

"Inspiration? Did you say inspiration?" Crase sighs and falls quiet; the unnaturally loud ticking of a pendulum marks the minutes of silent contemplation.

"Inspiration is a funny concept, and I think it gets in the way sometimes more than it does any good. If you think of those moments when you were really writing well and turning out something you are really happy with and that you're not ashamed to look at for the rest of your life, often you think it's inspiration because you don't know *exactly* how it got there. You look at it and think, This is so much better than I could possibly do. I must have been inspired.

"But if you then think back to that moment and try to reconstruct in your mind how the moment was contrived, how it was arranged, and what the conditions were for that so-called inspiration to happen, it seems to me that you can try to reproduce those conditions. And if you reproduce those conditions it seems to me you have increased the probability that the 'inspiration' will visit again just as certain chemicals combine under some conditions and not under others. Providing those same conditions increases the probability that you're going to get the combustion, the combination, the fertilization. An event just might take place."

This is not idle speculation on his part. Crase, a former law student, has evidence:

"You can go looking for things, even if you don't know what you're looking for, just by setting up the conditions you know yourself to favor. I had a poem once that was a tremendous problem for me. It just wouldn't—well, it just wouldn't. It was there and every time I reached for it, it moved a little bit further away. But it eventually turned out in a way that I liked very much, and there were ways that I think helped me to get it."

The poem, called "Cuylerville," appeared in *The Revisionist*, his much heralded first volume of poetry, at times so powerful that it can spark a pulse in even the stoniest of hearts.

"To begin with, I actually went to the place and just sat and looked around for a long time. Then I identified a piece of music that made me think of the place. It was a piece by Charles Ives which was kind of long and slope-y sounding, and the landscape is kind of long and sloped. As a matter of fact, I made a tape of it so that it would repeat over and over and over and over. I just put that on and listened to it. Eventually, by that means, I got the thing to stop moving away. And then finally, it came closer and I wrote the poem."

Paying attention to the conditions likely to enhance one's creative impulse is something that each person has to sort out for him- or herself. Throughout history the conditions have been as diverse as the creators:

During the Roaring Twenties many noted writers and artists believed Paris to be the only city worth living in. Katherine Anne Porter, on the other hand, spent those years in Mexico and credits it as being essential in cultivating her literary gifts. Geography wasn't Kipling's concern—he insisted on obsidian black ink. Kant wrote in bed, at the same time every day, staring at a tower out his window. When the trees grew to block the view, he had them sliced down. Dickens turned his bed north, believing himself to be enabled by the magnetic forces. Schiller favored the sweet scent of fermenting apples. Balzac swilled rivers of coffee. Proust had his cork-lined room. Beethoven stimulated his mind by pouring ice-cold water over his head.

For Crase, a man of careful tastes and elevated sensibilities, a sense of order and some quiet are helpful. He likes a calm, uncluttered atmosphere so much that for many years he preferred to write at night and sleep during the day.

Suggestive music, evocative landscape, a stretch of time idled away just listening and looking around—these acts seem so commonplace, so available to any of us. For Crase, they are helpful conditions in coaxing the appearance of a coquettish poem. He didn't feel he was wasting his time when he drifted about Cuylerville soaking up the particulars of the terrain, the richness of the history. He didn't feel awkward listening to the same piece of music, over and over again, or if he did, he didn't let it deter him. He made himself comfortable. He tailored an environment for himself that he thought might help in seizing hold of the poem that was as difficult to catch as fish with the open hand. He laid a trap, so to speak, and snared his quarry.

But one man's nostrums will never do for another. Crase now writes during daylight, but he still prefers a clean peaceful environment to do so. Another person, like filmmaker John Sayles, for example, wouldn't care if he was scrawling on the back of a used envelope while sitting in New York's Port Authority bus terminal. Sayles's powers of concentration are unparalleled. Calm is not one of the conditions he needs to work.

Now money, that's something else again.

■ 3 ■

LET'S FACE IT, the tangible tools of poetry—a writing utensil, a bit of paper—are both easy to find and to afford. Filmmaking, on the other hand, is hideously expensive. Salaries, film, music, lighting, cranes, costumes, props, automobiles to smash up in chase scenes, walls to knock down, set designs, transportation costs, security, accommodations, the meal truck for cast and crew, editing equipment, insurance, sound-mixing fees, promotion costs—just the beginning.

It's fine to talk about taking an active role in setting up the necessary conditions for creative work if all you're really talking about is sharpening twenty pencils and getting up with the first light of the day, as was Hemingway's habit. But what about money? It's the stumbling block on which a lot of good intentions fall.

Does this mean in order to do certain kinds of creative work, projects like medical research, for example, or ocean exploration, money is necessary? Is there a correlation between money and creativity?

Yes and no.

Obviously people need money to survive, and certainly some activities require much greater funding than others. But money cannot completely compensate for a lack of talent, for sloth or a flawed vision, or for a pedestrian frame of mind. And the absence of cold hard cash can't keep you from making movies if that's what you want to do and you're clever about it.

To think otherwise suggests not just a lack of imagination but also a failure of the optimism necessary for attracting good things. If you're paying attention, there are buoyant, cheerful accidents in life and strange twists of plot to help you on your way. And when you think about it, it's much nicer to have pleasant things happen to you than to work out every last bit of your life from a master plan, detail by detail.

Furthermore, given enough time—and if you're paying close enough attention—you begin to notice a certain symmetry to the syncopation of chance. The irregularities of chance are pliant; they fit themselves to your needs or you make them fit. Either way, these vague encounters are woven into one's efforts to arrange the proper conditions for creative work.

This isn't Panglossian optimism, by the way. This isn't banality with a prosaic truth tucked within, like the soft center of a chocolate. It's fact.

Let us take, for a moment, one of Sayles's earliest movies, *Return of the Secaucus Seven*. It was made for a paltry sixty thousand dollars from his own pocket—table scraps compared to the forty-million-dollar-and-up box-office extravaganzas that crown the industry sales charts. *Secaucus Seven*, a bittersweet film that looks at 1960s survivors turning thirty, was shot in Sayles's own neighborhood and starred a bunch of his friends, to cut costs. By all rights no self-important critic would have wasted his time reviewing a homemade low-budget film about a questionable subject. But as it happened, fate had another plan: the movie received considerable reviewer attention *precisely because* the critics couldn't believe that a film could be made for sixty thousand dollars.

The myth of money is powerful and cuts through discussions of creativity with a double-edged sword. On the one hand, it's argued that creative work isn't possible *without* money because it's very expensive to chase down ideas or to explore the frontier of one's field. At the other extreme is the argument that creativity isn't possible *with* money—that no good can come from its sheltering effects, which produce fat in the indolent, and a soft shame in the industrious who come by their wealth through questionable means.

The double-faced Janus head of money is reflected within the MacArthur Foundation itself: the fellowship program gives it away as part of the effort to foster creativity; John D. MacArthur hoarded it in the belief that "free" money curdles the brain and robs the industrious of motivation.

Which is it? What's the connection between money and the creative impulse?

Within the context of the MacArthur Prize, the award money is meant to act as a liberating device to free the Fellows to pursue the ideas and projects most exciting to them. Some of the forty people interviewed have banked it, others have used it to clean up debt, many have funded an ongoing or new project, a handful have given it away to causes or friends, a couple have created their own "mini-MacArthur" by using the award money to sponsor young people working in their field or a related field—and in all of these decisions there was a sense of liberation and gratitude. Certainly no one has considered it a bad thing and no one has refused to accept it.

But it's almost unanimous that far more important to creative work than the money itself is the validation that comes with winning the Fellowship—phone calls returned more promptly, an easier time fund-raising, one's pick among a delightful range of sudden opportunities, and the warm congratulatory sock in the arm from the boss.

Time and again the Fellows proffered the same advice: With respect to matters within your control, use your influence to arrange the conditions that you find most helpful to working creatively and don't worry about the money—either you'll find a way to support yourself, or you'll adjust your work to proceed without it, or it will fall into your lap from a beneficent hand like a MacArthur, but no matter what happens, money is not nearly as important a condition to doing creative work as maintaining the confidence and the courage to keep at it.

▪ 4 ▪

COURAGE AND CONFIDENCE become difficult enough to muster, though, when you consider yet another of the enabling conditions for creative work, namely the culture in which you live. Unlike concerns about personal comfort, the right stimulus, good friends, and all the other factors that are more or less within your control, the culture in which you live and breathe is largely beyond individual manipulation. At the same time, however, without a receptive culture your work would long go unrecognized and one easily could die the ignoble death of a man out of step with his times.

Whether something is accepted depends upon its fit with the collective wisdom and the shifting sands of taste. In these money-grubbing times it is easy to forget that an economic motivation may well prove to be ephemeral. Other societies have placed a greater emphasis on other values, such as tradition, tribal loyalty, family honor, patriotism. Societies to come may value still other motivations, such as ecological security or the reach for enlightenment. The point is that one's culture will decide what will be honored and what will be cast aside as parochial or transient.

It's an observation that many of the MacArthur Fellows addressed, among them, Dr. Howard Gardner, a Harvard-based psychologist who is working on questions concerning the nature of intelligence and creativity and other ghostly subjects, all mysteries of the mind.

"My ideas about creativity have changed a lot recently as a result of working with colleagues here at Project Zero and as a result of my recent trips to China," he explains. "I used to think of creativity as a single kind of thing, and as something very much inside the individual; people are creative or they're not. I realize now that that is wrong and, as my colleague Mihaly Csikszentmihalyi puts it, the appropriate question is not *what* is creativity but *where* is creativity. To formulate the question in this way recognizes that there are institutions and people who make decisions about what is going to get noticed and what is not. You don't have creativity unless you have a certain mind engaged in a certain domain of practice with other people looking in at it and saying, 'This makes sense, this doesn't, this is good, this is not, this is original, this is not.' But there is no statute of limitations on these judgments— they can occur immediately or two hundred years later.

"I think of the creative individual as a person who regularly within a domain solves problems or fashions products in ways that are initially original or unusual but eventually become accepted by a wider set of people," he continues, "and whether people are allowed to do something unusual and whether it becomes accepted or not is really a value decision made by the culture. Most cultures throughout human history have not liked creative individuals. They ignored them or they killed them. It was a very effective way of stopping creativity. And, as we have seen in the case of novelist Salman Rushdie, author of *The Satanic Verses*, the urge to kill the innovator remains very much with us today."

You could make the same type of observation with respect to intelligence, he adds. Whether a person's intellectual potential is achieved or not depends on whether it is supported in the culture. "So, you might have the most wonderful logical mathematical potential in the world, but if you aren't in a culture which allows you to pursue math or science or logic or chess, you're lucky if you can add numbers up to ten."

It's a valid point. Taking the long view of talent and gifted achievement, not all cultures have given rise to the same proportionate number of creative geniuses. How does creativity in America measure up against what is happening in Japan, for example, or in China, or in the Soviet Union? How will the twentieth century compare with the twenty-first century, or the twenty-fifth? What factors distinguish fertile times from fairly bland and creatively unproductive periods?

Scholars have pointed to lots of variables to answer this last question, including improvements in health that allowed people to live longer, increased opportunities for education, travel, and the cross-fertilization of ideas, greater wealth allowing for the freedom to pursue creative work, less emphasis on hero worship and the sedulous aping of mentors, and an endorsement by the power figures in the culture that it was permissible to try something different. By the same reasoning, an environment that places a strong emphasis on conformity will tend to squeeze out the exceptional, the deviant, and the innovative.

Coming to grips with one's culture can be a spiny problem even today, though we like to think of ourselves as not only tolerating new ideas but also rewarding and encouraging them. There is pressure to conform to societal expectations, and the maverick must walk a fine line between pursuing his heartfelt work and being fed by the culture in which he lives.

"I mean, once you stop doing things the way other people do them, you're likely to get into trouble," Dr. Gardner continues. "Even in the West, as opposed to more restrictive cultures, if you start taking cues from what interests you instead of what interests the field, you end up very non-mainstream, which could be a problem for the person who wants to be considered *the* eminent psychologist or whatever. You aren't likely to win the awards or the presidential commissions or attain the same strong endorsements and recognition awarded to someone who is working squarely within the field. Initially, anyway, people won't like you. They'll say nasty things about you. You might not get promoted, and so on. So it's a personal decision as well as a societal one."

Life in the margins. It can't be easy but it is exciting, and there are at least a couple of ways of addressing the potentially crippling aspects of an unforgiving culture.

The first clue concerns communication skills and is explained by MacArthur Fellow Dr. Robert Shapley, a scientist interested in investigating that jewel of organic structures, the human eye. Like Howard Gardner, Dr. Shapley confirms that if you're trying to do creative work, by definition you have stepped out of the normal channels for things and into the cracks—if not the void. He notes the dilemma of yearning on the one hand to go beyond the culture with some new idea or discovery or accomplishment but at the same time realizing that if the creative person leaps too far, the culture will probably crucify him.

Strong communication skills help, Shapley notes, in the effort to bridge the gap between what the culture will tolerate and the innovator's vision. The package of skills he's referring to includes the ability to explain ideas cleanly and neatly, the sense to know when and how to do it, and the wit and good manners to do it with charm. In Robert Shapley's experience, it is precisely these interpersonal communication skills that can mean the difference between funding for one's important but speculative project and rejection, even ridicule. Stated another way, as in all matters of the heart, timing and tactics are everything.

A second insight related to mending the rift between cultural expectations and one's own idiosyncratic creative vision comes from MacArthur Fellow J. Kirk T. Varnedoe, Director of Painting and Sculpture at the Museum of Modern Art in New York City. He will be introduced more formally later, but for now, his observations with respect to the societal element of a creative act are apt.

"I am absolutely convinced that creativity is not solely a brain function but a social function as well," he explains. "What's at issue is how something is received in the culture. One of the key things that I think about innovation in modern art is that in order for innovation to survive and be valued it has to have the power to mean different things to different people and to set up very different and often conflicting agendas."

The important point that Varnedoe has seized upon here is that it is utterly incorrect to presume, as many people do, that in order to create something startling and revelatory the creator must completely escape the bounds of society. In fact, just the opposite is true—society has to accept the new discovery or object for it to be valued at all. And acceptance, the argument continues, comes from the creation of a situation where a wide range of people can identify with the work, or at least with some fragment of it.

The immense power of this proposition is best appreciated by seeing it work in a context, and one of the best examples— indeed, "a paradigm instance," says Varnedoe—is cubism.

When cubism took root, between 1907 and 1914, some of the artists painting in this style, as well as some of their admirers, thought that what cubism was all about was smashing the world to pieces—and they liked that very much. They felt a sense of satisfaction in seeing familiar images fractured and reassembled in a bold new way. The idea of decomposing their rational and ordered environment was a welcome and refreshing turn of affairs.

At the other end of the spectrum, another camp of people interpreted this provocative new style in an entirely different way. For these painters and connoisseurs alike, cubism was not at all about breaking apart the world, but to the contrary, a way of geometricizing it. It had to do with rationalization and with making everything into right angles, which was the antithesis of smashing everything up. In fact, some argued that the logical extension of this surprising cubist style was to view it as a mandate for a new kind of Platonic geometry.

"So in the last analysis," Varnedoe continues, "the impact of cubism was so powerful because it could be used by so many different people to do what they wanted to do in often directly contradictory directions. *That* is a kind of defining instance of what makes a successful innovation in the history of art, I think: the provision of a tool or an opening that lets a lot of different people do and think a lot of different things. It doesn't depend on an instrumental transmission of one specific innovation or message, but rather detonates a series of possibilities. There is a creative act involved by the *receiver* as well as by the sender and *that* makes for innovation. Both sides are equally important."

It's a proposition that makes sense not just with respect to art but for the success of any innovation or discovery. New things put a tremendous strain on old opinions. People are slow to change; the resistance to throwing out one's entire stock of old opinions is iron strong. The public is likely to appreciate something creative that stirs up, even cracks apart, the status quo only when they recognize some tiny part of their own agenda being championed. And if the timing is propitious and enough people appreciate some part of the new work, it will be deemed Good and will stand as a creative new contribution to the culture.

Initially, this may sound like heresy. (I can hear a reader wonder, "Are you telling me that I have to compromise my work to make it palatable to the ignorant and fearful masses? Are you telling me I have to tolerate diametrically opposed interpretations of what I am trying to accomplish? Why should I bother to dilute the consequences of my new creation, or suffer the misinterpretation of the viewing public, or allow my work to be used to accomplish agendas or support conclusions that I never intended and may not even agree with?")

But there is another, more humanistic way of looking at it. When a work or idea is made or presented in such a fashion that it is *accessible* to the viewing public, not only does the work stand a greater chance for survival (in itself a powerful motivation to look kindly upon the varying interpretations), but there is also a ripple effect to enjoy—from your new thing a viewer gains the insight or the confidence to develop his new thing, and from his new thing another person goes off and discovers yet another new thing, and so on. Thus we progress as a culture, inch by inch.

LEARNING THROUGH DOING

(Three Scenes from the Art World)

■ 1 ■

AT WHAT POINT can a person call himself an artist?

Take painting. In order to call himself an artist, does a painter have to paint every day? Does he have to accumulate a body of work that shows a progression of style and theme? Is it necessary that he find an appreciative audience? Does he have to sell his paintings? Or achieve critical acclaim? Need he associate with other artists and discuss aesthetics deep into the night? Must he be invited to show in important galleries?

If the answers to these questions are yes, then at the precociously young age of twenty-nine, MacArthur Fellow Robert Irwin had attained the stature of an artist. With little difficulty he had sailed through art school, produced an impressive body of work, associated with other artists, and was having one-man shows of his semiabstract landscapes at Los Angeles's Landau Gallery, at the time one of the most prestigious and influential galleries on the West Coast. You might say he had it made.

But for Irwin, having all the *trappings* of an artist's life was not at all the same thing as *being* an artist. Though he might have looked like one, and acted like one, and suffered like one, he recognized that these were all superficial gestures that didn't amount to more than a façade, analogous, say, to the way young boys in a Little League game will imitate the pros in the way they chew gum in the corners of their mouths and knock the dirt out of their spikes.

For Irwin, the decision that he wasn't an artist was a realization that despite his training, the long hours of practice, and the early bloom of success, he still had everything to learn about art before he could really cultivate the depths of his creativity. Put another way, what Irwin realized is that ignorance makes us presume too much.

This realization was a major turning point in Irwin's progression as a visual creator. From this beginning he buried himself in an intense, highly personal, almost hypnotic self-tutorial that culminated in his work moving up, out, and beyond studio life—even beyond the canvas itself. Today he is occupied with environmental sculptures and numerous controversial works for public spaces. But how he got here is an exceptional story about how and why he penetrated the depths of his field, diving down to the very bottom of the well of knowledge. It's a story of intense dedication that underscores a simple truth: You can't do creative work unless you *know*—intellectually, or spiritually, or instinctively—what you're talking about. A glib approach to creative work rarely endures and almost never conveys the same power or importance as a work based on intimate knowledge, and the intimacy comes from the doing. Not the puritanical, closed-kneed doing of science or the aloof, fussy gilding of high art, but an honest kind of doing—for one's own self and in the service of accumulating knowledge.

◼ **2** ◼

IRWIN'S UNUSUAL STORY begins some thirty years ago. He was living in Los Angeles, then wide-open, freewheeling territory, land of the unblinking sun, light-years from the buttoned-down rules of New York. Irwin was in his early thirties, bobbing and weaving with the abstract expressionists, and enjoying a considerable reputation.

Increasingly, though, he was dissatisfied with this style of painting. Part of his discontent had to do with the notion of "an image" and how virtually anything in the abstract-expressionist mode could be made to stand for something else. It bothered him that an element of a painting could be made to "read" as an image: a squiggle suggesting a rainbow, for example, or a man leaning over, or a bridge. It disturbed him to think that—even if only for a split second—the painting looked *like* something else and was no longer simply the painting itself. (Taking this to the extreme, for a long time Irwin did not allow his work to be photographed because he felt that it robbed the painting of its physical immediacy.)

Mulling over the idea of image he began to question both what art was all about and his role as an artist. Eventually he came around to the notion that a simple horizontal line moving across a solid colored field was the least likely image to be "read" as something else. But the more Irwin worked with his line painting, the more complicated it became for him, the more questions it presented about the whole "art act," until eventually he withdrew from the distractions of daily life and confined himself to his studio, painting the same painting over and over and over again, trying with each effort to penetrate it and understand more fully the lengths of his perceptive abilities.

One month passed in this dedicated monastic existence, then two, then twelve, then twenty-two, and still Irwin continued to paint the same painting over and over again in his self-imposed isolation. Seen in retrospect, it was the behavior of a young, aberrant, devout man who was destined either to become great or to destroy himself.

Working seven days a week, often from twelve to fifteen hours a day, he concentrated on the same picture: a seven-foot-by-seven-foot bright orange or yellow field with two parallel lines running across it. At first, the placement of the lines became Irwin's primary concern. Then it became a question of examining his aesthetic judgment. He asked himself why he placed the line at the height he did and what that meant in terms of the values and morals he possessed.

(And one of the better ways to appreciate the seriousness with which Irwin *still* continues to question the values and morals that inform his art is to read the catalog notes of his exhibitions, the occasional published interview he has granted, and, above all, his own book, *Being and Circumstance: Notes Toward a Conditional Art*. To even the casual reader, it is immediately evident that there is nothing casual about Irwin's logic. Indeed, there is a certain gravity to the rhetoric that is emphatic, startling, pious, didactic, messianic, Olympian. Long a student of political theory, Irwin struggles to knit together all the pieces of his experience, from his study of the master painters and philosophers to his encounters at the racetrack where he used to spend considerable time. It's an ambitious task, made especially feverish when taken on by one so ardently committed to getting it right and expressing it precisely. In fact, in his effort to make sense of the world, Irwin often shakes everyday words loose from their meanings and attaches his own, specialized definitions. To understand the man, then, requires that one first learn the language he is speaking. But even then, his is a starched logic that is at once wild and vaulting, yet wilting to think on. The story continues.)

Back in the studio Irwin forced himself to stare at the painting, looking at it for hour after hour, nodding off from time to time for fifteen-, maybe twenty-minute naps. He slept without taking particular notice of it, and when he awoke he was neither tired nor rested but blank and fresh, like a white canvas.

When he came around, the same questions awaited him: Should he move the lines up a fraction of an inch? What did they say about his own cultural prejudices? Didn't they simply reflect his own social conditioning for order? If he moved them, would it prove that he had broken out of such conditioning or that he was merely being clever?

Staring at his much-meditated lines in this way had the effect on him of emptying them of content. The lines were just lines—there was nothing lyrical there to give vent to the soul. He was bored, which, curiously, he found liberating—and useful. Art for him, at this stage in his life, had less to do with inspiration, the Muse, and all that nonsense, than it did with rigorous self-discipline and an exploration of his sensibilities and his aesthetic process. When he got restless he didn't allow himself to get up and go do something—run an errand, raid the refrigerator, read the newspaper, buy a Coke. He sat and he concentrated. He asked himself questions, each question leading to another question, the seriousness of his inquiry saving him from jumping to shallow and trivial conclusions. Irwin wasn't interested in facile conclusions. To the contrary, he wanted to peel away his superficiality.

And at the end of two years there were ten paintings in all. Ten paintings, twenty lines—two years' worth of intense work. Irwin was thirty-five years old.

That was in 1962 through 1964, but it's hardly the type of activity that can be glossed over lightly. How much meaning can be wrung from such an experience? How much enrichment can an artist derive from moving the line on a canvas up an eighth of an inch, down a hair? If art (which is said to prove nothing, assert nothing, and exist only for its own sake) is as close as we get to a true account of the mind, what do Irwin's lines tell us? If you were walking through a gallery and happened upon such a painting, what would you think? What would you conclude if the curator's discreet tag classifying the work mentioned that the artist sequestered himself in his studio for two solid years working on these "line experiments" not necessarily for the sake of creating a Work for Sale but for his own evolvement as an artist? Fanatic or genius? Is there a difference?

As Lawrence Weschler noted in his biography of Irwin, entitled *Seeing Is Forgetting the Name of the Thing One Sees*, "When you think about Irwin's activity during this period, you keep expecting Rod Serling's voice to intrude, amidst a falling spangle of percussion, confirming that, yes, this man has definitely strayed . . . 'into the Twilight Zone.' The entire enterprise basks in irreality."

But for Irwin it was a period of serious discipline, of starting over and learning, *really learning*, his craft. It was a period that launched him into a new phase of work. Staring so long and so hard at the line paintings fundamentally changed both his perception and his ideas about perception.

He began to notice, for example, how a spiderweb-thin crack in the studio wall affected his perception and how, when he replastered the crack, the painting he was working on changed. This led him to realize that the environment itself deeply affected the work. And this realization touched off a personal revolution, which caused him to abandon the studio altogether and involve himself with a continuing series of experiments and explorations into a field broadly labeled "environmental art."

His dot works followed, then his luminous discs, the light and space projects, the columns, then the desert experiments where he strung a line of piano wire out toward an undefended horizon. From there he moved into public works, sculpture created for post offices, parks, college campuses, making use of all kinds of material including metal, glass, and a gauzy material called scrim that he discovered on a trip to Amsterdam. Abstract expressionism was long a thing of the past, as was the studio and the canvas.

Increasingly, Irwin was invited to inspect a public sight and design a work for it. Environmental sculpture is one name for this, but Irwin, with his penchant for redefining everything, began to specialize in what he called "site-generated projects." He would fly off to a city in order to study the space, form an impression about the area, develop a concept about what was needed, and then design a work to suit the site, a work that if removed from the site would no longer be the same work, or even any work at all. Take an Irwin site-generated sculpture out of the site and it's just a scrap heap of metal or a derelict mound of scrim. It no longer works as art.

Many of Irwin's projects die in the planning stage. Public works are layered with complications and he is the first to recognize that, as he wrote, "projects such as these are riddled with contradictions, risks, failures, successes, and even a kind of black humor." It's far easier, in some ways, to work alone in the studio where he doesn't have city politics to deal with, decisions by committees, unions telling him that he isn't allowed to weld his metal pieces together, janitors complaining that they can't dust it, patrons moaning that it's not comprehensible, city fathers maintaining that's not even art, bureaucrats irritated because the piece isn't, "um, quite what we had in mind, we wanted, well, something pretty, you know, like a Henry Moore. . . ."

Irwin doesn't seem frustrated by the inherent complications in the art he now practices. To the contrary, he seems comfortable in his art, challenged by it, excited and renewed through it. But to achieve satisfaction and intense creative output, he began by penetrating what it really meant to *be* an artist. It was a quest to get to the bedrock of knowledge, and from knowledge comes the exercise of control. To find it, he didn't choose to go back to school, to apprentice himself to a mentor, to study other people's art, or to converse with his artist friends. Instead, he got right down into the process and stayed there until he figured out the beginnings of a philosophy of art that he still continues to define.

Perhaps, to an outsider, it could be fairly argued that Irwin carried things out beyond the limits of what some might regard as "normally accepted social behavior." Let's just say that the isolation and discipline he exercised worked for him, though another might judge the experience excessive or even oppressive. Moving beyond this debate, however, it's *how* Irwin conducted his search for knowledge that the person interested in creativity should pay attention to: it was an approach to knowledge that came from the doing.

■ **3** ■

CREATIVITY THROUGH THE DOING.

J. Kirk T. Varnedoe is well familiar with the concept, but then, he has had the advantage of spending his entire academic and professional life in the art world, where the creative impulse is a daily concern. Having recently assumed the post of Director of Painting and Sculpture at the Museum of Modern Art in New York, Varnedoe occupies one of *the* most influential positions in the shaping of modern art internationally. What he says about art—in the acquisitions he authorizes, in the way he assembles a show, in the essays and books he writes, in the lectures and public addresses he gives—matters. What he thinks about an artist's work can be decisive in his or her career. But, as one might hope of a person in his position, Kirk Varnedoe is eminently well suited to the challenges.

His office on the fifth floor of the museum faces out over the sculpture garden. At the moment it houses only a bare desk, a gleaming credenza, and a couple of chairs. The blazing white walls are completely nude. In fact, the only artistic expression in the room comes from Varnedoe himself, impeccably dressed, which seems appropriate to the money-hued culture of a museum. The stark white backdrop, both framing and intensifying his poised, dark good looks, completes the startling but fleeting impression that here in the upper reaches of the museum is an astonishing still life done by a very successful artist. As if aware of the illusion his bare walls create, Varnedoe explains that in the next weeks of settling in, he will roam the museum's inventory in search of works to dress his walls. It's one of the choice perks of the post, and when one considers that the museum shows only ten percent of its holdings at any given moment, one can imagine the treasure-filled corridors at his disposal.

For now, Varnedoe clasps his manicured hands on the smoothly buffed surface of his desk and talks about his progression from art student to art historian to teacher to museologist. It's a progression that has allowed him to examine repeatedly the creative process from many related but dissimilar vantage points. It also forms the subject of a book of essays he is writing, his first foray into writing about art for a broad audience. It's a project he says he would never have had the courage to pursue without his MacArthur grant awarded in 1984. Varnedoe was thirty-eight at the time, a perfect age, really, when a man is mature enough to know himself yet young enough to do something about it.

"I'm increasingly impressed with the kind of innovation and knowledge that doesn't come from preplanned effort, or from working toward a fixed goal, but from a kind of concentration on what one is *doing*. That seems very, very important to me. It's the actual process, the functioning, the going ahead with it.

"Look, for example, at what arises in Picasso's sketchbooks. *Simply* through the act of repeating a drawing two or three times and comparing the variations that occur, something that wasn't in any of the three of them becomes the motif for the fourth," he explains, the faint vestiges of his Savannah upbringing in his speech. "Or, look at what Rodin did. Broken sculpture and casts were on the floor of every artist's studio. For everybody else, they were a way to get from point 'a' to point 'f.' But Rodin *stopped* at point 'c' or point 'd' and said, '*This* is something else. This is something in and of itself. I can make *this* into something.' He had a quality of *knowing* by *doing*. There was a process of discovering *in practice*.

"It's something my wife always stresses about what innovation consists of. A lot of it involves paying attention to what you're doing rather than aiming so fixedly toward some sort of goal that you don't pay attention to what's going on as you're trying to get there. It's in the process of working and by watching yourself work that innovation comes."

Varnedoe is married to Elyn Zimmerman, an environmental sculptor who, coincidentally, was influenced by Robert Irwin during his light-and-space period. Living and associating with artists, says Varnedoe, is a constant education in understanding the creative impulse.

"It's a *wonderful* thing to observe the artistic process up close. There is a mystification about how creativity works and what it consists of that when you are close to the process you lose. Zeus doesn't come through the ceiling and smack you in the head with a thunderbolt. It has to do with the newspaper that you pick up, the odd comment that somebody makes, the particular deflection. Watching an artist struggle through the problem about 'what am I going to do with the lower corner of the canvas here,' or 'what is the appropriate symbol for a public space of this nature,' shows me that it is a process that is closely related to the kind of thinking a lot of other people do. It's a process which, if observed up close, often comes down to very simple, very understandable, very commonplace things which seem very, very important to me. I am convinced that many of the most profound and profoundly consequential changes in the history of modern art depended on learning to trust or go with the less prepared, the less familiar, the less acceptable way of doing something and relying on a different aspect of one's ability.

"It's the idea of *doing* without a fixed purpose, *doing* with a sense of exploration, that lets you see the tension in something that everybody else thinks is inert, dull, traditional, gone, forgotten, not worth thinking about. It's the reformulation, the mileage that can be gotten out of changing where that part fits in the scheme. Look at Picasso's collages and the substances and techniques he used. These were perfectly banal things which, like the broken parts on the floor of the studio, were available to anybody. The idea was to see the potential in them—not, like some volcano, to eject some completely new thought, but to see the new possibilities in the things that other people take for granted. Just said that way, it sounds like a cliché but—"

Touching on the Wright Brothers and Darwin and the work of Stephen Jay Gould, all heroes of a sort for him, Varnedoe struggles for a still better example to illustrate the point that creative resolutions to the problems an artist faces often come through the doing. Finally, inevitably, he is drawn back to art and an example taken from one of Picasso's best-known paintings.

"They just had the exhibition of *Les Demoiselles d'Avignon* in Paris, and when you look at the way that Picasso worked up those forms and drawings, many of the standard pieces of wisdom about the exotic influences from Africa fall by the wayside. The simple willful *act* of schematization is what mattered. He tried everything out. He drew the figures in blocks, he drew the heads, he divided them with horizontal lines, then diagonal lines. He just kept *generating* systems that defamiliarized the body or made it into something else. And by generating those systems and by watching himself as he did it, he began to see new possibilities come out of that practice. It wasn't as if something flew in the window at him. It was in the process of working and by understanding what his process was doing for him that a lot of these innovations took place."

It's an explanation that helps to make sense of Irwin's experience. Robert Irwin woke up one morning and for reasons he is still, all these years later, unable to articulate, he decided that though the rest of the community thought of him as an artist, he had an awful lot to learn. Consistent with what Varnedoe has observed throughout his several incarnations in the art world, the learning and the discovery came through the doing.

■ **4** ■

IT'S ALSO THE WAY that art historian Henry Kraus, the third subject of this art trilogy, sought knowledge of his field and the way in which he came up with startlingly new interpretations for works viewed by the experts tens and hundreds of times over. He didn't read books or enroll in school—he prowled the museums of Paris, simply looking and making notes on what he observed.

Seated in the restful calm of his Paris apartment not far from the Ecole Militaire, he reflects back on this period of his life, now a long time ago. His first trip to Europe was just after he married his wife, Dorothy. She was eighteen, he was twenty-three. At the time he didn't have an interest in art. When asked, he told people he was leaving his boyhood home in Cleveland and going to Paris "to develop a philosophy of life." Ridiculed for such naïveté, he changed his story to say that he was going to pursue a degree in French literature at the Sorbonne. And for six weeks he did, until an unpleasant encounter with a high-browed, narrow-minded professor convinced him that he was wasting his time. He quit and never again sought an alliance with any academic institution.

"So, Dorothy and I talked it over," he explains in a voice as delicate as sea foam or old lace. "Should we go back home? What was here? We missed Cleveland, the orchestra, and our families. So we thought maybe we ought to go back and do some work there, but that we had to do something here first or the whole thing would seem like one big failure. So we thought, What does Paris have to offer, anyway? Finally we thought of the arts. *That*, we decided, was what we could take home from our great European adventure."

With that, the pair began to go to the Louvre, at first on Sundays because it was free. At the time they lived on one dollar a day, eating only once a day, but the Louvre really thrilled them and so they carved the admission price from their thin budget and went every day. "The whole time, six months, I took notes. Writing, writing, writing. I was always taking notes. Never reading anything, just making my own observations. Noting what I liked and why. I liked, for example, Caravaggio. I had never heard of him, but I liked him. I thought he was great. I saw a depth in him, a sort of basic humanity, and a roughness, even, that I thought was fantastic."

Henry and Dorothy Kraus stayed two years on this first journey to Paris. They spent the days on their self-tutorial, looking at art, eventually stumbling into the medieval period, which hit them "with the force of an explosion." Kraus began to form theories about works he saw and backed them up with forays into economics, sociology, political history. But before he could cultivate his thoughts, family beckoned and they returned to America with the country deep in the Depression.

For the next dozen years events pulled and pushed them in directions far from art and from the writing that he longed to pursue. They found a tiny apartment for ten dollars a month and furnished it with Goodwill castoffs. Henry did translation work for the Cleveland Clinic while writing a novel (*Acquisition of Courage*, which he pronounced self-centered and promptly buried away in a desk drawer). Dorothy taught dramatics at a YWCA. Their combined income was twenty dollars a week.

Still hungering to write, Henry one day noticed an article in the newspaper about a union's organizing and thought that it sounded interesting—something he might write about and, in any event, socially useful. He went down that day and offered his services as a reporter. Before long, he started a newspaper called *The U.A.W.*, which became very popular. There were strikes, and pickets, and sit-downs, and mean politics. Henry kept at it as a reporter, organizer, and chronicler while Dorothy manned the strike kitchens. Through the next six years, from 1933 to 1939, Henry collected some ten thousand documents about it, from which he wrote his first book, *The Many and the Few*.

("And I had to teach myself to type," he laughs, his frail eyes widening under the canopy of thatched white brows, "but I typed the whole thing. Three hundred and fifty pages by the time I was done and I didn't like it! So I ditched it and rewrote it, toned it up, straightened it out. In answer to your question about creativity, *this* is how an idea changes: in the works, *working and doing*, you know.")

He finished it just as World War II was gearing up in Europe and decided not to publish it for fear that it would stir up antagonism at a time when the country needed to pull together. Eight years later, in 1947, the book was released, but by that time he and Dorothy had already moved to southern California, to the port town of San Pedro. Dorothy wanted the warmth, Henry wanted to write.

To support themselves, Henry took a job working in the shipyards. Their home was in a low-income, interracial housing project, a tinderbox of trouble. Consistent with what had by then become their style of living, they called their neighbors together and in their innocence organized a council of residents. Through it, they solved many of the racial problems, cleaned up the area, created a medical plan, a transportation system, and a nursery. It was a bold act of organization for the common good at a time when the first tremors of McCarthyism rumbled.

Henry wrote of his experiences with the housing project in a book titled *In the City Was a Garden* (1951), moved to New York to take a job translating, and then in 1956 was transferred to Paris to become bureau head of an American medical journal.

"It had been twenty-five years since we were there, and we couldn't wait to go back and continue our study, our true study, our deep study of art."

He and Dorothy picked up where they had left off—going to museums, studying architecture, "looking, looking, always asking why, why, why?" Not long after his return to Paris, he quit the translating job and devoted himself to the study of art full-time. That they were still living frugally and didn't have high prospects of earning money from their art studies did not deter them.

"Money is something we just never worried about. It was more important to keep working at what mattered, to make life worthwhile. And in that we have always been blessed—my God, who could want more than that?" Even with the MacArthur money, which Kraus did not receive until 1984, at the age of seventy-nine, the couple did not change their ways. A lifetime of modest living had cured them of the desire to acquire things. Most of the funds were passed along to artist friends in need, some of it was tucked away with the thought of buying a place to live when and if they returned to the States, and the rest was spent on the occasional luxury of taking a taxi—"when it was raining, of course."

As always, he followed the same course of study he had laid out for himself some twenty-five years ago: he would look, and from the looking he would learn. He taught himself to notice "the offbeat, the interpretative, the overlooked." He'd make notes about the things he discovered, but studiously avoided reading up on the work until he had formed his own impressions. He never kept congress with any crowd, any school, any particular huddle, and in this way avoided seeing things in a practiced fashion. It was a perspective that afforded him a certain naïve latitude to reach his own conclusions to the question: Why?

It's a manner of pursuing knowledge that allowed his work to unfold on many different levels. Falling in love with a beautiful piece of art, he would eventually come around to investigating the group of circumstances that conspired to create such a thing of beauty, a thing that glowed with the courtesy, clarity, and harmony that mark great art. That, in turn, led him to explore the broader social themes of the time and to look even further afield for representations of his theories. In this way he became phenomenally adept at placing works of art against their social and historical backdrop.

And it was through this approach that he began to make his many discoveries. Like the panel at Notre Dame all the great "pooh-bahs" claimed depicted the life of a saint when, in fact, it was secular art. Like his discoveries concerning the misericords, that is, the carefully chiseled carvings found beneath the choir seats once occupied by the fannies of puffy dignitaries, a fantastic world of sculpture no one had thought important enough to comment on. Like his discovery and restoration of the Gothic choir stalls of Oviedo, Spain, that current widsom held had burned or otherwise disappeared during the Spanish Civil War. Like his sociohistoric interpretation of how cathedrals were built. And one of his earliest discoveries—his identification of anti-Semitism in medieval art.

"Anti-Semitism in medieval art?" gasped a shocked Professor Jean Adhémar, Director of the Bibliothèque Nationale, and editor of the *Gazette des Beaux-Arts*. "Where?" Henry ticked off five or six examples he found in Paris alone. Adhémar was so impressed, Kraus's article on the subject was published immediately, short-circuiting the usual two-year lead time.

From 1967 through 1985 he published four art books, all of them beautifully written and well received. And still he continues to work, with his wife, with the same habits he has spent a lifetime cultivating.

■ **5** ■

IRWIN, VARNEDOE, KRAUS: artist, museum director, art historian. Three highly creative lives, each wholly dissimilar from the others in personality and in taste, all completely different in style and in time of life.

Yet in listening to them talk about their experiences with the creative process, I heard a common theme, which turns out to be a centrally important observation about the nature of creative work. Stated simply, it is that creative efforts are neither glib nor ignorant, but rather stem from a solid base of knowledge, and furthermore, though the traditional way to accumulate knowledge is to pursue a university curriculum or to fetter oneself to a rigorous program of stylized, meditated, preordained intellectual endeavor, there is another powerful source for the valuable stuff of knowledge, which is simply to roll up one's sleeves, jump into the work, and *do*.

It's from giving oneself over to the doing that the creator accumulates an *intimate* fund of knowledge that will inform his efforts. It is through the doing that he exposes the knotty tangle of relevant questions that will make up the capital of his lifetime work. It is in the act of doing that he opens himself up to the unanticipated directions that may lead him to something new, something useful, something beautiful, something creative.

The act of doing is an act of faith. If the creator is capable of the seriousness of this commitment and approaches it with an unclouded mind he may be rewarded with the store of knowledge that will enrich every one of his creative urges.

Knowledge comes through the doing—this is true—but there is a postscript that must be added: you do not have to use everything you discover. In fact, it's the knowing that allows the creator to skip over things in the mad rush to distinguish himself. But if, on the other hand, he skips over things because he is unsure or unaware of them, then he leaves gaping holes in the work, obvious to even the most casual observer.

Hemingway put it well when discussing *The Old Man and the Sea* in an interview he gave about the writer's art: "I've seen the marlin mate and know about that. So I leave that out. I've seen a school (or pod) of more than fifty sperm whales in that same stretch of water and once harpooned one nearly sixty feet in length and lost him. So I left that out. All the stories I know from the fishing village I leave out. But the knowledge is what makes the underwater part of the iceberg."

■　　■　　■

The dangling threads . . .

Here, at the end of Part One, I'd like to pause a minute in deference to a natural inclination to summarize how far we've come in our understanding of the creative process. Cutting through the stories, eight simple principles emerge from the preceding chapters, which, like a grocery list, can be itemized and contain things as fundamental and necessary as milk, eggs, leafy greens:

1. *Find your talent.*
2. *Commit to it and make it shine.*
3. *Don't be afraid of risk. Or even failure, which if seen in its proper light, brings insight and opportunity.*
4. *Find courage by looking to something stronger and better than your puny vulnerable self.*
5. *No lusting after quick resolutions. Relax. Stay loose.*
6. *Get to know yourself; understand your needs and the specific conditions you favor.*
7. *Respect, too, your culture. We can't, any of us, escape the twentieth century. It's tucked up around our collective chin as snugly and as firmly as the bedsheet.*
8. *Then, finally, break free from the seductive pull of book learning and research and the million other preparatory steps that could delay for the entire span of a life and immerse yourself in the doing.*

Eight simple points . . . and no mention of the dangling threads. Hardly surprising given my penchant for order and for the neat, clean lines that characterize the well-polished, tightly reasoned works I admire. Yet something is missing—does it show? In the making of any creative work—mine, yours, or anyone else's—there are always the dangling threads. And whether they enchant or simply annoy depends upon the person and the project. But either way, the same question must be answered: Which threads should be pulled, and which snipped off?

For instance, back in June 1988, I had an interview scheduled in the hills outside Berkeley with an anthropologist and, like all these MacArthur people, she was incredibly busy. It took some doing to find a time and place to meet, but finally we agreed on her house, tucked up high on a narrow, twisted road, very early in the morning.

I showed up in my tin rental car just as the sun was easing into the day, but there wasn't a sign of life in the place except for some big, old mangy dog lolling around the front stoop. I knocked. I knocked again. I sat and talked to the mutt a bit and then knocked again.

At last the anthropoligst appeared, slightly swollen and damp with sleep. Pulling on socks, she showed me to a couch near the coffee table that was strewn with the dessert plates from the preceding night's dinner party. Then she disappeared into the kitchen, with the dog right behind her. I heard her chatting with him while she fixed herself some coffee and toast. She crooned to him in the high, sweet voice a mother reserves for her baby: "Aren't you a beautiful thing, oh yes, yes you are."

And, in time, she got around to chatting with me about creativity, but it was hard to concentrate because that bearlike creature was being a nuisance in the way that big, smelly animals can be, rubbing up against her good furniture, rolling over in a play for attention, poking its muzzle into fragile wineglasses. So finally, as gingerly as possible, I asked her if we could let her dog outside for a while, just until we finished. "My dog?" she says. "You mean he's not your dog?"

(Now really: I travel all the way across country to see this woman, at my own expense, and after no small amount of preparation, and she thinks I'd arrive at her door with a wretched, lumbering dog at my heels? This is the kind of misunderstanding that could happen only in Berkeley; never, I assure you, in New York.)

We threw the beast out, but by then it was too late. The household was in motion, doors slamming, showers running, the arrival of the maid who began to collect the dishes, the arrival of the landscape gardener wanting to know how to plant the area around the hot tub . . . if this were on film, it would star Diane Keaton, in one of her brainier roles, and Woody Allen, upstaged by a shaggy dog. But what, I stopped to wonder, do I do with something like this in a book? Use it? Forget it? Simply note it and move on?

Please, don't misunderstand me. It's not that I'm reluctant in the slightest to cast aside material that seems inappropriate to the finished piece. Rather, it is that each one of these MacArthur Fellows has something to add and every clue is valuable when you're stalking such an elusive quarry. Understanding creativity is a mosaic-kind of undertaking—I need all the pieces I can get, and still the chances are good that whole chunks will be missing.

It is for this reason that I consider these loose threads. Should I have spent more time dissecting that whole wacky morning with the anthropologist?

So, too, I wonder if I should have lingered longer over my file marked "Rosenberg, Tina." Inside, this nest of notes: "A journalist who hates working alone. An American now based in Chile. She got off the plane, planted her feet firmly on South American soil, and knew that she had 'come home.' Does the relief that comes with this sense of belonging affect her creative output? She's young. Still on the cusp of thirty years. And yet she knows what it is like to go up into camps of guerrilla rebels. She has wondered whether to wear, if offered, their uniform. She has felt the press of flesh in a rally gotten out of hand. She knows the sting of tear gas. Creativity is mostly luck, she says."

Another fat file, rife with possibility, labeled "Keightley, David." The stray facts within: "A serious scholar. An admired professor. A one-note historian with an interest in cultures that existed some 8,000 to 1,000 years before Christ. 'Ancient' seems too anemic a word. Travels often to China. Easy to picture his long spider legs pacing the floors of some endlessly dusty excavation. Yellowed bits of Paleolithic turtle shells and cow scapulae gathered. On them are the intriguing inscriptions of long-gone tribes. 'Bone oracles,' they are called, and for a long time no one understood their message. But Keightley can read them and can tell us what man had on his mind, thousands of years ago."

The anthropologist, the journalist, the sinologist—all dangling threads, loose ends, wayward opportunities not fully realized. Their stories make up part of the great clamor of experience that characterizes this investigation, the tantalizing din of genius that comes with exposure to the MacArthur Fellows.

What is the best response to these loose ends, the avenues left unexplored? Does one sweep them out of sight, or is it better—as you sometimes see in paintings—to leave them in for the observant viewer to think about, like the faintly rendered figure that the artist in a change of mind abandoned but didn't completely obliterate from the canvas? Wandering through the museums, feasting on the works of the Old Masters, how the eye lingers on those ghostly figures, missing yet not altogether absent from the landscape.

"You're missing something," the writer Ved Mehta confirms. Outside his office window at The New Yorker *a furious summer storm rages, a suitable setting for his nostalgic drift of memory and for his remarks on the critical importance of irony to the creative process:*

". . . I should tell you the one thing that makes being a writer bearable, I think, and it is also the thing that I most look for in life and literature. It is irony. I don't know quite how to explain that to you quickly, but that applies to what I think creativity is—things are never what they seem. The constant battle is to try to get at the truth behind what they seem and then one is constantly surprised because the truth turns out to be the opposite to what you imagine it is. The surprising and the unexpected is what makes me have an interest in wonder. I am wonderstruck by so many things and then interested in the explanation, but the more you explain, the more there is to explain. And so on. I think you should get into irony because that has an important creative thrust to it."

Now there was the provocative thread of an idea that I found impossible to ignore. Irony linked to creative thought? What did he mean? If I pursued it, surely it would lead to something revelatory, yet at the same time yanking on loose ends was a sure way to unravel the fabric. Perhaps it would be better simply to snip it off, and toss it aside, taking my chances that I hadn't discarded something of irretrievable value. It's a gamble, but all creative work, no matter one's field, presents plenty of these sorts of judgment calls.

If this makes you a little nervous, let me pass along a word of advice picked up through the course of the project: try not to worry about the loose ends because the chances are very good that in the next project, or perhaps in the one after that, you will have an opportunity to address them again. "It's that old idea," the poet John Ashbery notes, "of each of us having only one or two ideas in life and spending our years expressing them, and expressing them, and expressing them." If he's right, then there will be time enough in the future to lay these loose ends to rest.

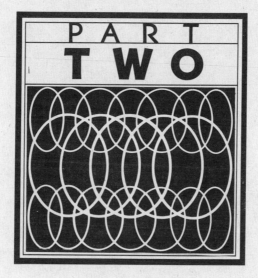

PART

TWO

INVESTING YOUR WORK

WITH A VISION

WE ARE ACCUSTOMED, all of us, to reasoning in a certain fashion, which proceeds something like this: a storm came, a law was overturned, my mother named me Napoleon, and therefore such-and-such happened. It's a linear kind of thinking, crisp and clean, direct and causal. It holds within it an element of inevitability, that is, the assumption that past and present events determine our future.

Less obvious is another, more subtle kind of reasoning, which goes along like this: we need a new town hall, I have a fantastic new idea, wouldn't it be wonderful if we raised our sons to be feminists, and therefore let us do this, this, and this to effect a new order of things.

This is also a kind of linear thinking, but it reverses the causal relationship. It squints into the future; it looks ahead instead of behind. Instead of concentrating on picking up the pieces of our yesteryears, it allows a concept of tomorrow to shape the decisions we make today. There is no sense of inevitability. In fact, often this sort of reasoning holds at its core an image of something desirable but considered wildly impractical, audaciously speculative, or flatly unattainable.

It's the thinking, in short, of a visionary.

There is a link between the creative impulse and vision that goes far beyond the simple (but truthful) observation that in our effort to get people to notice and applaud a new idea, we should package it in the most appealing and creative way possible. We know this already: the eye lingers on something shiny, but quickly passes over the lackluster and inert.

The link between vision and heightened creativity is stronger than this, and more valuable, too. It is, simply, that when motivated by deep-seated convictions that address a new and far-ranging order of things, the tendency is strong to think more creatively. Consider: a person caught in a stagnant phase of life will, in time, dry up and then wait to die. Boredom kills. So does alienation and loneliness. But give an unhappy, listless person a cause that embodies a vision of proportions greater and more worthy than himself, and once again the life-sustaining juices begin to flow. Give man a purpose, and he will go forward, again and again, heartily, steadily, and creatively.

<h2 style="text-align:center">▪ 2 ▪</h2>

THE OFFICES OF the Worldwatch Institute in Washington, D.C., are just off DuPont Circle. The building is one of a row of stately structures with clean and solidly defined lines that well suit the dignity and power of our country's capital.

Inside, a grass-green carpet anchored with earthen-colored furnishings gives the place the look of an open meadow. Photos of game and wildlife hang on soft cream-colored walls. Working quietly, the staff readies the place for a press conference.

Within the hour the press arrives, two and three members at a time. *Newsweek* shows up early. United Press, World Bank, *Fortune*, and *The Christian Science Monitor* are right behind him. The reporter from Voice of America is the next to step out of the elevator and behind him still others follow, the men sporting stiff white handkerchiefs, the ladies wearing prettily knotted silk scarves.

Most of the arrivals orbit around the makeshift bar. A few disappear into the library to set up their expensive recording equipment and, not incidentally, to stake out a seat. The hungry ones hover with forks poised over a buffet luncheon. They

are helped to ample portions of oranges and avocados on water-
cress, curried rice salad, chicken in a Roquefort mayonnaise.
They discreetly help themselves to assorted dips and greens,
fruits and cheeses. It's a well-tailored, well-mannered, well-
fed crowd.

Over bites of Brie, introductions are made, hands shaken.
A buzz of global politics and world ecology ensues. "Just got
back from Africa, covering the AIDs situation . . ." "My husband, a friend of the late ambassador of Zimbabwe, observed . . ." "Yes, I was doing fieldwork in Nepal and from
there I crossed into China for six months, and then India
before . . ." "As anyone familiar with acid rain can tell
you . . ."

At precisely the appointed hour, a tall, lean, curly-headed
man in casual gray corduroys and an open-necked blue shirt
breaks loose from the scene and invites the crowd into the
small library that doubles as a conference room. He doesn't
look much like an intellectual, an analyst, a zealot, or a man
in his fifties, yet he is all of these things. He is Lester Brown,
the founder and President of the Worldwatch Institute.

Worldwatch is a think tank concerned with the condition of
our planet. The loss of forests, the rising of oceans, the hole
in the ozone, the contamination of groundwater, the effect of
ultraviolet radiation, the crop yields in Third World econ-
omies—these are among the concerns that wrinkle the brows
of the research staff. Overseeing it all is Les Brown, a man
fluent in the language of fossil fuels and water tables, the
greenhouse effect and irrigation. While the rest of us worry
about the tedious particularities of daily life, Brown is pre-
occupied with the habitability of the earth in a hundred, two
hundred, five hundred years. While the rest of us have an ear
to the stock reports, Brown has his ear pressed to the ground,
listening to the heartbeat of Mother Earth. It's a reputation
that has earned him the nickname of God's Scorekeeper, and
that seems fair enough.

The distinguished members of the press scramble for a seat.

The unlucky ones lean in the doorframe. Only now do the staff help themselves to the buffet and linger within earshot. If you're young and brainy, committed to world ecology, and unencumbered by a Ph.D., the Worldwatch Institute would be a wonderful place to work. Brown rarely hires people with doctorate degrees; they're too rigid in their approach to problem solving, he claims. They just can't seem to break out of the narrow focus they spent a career cultivating in order to assess the big picture.

Brown, on the other hand, is brilliant at that and has fashioned an entire stellar career around his facility for integrated thinking. It's an approach that grasps an essential truth: everything is connected to everything else. Overpopulation, for example, contributes to a deforestation of the land, which, in turn, causes the loss of plant and animal diversity, overgrazing, soil erosion, and the migration of people out of the area into other, already heavily taxed areas. This, in turn, causes one to wonder how the economics and politics of the area will shift and how that will play out in the world at large. Les wonders. Les anticipates. Les postulates, proposes, and disseminates his disturbing, unsettling conclusions.

Imagine: The Third World spends four times as much on defense as it does on health care.

Imagine: As much energy leaks out of windows of American homes as flows through the Alaska pipeline.

Imagine: At the current rate of deforestation, India will be devoid of tree cover by the end of the century.

Imagine: The planet now has an estimated five billion people, twice as many as in 1950.

In order to reach such startling conclusions, Brown has culled a phenomenal amount of information starting with the newspapers: he reads five every morning, standing up so it takes less time. He also listens—to his staff, to people who write and call, to members of the press, to heads of government, to scientists, to activists. Garnering information from around the globe, he thinks about what he learns, and then

formulates opinions. Seeing linkages and far-reaching consequences is what he does best and he does it with the unshakable
enthusiasm of a visionary.

What marks a visionary is dedication to an ideal, a dedication
so strong that it rejects outright the complacency of those who
prefer the status quo and insists that there has to be another
way. It is this insistence that causes Les to ponder alternatives
well into the night. Instead of reaching for the nearest, most
convenient conclusions, his important ideal of a sustainable
society causes him to push hard against the limits of what
others believe is possible. If he didn't care so much, he
wouldn't invest so much of himself in this effort. Nor would
he be so determined to draw others into his effort.

Most of Worldwatch's findings are written up in an annual
series of books titled *The State of the World*, the first of which
appeared in 1984 with a printing of sixteen thousand copies.
Acting as a kind of report card on the earth, the almost biblical
series takes a close look at various dangerous trends in the way
we live and spend our resources. Today it is published in some
sixteen languages, with a first printing in a one-hundred-
thousand range, is disseminated in more than one hundred and
twenty countries, and is used as a textbook in more than five
hundred and seventy-five college curriculums. Over half of the
institute's income derives from publication sales, unlike that
of most research centers, which require grants to continue their
work.

In addition to the *State of the World* series, Worldwatch generates an estimated fourteen articles daily in major periodicals,
presents seven to eight comprehensive research papers a year,
and has just published a new magazine. The press conference
today is to announce the availability of the latest Worldwatch
paper, number 80.

In the library, at the head of the conference table, sits a
poised, faintly nervous young woman. Lined up in front of
her is a row of microphones. Les Brown occupies the chair at
her side. He hugs one knee to his chest and leans on it in a

down-home, comfortable gesture. "Welcome to Worldwatch," he says in his typically soft, unruffled voice, and the red needles on the recording equipment begin to swing. "As you know, there are a couple of *major* events in town this week and a few of you will probably have to leave after this one is over to go work on the other one."

Smiles break out all around. Everyone in the nation, let alone in the city of Washington, knows that Soviet leader Mikhail Gorbachev is in town to confer with President Reagan. Les is only kidding, of course, in ranking the Worldwatch press conference on a par with that momentous visit. Of course, it's just a joke.

With that, he introduces the young woman who authored the eightieth Worldwatch paper, this one on the effects of an ever-growing world population. He will not be heard from again until the end, when he will step in to get the question-and-answer period off to a good start. It's something his staffers really like about him. With Les, an upstart has a chance.

The young lady begins her talk; reporters' pencils start to fly. Lester Brown keeps his head down and listens.

▫ **3** ▫

MEANWHILE, across the Potomac in Arlington, in a towering glass high-rise that could blind you with the glare, are the offices of The Conservation Fund. The carpets here are wheat-colored. The photos are of ducks and farmland.

In the corner office, Patrick Noonan is on the phone. He paces back and forth behind his desk, his sturdy profile casting a beefy dark shadow on a wall covered with awards, certificates of merit, and photographs of Noonan in forests, on farmland, on white water, and in parks.

Pat Noonan's concern for America began when he spotted a small newspaper article about The Nature Conservancy, an organization dedicated to protecting America's natural pre-serves. He liked what he read and signed on as a trainee in

1969. At the time the organization was saving roughly one hundred parcels of land a year. With Noonan's assistance, by 1973 the acquisition rate had doubled. Shortly thereafter, he took on the presidency and held the post for the next seven years.

During his tenure at the helm of The Nature Conservancy, the numbers by which we measure an organization's success far exceeded even generous expectations: the establishment of twenty-five state natural-heritage programs, the acquisition of more than two thousand parcels of land valued at more than five hundred million dollars, the creation of a revolving fund to finance acquisitions, and the establishment of the largest private sanctuary system in the world, encompassing some seven hundred nature preserves.

The objective of The Nature Conservancy is to identify America's nature perserves and then to secure their protection for the benefit of the public at large. Almost always, this is a costly proposition that has caused Noonan and his staff to dream up creative mechanisms for funding the means to their goals.

One solution was the revolving fund—a kind of internal bank built from private, corporate, and foundation funds that makes dirt-cheap loans quickly so that jeopardized lands can be saved. Today the fund is valued at nearly one hundred million dollars.

Another solution, far more controversial, was to appeal to the very same "bad guys" who have been accused of putting the land in jeopardy in the first place. Through careful research, staffers would study the endangered area, identify a way that a corporation might help, and structure a business proposal much like any other proposal for a joint venture. Then they'd pay a visit to the organization—Getty, for example, or Standard Oil—and say, in effect, "Here's your chance to do something great for America—save a wetland, save a forest, save this bird sanctuary, recycle this abandoned piece of land, and not only won't we criticize you for your past evil deeds, we'll give you an award and let America know how proud we are to be working with you in this conservation effort."

In this way Noonan quickly and consistently dissociated himself and The Nature Conservancy from the conflict posture taken by predecessor conservationists and established an extensive network of partnerships with the business community. The idea was to create win-win situations—everyone coming out ahead.

When Pat Noonan first began to implement his work-with-them-not-against-them strategy, it was considered a new and clever response to solving ecological problems, especially given the relatively short history of the conservation movement in this country (which many believe started with President Theodore Roosevelt in 1907). It marked a shift from the conflict mode to compromise, from activism to cooperation. But like all creative ideas, it attracted a fair measure of criticism along with applause. On the one hand, Noonan's team has been remarkably effective in prying loose huge amounts of money to benefit conservation goals. On the other hand, critics suggested that litigation, not deal-making, is the correct posture to take when confronting these corporate offenders. His response to the criticism has been consistent from the start: "You say it's tainted money? I say it t'ain't enough."

After several years of involvement with forests, parks, and wetlands, Noonan expanded his interest to include the plight of the family farm, and he also served on President Reagan's Commission on the Outdoors. Appropriately, the committee he chaired was responsible for the creation of new ideas.

His methods in all these activities have been consistent from the beginning, he explains when he gets off the phone. His face is flushed with exhilaration at the news that his staff has just secured a twenty-one-million-dollar corporate gift, a large part of which will be put toward the creation of a new national park. It sounds terribly complicated, practically impossible, but to Noonan, it's all really very simple:

"I believe in the free-enterprise system and in harnessing

the free-enterprise motive to benefit conservation. Establishing partnerships with the business community is a nifty way to leverage our conservation purpose. We just keep hammering away at our very simple focus to protect, preserve, and manage the very best of America's natural terrain, and we provide people with the incentives to help us. To do this, we have created a team of interdisciplinary thinkers who can devise creative ways to fix our problems. And I take pride in our teams of workers who function not as specialists who can't see the big picture, but who operate from a many-sided perspective."

Like Lester Brown, Patrick Noonan realizes that the future belongs to people who can integrate across disciplines, a sentiment that closely echos the "surprising connections" definition of creativity, the idea of colliding frames of reference that produce an unexpected twist. "There are so many tightly focused people who can't make two and two equal seven if seven's the number you need," he says. "Bringing together a diverse set of talents to work out a problem from varying perspectives is how we will get creative solutions."

He pauses a moment, his attention drawn to the panorama of airplanes, gleaming obelisks, and other feats of engineering outside his windows, a scene about as far away as you can get from a natural bog or leafy forest. It's why Noonan is on the road a lot—not just to juggle the innumerable details and stresses of the deals he oversees, but also to walk the land, talk with the farmers, sit in on the town meetings, and listen firsthand to the concern and the fear.

"I get frustrated by the way we treat our lands and waters as commodities to be bartered or sold with no regard for the carrying limits of how much pollution a river can handle, the amount of pesticide the soil can tolerate, or what this will do to the wildlife, or how it will affect the groundwater. And I get especially frustrated here, inside the Beltway, where it seems that people who work on the top of these big glass buildings simply don't have their feet on the ground and can't feel the pulse of concern. They don't know what's wrong, and the few that do can't think of effective ways to fix it."

Noonan knows what's wrong and he is brimming over with creative ideas on how to fix it. Like all visionaries, he looks well beyond the status quo and imagines what the country would be like if certain things were changed, if public opinion were swayed. He's a dreamer of the highest order: he dreams in a socially useful way. As with Les Brown, dreams takes over where facts give out. Fact: man has walked on the moon. Dream: I believe that one day we will travel freely from planet to planet. Fact is what a visionary builds on; dreams are what pull him forward and get him thinking creatively about how to accomplish the images and ideas swirling around in the mist inside his head.

▫ 4 ▫

A LONG WAY from the urbane chatter of press conferences and the glare of urban high-rises is an old red barn tucked out back behind a white clapboard house on the edge of the woods. Thoreau country: Lincoln, Massachusetts.

Flashlight in hand, flannel shirttails sticking out from under a woolly warm sweater, a mean wind stirring up his tangled gray beard, Roger Payne crunches his way across snowbanks, into the barn, and up the stairs. It is unusual to find him so far from the ocean spray, landlocked on all sides, but here in this converted attic space more like a nest than an office is the modest headquarters for the World Wildlife Fund.

Payne is a research scientist and conservationist interested in the behavior and preservation of whales—a cetologist. It's a concern that has caused him to travel the world trailing the whales on their winter migrations, spending long periods of time in India, Sri Lanka, and Argentina. With such a long-standing relationship to the whale community, Payne not only recognizes the mammals by sight, and by the names he has given them; he also recognizes the offspring of whales he first encountered two decades ago. Watching their habits, studying their behavior, Payne has worked feverishly gathering the data that would contribute mightily to the field's important discoveries, each more startling than the next:

Insight: when whales moan and sing their haunting chants, they can be heard by other whales thousands of miles away, across the ocean basins.

Insight: whale song is not arbitrary but actually follows specific predictable rules of musical composition.

Insight: whale song is passed from generation to generation, just as we might pass along stories of our grandparents to our children; and, further, just as we elaborate on the tales we tell, the whales also improve upon the songs they pass to their young, theme and variation passed down from parent to child.

If pressed, Dr. Payne admits that he simply can't understand why everybody isn't quivering with excitement over whales. Indeed, perhaps far too much is made of man's relationship to the ape when, in fact, the gentleness and sociability of these sea monsters provide an equally worthy basis of comparison, the uncharted vastness of their brains as mysterious as our own. It seems inconceivable to Payne that right here on earth is a living phenomenon that we know next to nothing about, a species that has survived longer, possibly millions of years longer, than man.

He'd like to learn enough about the communication of whales to interview them eventually—"to ask them, Do you remember back when you lived in the wild, before you started to work with us, were you afraid of sharks? Do you have a religion? Was your mother faithful to your father? Were you concerned when you heard us talking about the atomic blast? If people continue to harm the whales, we're going to endanger the mystery, and an endangered mystery is a very sad thing to have."

To hear him express his concern for the giant blubbery mammals is tantamount to being privy, in a moment of unaccountable intimacy, to a man describing the most profound and pivotal experiences of his life. He talks about the extraordinary creativity of whale song and the strange, bewitching power it holds, causing many who hear it to weep uncontrollably. He refers to F. Scott Fitzgerald's remark about man's coming face-to-face with something commensurate with humanity's capacity for wonder. He asserts that whales are a fantastic window not only into the sea but into one's own heart and soul.

And as he gazes out the barn window at the strange, gray, pearly light of a winter moon illuminating spare, stark trees and the snow falling in thick tufted flakes, he admits that the secret, private wish of his soul is to go out to sea, to live there for huge, unclocked stretches of time, one year blending seamlessly into the next, in the tradition of the long hunters of yesteryear, but not to kill these moist, oily-eyed creatures, certainly not, only to observe them, to befriend them, and who knows, maybe even to die among them.

■ 5 ■

ARDENT? Vehement? Serious? Intense?

Certainly.

And perhaps before we go any further, something should be said generally about the fervor of a visionary's dreams. Apart from their enduring concern for the earth, what Lester Brown, Patrick Noonan, and Roger Payne share is an unshakable commitment to a vision of magnificent proportions. It's a zealous undertaking fueled by a sober, serious passion. Are they more passionate about their work than the executive down the hall, more intensely involved than the researcher in the lab next door? Maybe, but certainly not to such a degree that their soundness of mind would be questioned. Their social poise and mental equilibrium have not been sacrificed, which is to say, the appropriateness of a man's fervor is a question of degree.

Increasingly, though, there is a body of information generated by psychiatrists and psychologists involved in investigating the *outer* limits of passion, technically called "the psychopathology of a creative mind." Among these studies, the findings of Dr. K. R. Eissler (writing for *American Imago*) are enlightening. Dr. Eissler has observed that the dreams of a creative person are marked by a longing to construct an order that cannot be unthought—that is, an order of things that possesses a *higher* degree of reality then the tangible, visible reality around us. In order to fulfill this urge, the visionary has to embrace the world as he finds it and then reject it outright in his effort to fashion something new. He is at once a clear-sighted realist and a misty-eyed dreamer.

The result of his effort, continues Eissler, is a product that possesses its own psychic reality, a product that is above the creator himself, sacrosanct, inviolable, and perfect in a way that he, a mere mortal, is not. Who would presume, for example, to rewrite a play by Shakespeare? Who would dare to alter Picasso's *Guernica* or Vivaldi's *The Four Seasons*? Don't we mourn more grievously the savage attack on Michelangelo's *Pietà* than we do the victims of the latest terrorist attack? Is it simply that great art is irreplaceable and human life is cheap?

Eissler has demonstrated that it is more than that. His suggestion is that these works hold a certain power over us because they have taken on their own impenetrable reality. Somehow we have been drawn into the intensity of the creative vision in much the same way that the creator himself has experienced the intensity. For the creative genius, he argues, the work has taken on its own very real, immensely powerful existence: Goethe is said to have burst into tears when Mignon died; Rousseau had to run to the window for air, he was so terrified of the dense jungles and fierce animals he painted; and countless novelists have assured us again and again that their characters act and speak for themselves.

It is the ardor of this vision that overpowers both the creator and the viewing public. But as much as the intensity of the work can bestow pleasure to those of us who encounter it, when the intensity has gotten out of hand it can cause tremendous distress for the creator. For one thing, he often feels compelled to produce the work, so much so that he feels he has no choice in the matter—an experience analogous, says Eissler, to the way a schizophrenic feels he has no choice in the delusions he experiences. For another thing, the finished work inevitably falls short of the creative vision, which plunges the creator into a roller-coaster ride of hope and despair, elation and crippling disappointment. As Vera John-Steiner, another researcher in this field, has observed, the very conception that gives rise to the work at the same time defeats the creator to such an extent that many an onlooker would be tempted to label him neurotic. Such is the price a visionary pays when swept away by the tidal waters of his own passion. Exercising control over one's fervor, however, creates another situation altogether.

▪ **6** ▪

WHAT HARNESSES THE IDEA of vision to the creative impulse is the notion that dreams unleash the imagination. And taking this one step further, where the dream addresses some greater good, there is an even stronger tendency to take risks and make the innovative leaps necessary to accomplish its goals. Limit yourself to your own private world and you've limited your creativity by worrying about how to protect what you've got and how to get what you're missing. Get yourself out of the way in pursuit of some greater good, in response to a strong pull of mission, and you've liberated the mind.

This is a principle that Les Brown, Pat Noonan, and Roger Payne understand well. I elected to discuss these three because I am grateful for the way they stand as protectors of the earth, the place I live. But they are only three among the scores of visionaries who make up the MacArthur population.

For example, many of the Fellows interviewed talked at length about the need to strengthen democracy, something one might expect to hear from a political scientist perhaps, but from a poet? from an art curator? from a schoolteacher in Harlem? Many also have staggeringly large visions: The writer Brad Leithauser, for example, who doesn't merely want to write a great book of poems but seeks to redefine the essential nature of verse. Community organizer Andy McGuire, who has no trouble scaling up his concerns from stopping smoking to stopping war. Two theater directors, Peter Sellars and Ellen Stewart, who crisscross the globe in their efforts to understand the connection between art and culture. Lawyer–abstract painter–songwriter Joan Abrahamson, who has founded an institution involved in everything from curing AIDS to enhancing creativity. Woodworker Sam Maloof, who freely passes on his secrets in the hope of preserving the crafts tradition for America. The examples run on, and in each case it's the *vision* that generates the ideas and carries forth the work, not the hope of praise, reward, or glory.

▫ **7** ▫

THIS ISN'T TO SAY, though, that everyone is going to fall into step with your clamorous dreams and adopt your personal imperatives as their own, no matter how persuasive and creative you are.

Once upon a time, a while back, a young Patrick Noonan traveled to Florida to meet with one John D. MacArthur, the eccentric billionaire who counted among his holdings a sizable portion of the state. It's a pilgrimage Noonan had in common with a trail of congressmen, senators, governors, presidential hopefuls, chairmen of the board, con men, hucksters, sharks, knockabouts, and deadbeats, each with his own interest to promote. Noonan's concern, as always, was with the earth— specifically, a chunk of Florida land he wanted to have preserved as a wildlife refuge.

The meeting was at the Colonnades Hotel, in the coffee shop MacArthur treated as his office. Pat Noonan came dressed in a pressed suit and fresh tie. MacArthur was unshaven and clad in a grubby T-shirt. Scattered about him were the remains of his twenty-cup-a-day coffee habit and overflowing ashtrays.

Not wasting any time, Pat Noonan launched into his standard pitch: "You know, Mr. MacArthur, sir . . . saving the parklands . . . important wetlands . . . national heritage . . . ecology—"

The billionaire cut him off in the middle of this delivery: "Young man, I've never given anything away in my life, and I'm not about to start now. Is there anything else on your agenda?"

"No sir," answered Noonan.

"Well, then," MacArthur replied, "pay for your coffee on the way out."

To date, Patrick Noonan is the only MacArthur Fellow who ever had the pleasure of meeting face-to-face the man who endowed his fellowship. And if that isn't irony enough, the very parcel of land Noonan sought to protect was in fact given over to benefit the public, and dedicated in 1989 as the John D. MacArthur Beach State Park.

A CHANGE OF PERSPECTIVE

A STORY ABOUT Picasso tells of how when he was a schoolboy he was terrible at math because whenever the teacher had him write the number 4 on the blackboard, it looked like a nose to him and he'd keep doodling to fill in the rest of the face. Everyone else in the class saw a number on the blackboard; Picasso perceived a face.

The link between perspective and the creative process has to do with habituation and saturation. Overfamiliarization with something—an idea, say, or a method, or an object—is a trap. Where creativity is concerned, that is the irony of skill: the more adept you are at something, the less likely you are to appreciate a varying interpretation; the greater your mastery of the skills and routines associated with a particular discipline, the less you will be tempted to generate new approaches.

Creativity, no matter which of its many definitions you favor, requires something new, a different interpretation, a break from the twin opiates of habit and cliché. Sometimes acute boredom or a period of prolonged, debilitating frustration will force a person to throw up his hands in despair and trundle off in search of a fresh approach. But a more lively mind will act sooner and deviate from the norm whether for his own amusement or out of curiosity—just to see what happens if he shifts his inclinations. Thanks to a growing body of thinking technology (consolidated in the 1950s and improved upon ever since), a novice determined to experience the rush of adrenaline and creative surges that accompany a shift in perspective can dabble with an assortment of packaged formalized exercises as varied and as inviting as a sampler box of chocolates. We will taste only four, certainly enough for anyone to digest at a single sitting.

EXERCISE No. 1: PLAYING WITH HYPOTHETICALS

This first exercise, an easy one, relies on the use of a series of hypothetical questions that are meant to shake up our ideas about how we define a problem and where we look for the answer. When we are trying, for example, to resolve a particularly obstinate issue, the teaching of this exercise is to stop a minute and ask ourselves: Can this problem by phrased more broadly? more narrowly? more abstractly? using other verbs? other nouns? other adjectives? Can it be broken in half? or can its various pieces be consolidated? Is it possible to relate it to something I might have done in the past? Can it be diagramed?

Similarly, if we have invented something that doesn't satisfy us, the following hypotheticals might yield a better mousetrap: Can we change the color? the material? the texture? the smell? the density? Can it be turned inside out? made larger? smaller? stretched? divided? rearranged? Can it be made more durable? more expendable? more efficient? more economical? more beautiful?

And so on. Though hit or miss in its application, any one of these hypothetical questions holds the potential of nudging a stale perspective in the direction of something new, something more imaginative.

EXERCISE No. 2: SHARPENING THE EYE

This creativity exercise focuses on sharpening vision in order to break through the mental saturation. Art students, for example, when asked to draw a familiar object from memory, find that they have only a rough idea of what a telephone looks like, or a favorite reading chair. But when asked to draw an object or scene from an upside-down perspective, head hung between knees, a person is forced to notice shapes and relationships one slurs over from a more familiar vantage point. The same is true when one is required to draw with the less dominant hand—the left hand for most people. Or to draw the same object but from a variety of angles. Or not to draw the object at all but to concentrate on depicting the spaces around it.

One of the more effective teachers of these visual-perception exercises is Betty Edwards. The Edwards books—*Drawing on the Right Side of the Brain* and the sequel, *Drawing on the Artist Within*—like so many contemporary explorations of creativity, uses as a launching pad the discoveries of psychobiologist Roger Sperry and his colleagues at the California Institute of Technology. His Nobel Prize–winning work has established that the human brain consists of two nearly identical hemispheres (anatomically speaking) that perform different functions. The left hemisphere, we are told, plays a dominant role in comprehending language and in classifying and categorizing objects. The right side receives credit for discriminating sensory differences, which includes performing tasks of a spatial, musical, emotional, sexual, spiritual, and imaginative nature. Creativity is widely perceived to be a right-brain phenomenon—but that's educated speculation. How the brain manages intuition, consciousness, personality, and artistry is still a profound mystery, to say nothing of determining which hemisphere is dominant in these matters.

EXERCISE NO. 3: EXPERIMENTING WITH METAPHORS

A metaphor is a figure of speech in which a word or phrase that means one thing is used to describe an object or idea to which it is not literally applicable—a ship said to plow the sea, for example, or a lover's lane described as a ribbon of moonlight. The ability to express a problem as a metaphor increases the likelihood that one can appreciate it in a new light, which, in turn, may lead to solutions that might not otherwise have been anticipated. As an experiment in perception, the exercise can be stated in a single instruction: can you express the matter at hand—be it a problem, an annoyance, a point of confusion, a theory, whatever—as a metaphor? The better you get at this, the greater your opportunities for a fresh perspective. So powerful is this device that it merits more than a passing discussion.

Leaving aside the intuitive, tender, poetic beauty of a metaphor (if beauty can ever be dismissed so lightly), what is useful about this sort of wordsmithing is that by comparing dissimilar things we are able to comprehend the unfamiliar in familiar terms. There, precisely, lies the *creative* power of metaphor: it uses something we know well to explain what has eluded us.

This is easily appreciated in the sciences. Darwin's most fertile metaphor in his efforts to comprehend evolution, for example, was the branching tree. Friedrich Kekulé described his understanding of the ring making up the benzene molecule as a snake biting its own tail. Einstein, in articulating his theory of relativity, relied on an image of himself riding on a beam of light holding a mirror in front of him. More recently, the American research team struggling to understand the theories of superconductivity worked in conjunction with a dance troupe to see if it could grasp the choreography of how subatomic particles paired and interacted. And MacArthur Fellow Edward Witten explains what he knows of "string theory"— possibly the most revolutionary idea in physics in more than half a century—by replacing the billiard-ball image of particle science with the image of tiny loops or closed "strings" likened to, say, doughnuts. The imagery is clumsy, perhaps, but then physics has long had to rely on metaphor to make itself understood. Niels Bohr, the father of quantum theory, put it best once with the remark "When it comes to atoms, language can be used only as in poetry. The poet too is not nearly so concerned with describing facts as with creating images."

Apart from the sciences, however, the creative power of metaphor can be equally appreciated in the arts, and it is here that the work of theater director Peter Sellars, a MacArthur Fellow at the age of twenty-seven, deserves an extra moment of attention.

■   ■   ■

THE LOBBY OF Boston's Copley Plaza Hotel is an elegant, high-ceilinged affair carpeted in royal blue and deep golds. Columns soar. Frescoes grace the upper reaches. Plenty of cut crystal glitters overhead. Chinese ceramic vases show off long sprays of delicately hued orchids. It's the kind of preciously decorated place you might expect to play host to dignitaries or heads of state. Instead, the discombobulated Peter Sellars comes racing down the long hall; he is dressed in worn blue jeans and a wrinkled shirt, his trademark Japanese Happi coat flapping like tail feathers.

Nobody minds. He is recognized at once. The staff is used to him treating the lobby tea court as an extension of his place of business and seats us at a diminutive breakfast table near a column. In no time I begin to appreciate his particular genius for metaphor.

"Fantastic! Will you look at this, please? This. Is. Fabulous! I love this! This is FABULOUS! Now if I did this in one of my productions—"

Peter Sellars cuts himself off in mid-sentence, laughing so hard he is in danger of choking on a spiced pumpkin muffin. He downs a huge swallow of milk before he can continue with his exuberant outrage. Exuberance and outrage come easily to him.

The occasion for this particular outburst is that a hotel employee is driving a noisy service vehicle down the hall of this elegant room, a kind of oversized go-cart clanking and grinding to the music of metal in agony as it inches down a stretch of royal carpet. It pauses, motor groaning, before a golden clock hung high on a wall. A metal accordion-style ladder unfolds and a Chinese man in a white lab coat gingerly scoots up a few rungs, advances the hour hand of the clock, and retreats down the steps. With the clunking of gears, the vehicle crawls off.

"What an image," Sellars hoots. A wild, whooping laugh punctuates his sentences. He has to shout to be heard over the racket but, piece by piece, he dissects the scene:

"Here we have this genuine Enlightenment clock with the little sun at the top and the little putto on the bottom. And this Chinese person dressed in a white technician's coat! In order to move the clock ahead one hour, it requires a Chinese person on a ridiculous tractor trailer moving at a snail's pace through the Copley Plaza. You see, if *I* did this in a show, people would be *so* upset. I would stage it with these very same marble columns and charming furniture and drive this crazy thing through the middle of the room and people would say, *How* can he do this? In fact, here we have it. In real life! If I did it in the theater, they would accuse *me* of being destructive or arrogant or a lunatic."

That's true. But it's not without cause.

Peter Sellars is a brilliant image-maker: metaphor and analogy are the warp and woof of his best ideas, his ability to perceive similarities among the dissimilar the very fiber of his most creative work. Bringing his knack for seeing the correspondence between things to his work in the theater, he reinvents stale plays and revives long-dead operas. Culling from an astonishing multiplicity of sources, he thinks nothing of combining rock videos with myth, martial arts with deaf signing. With this ability to finesse huge swings in perspective, he resuscitates works long fossilized under the weight of time and the pressure of custom.

Take, for example, his rendition of George Frideric Handel's opera *Julius Caesar*. When Sellars staged it, he set the action in the Middle East at the Cairo Hilton. Caesar is modeled after a head of state who never misses a photo opportunity. Cleopatra is portrayed as a spoiled poolside princess playing with her rubber toys in the swimming pool.

In each of Sellars's productions he shakes up an audience's perspective by exposing them to a completely new interpretation of a familiar work. In Mozart's *Don Giovanni*, the lead chomps down on Big Macs, pulls a switchblade instead of a sword, and shoots up during the champagne aria ("an aria of oblivion"). In Shakespeare's *King Lear*, His Highness has a Lincoln Continental center stage, a symbol of his authority that is dismantled at every performance. In Gilbert and Sullivan's *The Mikado*, Nanki-Poo rides a motorcycle, charges a bribe on a credit card, and lives in a Japan littered with Coca-Cola signs and car advertisements.

Marrying Handel to the Middle East crisis, Mozart to *Saturday Night Live*, Shakespeare to Detroit—is this creative or smart-alecky? The reviewers can't agree. There are those who believe that Sellars is a genius, a blazing meteor, a *Wunderkind* who directed forty of his own productions while still a student at Harvard, opening ten in a single month at the peak of his frenzy. His detractors take another view. Some see his updating as cheap and gimmicky—little more, they claim, than a series of sight gags. Mozart's *Così fan tutte* doesn't need a modern vocabulary, it's argued, and loses its potency when set in a neon-lit diner, the heroes modeled after the Blues Brothers. Setting Haydn's *Armida* in Vietnam, they complain, turns it into a political farce, and portraying Verdi's Duke of Mantua as a member of the mob is shameless and insulting.

Peter Sellars, inevitably, perpetually, and forevermore, creates controversy, leaving in his jet stream a litany of accusations like "sophomoric," "emotionally false," "unconvincing," "boring," "musically destructive," "petulant," and "brash." But if Sellars was once guilty of a reckless juvenility, few signs of it linger today. Perhaps that is the effect of having been fired from some fairly glamorous jobs. Or maybe it has more to do with the impact that turning thirty has on some people. But whatever the motivation, Sellars is very serious on the subject of why and how he relies so heavily on metaphor as a means of breaking out of tired, jaded, petrified preconceptions.

"What we face in America is a crisis in culture that has never previously existed," he explains, sufficiently recovered from his attack of laughter during the crane event. "In terms of the daily image bank, what we are handed every day in movies, in television, and in advertising is packaging that is devoid of meaning. Our wrapper has superseded the contents. Just to get an image to mean something again and to have power and resonance, and that provokes a genuine reaction from people instead of the prefabricated reaction they have been trained to have, is very hard work.

"What I'm trying to do is to take our modern-day vocabulary and enrich it," he continues. "Our vocabulary is pretty pale with respect to content, but is livid with event. You can't, for example, top the average car chase in some crummy movie except that it expresses nothing: good technique, blank content. What I do is to try to take our modern vocabulary and enrich it with references to other vocabularies—the Kabuki stage, or the tradition of eighteenth-century opera, or Greek theater, or a mood captured by a painting, or any other of a thousand possible references. By drawing these analogies and creating these metaphors, I'm trying to convey a deeper meaning, a meaning which is not just on the surface of things."

This is where a change of perspective figures into the creative process. A shift in perspective is a break with habit, a departure from cliché, a deviation from convention. A shift in perspective opens you up to something new, something you haven't considered before, something startling, something important. The realizations that flow from a fresh frame of mind are fuel for the creative impulse, the firecracker explosions of new ideas.

"These juxtapositions in my work that everybody makes such a fuss about—we do, in fact, live with them every day. They are the texture of our lives, and it's just a question of looking around and noticing that certain things exist right next to other things, like the Chinese man on the crane advancing the clock. That's real observation. If we broaden our perspective, we would see it. We don't need the arrogance of Hollywood or of Broadway to flatten it out in order for us to understand it."

He's right. In order to change our perspective we have to let go of what we are being fed by our culture, our politics, our socioeconomic conditioning. Sellars is a master at shifting his frame of reference. He does it by keeping his eyes open and seeing the similarities among dissimilar things—a technique available to any of us. All we need do is cultivate a taste for metaphor.

EXERCISE NO. 4: EXPERIMENTING WITH VISUALIZATION

The pivotal role that metaphor plays in Sellars's creative process leans heavily in the direction of still another device— the fourth and last I'll discuss—for breaking out of a stale perspective. This one concerns visualization.

In the generic sense, visualization is a kind of mental movie. Rather than imagery on stage, what's involved is a theater of the mind. The tailoring of scene, the shading of character, the witty dialogue, the suspenseful plot—every aspect of a visualized experience is controlled by the individual. He can work alone or in concert with another who, by the power of suggestion, "guides" him through the experience, hence the term "guided visualization"—a phrase commonly associated with a mental, meditative activity. For our purpose, the reason to engage in such an exercise would be to fish in a deeper pond of creative potential, but visualization exercises can be used for more mundane things as well—like enhancing one's self-image, improving performance at work, sharpening a tennis game, or even, it is said, attaining material wealth.

How does it work? Mike and Nancy Samuels, in their book *Seeing with the Mind's Eye*, relate an experiment that applies visualization to improving a basketball player's free throw. The study (conducted by Australian psychologist Alan Richardson) centered on three groups of students chosen at random, none of whom had experience with visualization. The first group practiced free throws every day for twenty days. The second group practiced only on the first and twentieth days, loafing in between. The third group also practiced on the first and twentieth days, but in the interim they spent twenty minutes a day *imagining* that they were sinking shots. The visualization they practiced was as rich in texture as each player was able to conceive. They were encouraged to feel the hard, rubbery round shape of the ball, to picture stepping up to the free-throw line, to feel the spring in their knees, to hear the *whoosh* as the ball passed through the net—or to adjust their aim on the next imaginary shot if, instead of a clean *swish*, they heard a metallic *thunk* when it bounced off the rim.

The results of the Richardson experiment were intriguing. The first group, the ones who practiced, improved twenty-four percent. The second group, the loafers, showed no improvement. The third group, the visualizers, improved twenty-three percent. Not bad.

And, apparently, the successful effects of mental imagery are not without historical precedent: Conrad Hilton imagined himself owning a hotel years before he bought one; Napoleon mentally practiced being a soldier well before he stepped onto a battleground; and Stanford University professor Robert McKim was so taken with the possibilities of mental imagery that he built the Imaginarium, a geodesic dome where students lie about on floor cushions and are treated to a controlled sensory experience with pictures flashing on the ceiling, sound effects surrounding them, vibrations felt through the floor, and odors piped in through the ventilation system. The idea, of course, is to free the imagination, to let it roam where it will, experience what it may.

This swiftly emerging pool of information on the creative benefits of visualization inevitably set me to wondering. Did any of the MacArthur Fellows have experience with visualization techniques? Was mental imagery a part of their creative process? Did any of them rely on mind pictures to cultivate their best ideas? Did any of them use visualization techniques in their work?

During the first couple of months of my interviews, most of the Fellows looked at me with a blank stare when I got to the questions involving the use of visualization and imagery as a means of breaking out of an old perspective. In fact, I was just about ready to drop this line of inquiry altogether when I met a man who not only knew what I was talking about but also had used these techniques in his work with cancer patients and children in distress. The MacArthur Fellow was Michael Lerner, a self-described "half-Jewish East Coast intellectual who was meant to be a college professor and by accident slipped into something else." The something else is an organization he founded called Commonweal.

■   ■   ■

THE DRIVING INSTRUCTIONS from San Francisco to Bolinas, California, home of Commonweal, were a page long and ended with the advice to allow two hours for the ride despite the fact that, if you knew the way, it was an easy fifty minutes. The local residents protected the privacy of their precious town so closely, a native explained, that signposts regularly disappeared or were turned around to confuse any infiltrators.

Actually, I had some some sympathy for the residents' behavior when at last I set eyes on the place. Arcing forests, springy green pastures, eucalyptus-scented air, wind-ravaged cliffs, pale beaches, the sparkling jewelry of sunlit ocean spray—if the best of anything belongs to the deities, this was God's country.

The Commonweal compound, a neat cluster of cool cream and pink houses, is set within the thousand-acre park of Point Reyes National Seashore. Apart from the felicitous beauty and healing solitude of the land, the area is further distinguished as the westernmost point of the United States, a site once inhabited by RCA and Marconi workers responsible for radio transmissions across the Pacific. I mention this only in case you should wander out here and wonder about the peculiar graveyard of telephone poles filling a vast meadow—hundreds of these weather-beaten crucifixes, standing stiff and idle, out of service now that peace rules the land.

With a knack for keeping one foot in staid academia and the other in an unorthodox alternative, Michael Lerner defies easy description. He started out as an Ivy League success story complete with all the trimmings: a doctorate in political philosophy, a joint appointment in the political theory department and the medical school, and plenty of research grants. But with his keen ability to pose useful questions and the raw courage to go in search of the answers, somewhere along the line he fell out of step and ended up on the West Coast, where, among other things, he became—what, exactly?

"Dear Dr. Lerner," I wrote in exasperation. "I'm having trouble describing your multiple talents and interests. Even a simple statement of your chosen field eludes me. Can you help?"

"Dear Denise," came the reply. "It's a hard question. Here are several answers: (1) I am a social scientist concerned with issues such as the recovery in modern medicine of perennial wisdom about psychospiritual approaches to health and healing; (2) I am trying to develop a field for the objective study of unconventional or complementary cancer therapies; and (3) My three central interests are helping exceptional cancer patients, helping children and young adults with learning and behavioral problems, and supporting youth prison reform."

Pursuing these interests, in 1976 he founded Commonweal, described in the literature as "a center for service and research in health and human ecology." Others have described it as the epitome of the art of caring.

Commonweal's longest-standing interest is with children in trouble—legal trouble, health trouble, family trouble. This work finds expression in many forms, including efforts to prevent the dissolution of families, to improve the conditions of incarcerated youths, and to help young people focus themselves in constructive ways to bring out the best within them.

The other major arm of activity, the Cancer Help Program, was started in 1985. In response to his father's bout with cancer, Lerner traveled all over the world in search of alternatives to traditional Western medical practice. What he discovered were dozens of alternative complementary therapies ranging from work with the psychological aspects of illness to nutritional, herbal, immune system–related, behavioral, technological, and spiritual approaches. This research, coupled with his own highly evolved philosophy of health and right-minded living, led to the establishment of the cancer program. Its threefold purpose is to reduce the stress of the cancer experience, to educate participants about options in lifestyle, and to explore the physical, mental, and emotional conditions under which healing takes place.

"The goal of the program is to support people who are navigating the life passage called cancer," affirms Lerner, sitting on the very edge of his office chair, his erect back a testament to his long-standing commitment to yoga. He is a man of imposing intensity, with a rare ability to be both spontaneous and highly articulate at the same time. His face is noticeably placid, remarkably inscrutable, belying the pressures of running such an important institution—and one likely to be widely misunderstood. The state of Western medicine is such that it does not openly embrace notions of mind over matter, or states of higher consciousness, or the role of personal responsibility in an illness.

"The key question for someone who is ill is not 'How did I get this cancer and how can I get rid of it?' but 'What is the unique song that I'm supposed to be singing?' " Lerner explains. "We are here to present options and assist people in choosing a course of action that seems most life-engaging and rejuvenating, no matter how curious it may appear to someone else. The people who come here become active participants in their well-being. We support the healing process and we firmly believe that healing can take place in living and dying. For all those who seek to sustain physical life, we vigorously support their effort, no matter how advanced the cancer. For those who see themselves as moving toward death, we support the healing that can take place in that surrender with equal strength."

Healing for Lerner does not necessarily mean curing; it means becoming whole again—which, in turn, involves a kind of upward movement toward our higher selves. This concept is part of the "perennial philosophy," a term coined by Gottfried Wilhelm Leibniz and popularized by Aldous Huxley. Huxley's writings have had a deep influence on the scholarly mind of Lerner, who has integrated certain of Huxley's views on illness and healing into his own work.

For participants in the Cancer Help program this translates into a daily schedule made up of healthful meals, yoga classes, guided meditation sessions, massages, relaxation exercises, information exchanges, discussion groups, and work with various forms of mental imagery, including fantasy sessions with the sand tray, a Jungian tool for self-exploration.

At the start of an encounter with the sand tray, the surface is raked smooth and clean. Surrounding it are literally hundreds of bright objects: tiny pretty dolls, colored marbles, shells, feathers, bits of wood, plastic toy soldiers, a miniature bride and groom, fake dinosaurs, ugly rubber snakes, mean sharks, toy pistols. Choosing whatever he fancies, the participant builds a scene in the sand. In this nonverbal form of self-expression, undertaken in a protected environment, the symbols that emerge often surprise the maker and may reflect everything from an insight about an unarticulated experience to a profound statement of what is needed for healing.

Such is the power of imagery; such is the creative power of a shift in perspective.

"We have a special interest in imagery and creativity," says Michael Lerner, "and consider the two to be intersecting inner forces that support psychological healing as well as enhance whatever movement is possible toward physical recovery. In addition to sand trays, we use art (sculpture, drawing, painting) to help people to discover aspects of their experience of which they hadn't been consciously aware. Relaxation in a safe environment is an excellent induction technique for the exploration of imagery because it leads into deeper states of consciousness in which both guided imagery and internally generated imagery can be vividly experienced."

Visualization is only one of the many activities that make up a stay at Commonweal but it is a powerful one—one that opens up perspective in pursuit of peace of mind and personal growth. The ability to shift perspective is the pivotal concept.

▣ 2 ▣

THESE FOUR EXERCISES—the mechanical quiz of hypotheticals, the experiments with sight, the construction of metaphors, and the wide applications of visualization, which can range from improving a basketball score to improving peace of mind—all share a common objective: expanding your creative potential by changing your perspective. The nature of one's own specific concern is not at issue. Building a better widget, eliminating waste in a production line, painting a better picture, reinterpreting a play or an advertising campaign, writing a better business plan, reducing stress, getting well, learning to say no—any mechanism that can shift perspective can shift your prospects. And sometimes the change can be dramatic:

Once upon a time, after John D. MacArthur's third airplane crack-up in two months while he was in training for the British Royal Flying Corps, he fled a Toronto hospital to escape the court-martial that surely awaited him and went to New York. Though AWOL, that didn't stop him from partying for a couple of days, promising marriage to a girl he picked up, and then stowing away on a troop transport ship destined for the front lines. Evidently he thought he could rectify his ailing service record—to say nothing of his desire to avoid a return either to his father's or a brother's home, neither being a desirable place to live as far as John was concerned.

It didn't work: he was discovered within the first half hour on ship and bounced out to await his just deserts. Meanwhile, his girlfriend and drinking companion for all of three days was a reporter and very much taken with the confident young MacArthur. In an effort to rescue him from his troubles, she wrote an article for a New York City paper profiling him as a brave young man so profoundly dedicated to his country that he ignored his serious injuries and stoically stashed himself aboard the ship so he could continue to serve in the war effort.

It worked: the War Department made him a hero and sent him on a tour around the country to march in parades, sell Liberty Bonds, and inspire patriotism in other young men. Everywhere he went, veterans were moved to thump him on the back, praise the father who had raised such a fine young man, and wish their own sons were more like him. Incredibly, his biographer writes, he expected to be cashiered and was lionized instead. In the end, he was fully exonerated, given a medical discharge and even a pension for his injuries.

It's all, you see, a matter of perspective.

A SHIFT IN THE SCENERY

October 10, 1987

Dear Ms. Shekerjian,

I would be happy to be interviewed. The question is: when to get together! I'm flying to Washington October 20, staying at the Cosmos Club, usually room 321. The desk is good about taking messages. Then, I'm not positive yet but will probably go to Chicago November 5 for the MacArthur reunion. November 8th I'll be at my brother's house in McLean, Virginia, or possibly their beachhouse at Nags Head, North Carolina. Then on Friday the 13th I fly to London. . . . So, we'll meet, I trust.

Best wishes,
Richard Critchfield

"Is Ellen Stewart in?"

"Ellen's in Istanbul. Who's callin'?"

"This is Denise Shekerjian. I'm the person who is working on—"

"Uh-huh. I remember you, doll. You bin callin' for a couple weeks now. Ellen's not back for a while, honey. There's Istanbul, then she's goin' to Greece, then Korea—hey Jimbo? is Mama goin' to Korea?—yeah, it's Korea next. They love her in Korea. After that she's goin' to Spoleto to check on her castle. You know about her castle?"

November 27, 1987

Dear Ms. Shekerjian,

My apologies for taking so long to reply to your letter. I would be happy to speak with you about creativity—or whatever else you think might be of use to you in your project. Although you are right in thinking that I'm often out of the country, these days—alas—I'm apt to be very much in the country in two senses. Which isn't to complain about South Hadley, but merely to suggest that I miss London, where we lived last year.

Warmest regards,
Brad Leithauser

Sky-blue aerogramme postmarked India:

April 7, 1988

Dear Ms. Shekerjian,

I'm sorry about the delay in answering your letter but it took some time to reach me. Unfortunately it will not be possible for me to be part of your series of interviews—from here I have to go to England and really don't know when I shall be in New York again this year.

With good wishes for the success of your project,
Ruth Prawer Jhabvala

March 31, 1988

Dear Ms. Shekerjian,

Thanks for yours of March 18. Unless I hear further word, I shall just materialize at the appointed hour at the Basil Street Hotel. But I think you should consider meeting me in Richmond, which being hilly and on the Thames, is, I think, the most scenic part of London suburbia. It's straight out the District line, last stop.

Looking forward to seeing you,
Richard Critchfield

When I started this project it never occurred to me that I would be writing a chapter that explored the relationship between creativity and travel. If I touched on it at all I thought it would be as part of my remarks on perspective. That was before the statistics of the enterprise were in.

Of the forty fairly randomly chosen MacArthur Fellows with whom I spoke, three lived abroad permanently—Paris, London, and Santiago—seven intermittently took up residence overseas as often as could be arranged, three traveled at least a couple of months a year on business or on pleasure or on some trumped-up excuse that combined the two, one confessed to getting to the airport several hours ahead of flight time because he claimed to work so well in charged bustle, three had been to China within the last six months, and at least two, I suspected, were afflicted with what Baudelaire called the Great Malady—namely, horror of home.

▪ 2 ▪

"Is the sun in your eyes?"

"No, I'm all right."

"Are you sure? Because if you want, we can pull this table back some."

"No, really, I'm fine. The sun feels good after all the rain we've been having." And besides, if the table were away from the window I wouldn't be able to see the view of the Thames that was, as promised, perfectly, splendidly, tastefully English.

It's a breezy spring day and Richard Critchfield and I have just come in from a long amble through Richmond's meandering streets. As one might expect from a crack journalist and former war correspondent, he possessed a dazzling rainbow of past and present detail about the town, which he delivered with unabashed enthusiasm: "That castle in the valley is Hamm House, built in 1610—rather gruesome, don't you think? Up this lane is the little hill Henry the Eighth stood on. Watch that car! Put an ordinary man behind the wheel of a car . . . There's our movie theater, the Odeon, four screens.

This copy center charges an outrageous forty-four pence a page, which is about a quarter! Down that row you come to the port where Catherine threw herself in. Here's the old Arms Tavern—pretty good ale—and the Italian restaurant, and the Lebanese place. Out that way was Sir Joshua Reynolds's house. That jackhammer noise is a renovation going on—now, why can't the Americans do that with their old buildings—it looks good, don't you think?"

I quite agreed but didn't have a chance to say so as he moved right along in a steady chirp of detail.

The table he has offered to move farther back into the shade of his living room was probably meant for dining, but serves instead as his desk. Pages and pages of densely packed type lie about, single-spaced, the way he talks. A beat-up Olivetti relic, a manually driven tool in this age of electronics, is within reach. Every now and then, a sideways breeze blows in from the patio and rattles the piles, causing a letter or two to flutter to the floor. They are notes related to the new book he's working on, entitled *An American Looks at Britain*, a kind of omnibus work on how Americans view the English.

(We already know, of course, how the English view the Americans. Pulitzer Prize–winning poet and MacArthur Fellow John Ashbery put it neatly once: "It seems that the English expect Americans to either sound the barbaric yawp or be sophisticated and move to England and become T. S. Eliot. When one does neither, or both, it produces a certain amount of consternation.")

The flat we are in is another rental in a long line of makeshift accommodations. The closest thing Critchfield has to a home is a spare room kept for him at his brother's house in Berkeley. It's not that the settled life doesn't suit him; it's that it has never really occurred to him to give it a try.

Richard Critchfield's first job in journalism was as the farm editor for the *Cedar Rapids Gazette* in Iowa. Modest beginnings for a man who evolved into an award-winning foreign correspondent. The early years of his career were occupied with war—the Asian species, starting with the China-India conflict in 1962 and ending with the better part of four years in Vietnam. His notes during the latter period filled four hundred and fifty steno pads. He got them out of the country by sending them home in batches as Christmas presents. He got himself out through the timely help of a friend, who secured a seat for him on *Air Force Two*, in the company of Hubert Humphrey.

Inevitably, Vietnam left scars: "You knew this was going terribly wrong. All these life-and-death situations. There was nothing like it. It was the most intense, most important experience of my life. It really finished me. I lost faith in everything. Such a nightmare. I wouldn't go out of doors at night for a long time. If there was a sudden noise—" Sighing deeply, exhalation being the breath of surrender, he breaks off into a momentary moldering fog of silence, his cloistered eyes sweeping the room like a stranger.

But if there was anything positive to say about the howling malaise of Vietnam insofar as it affected the shape of Richard Critchfield's life, it might be the fact that it led him to pursue a body of work that would cause him to wander the earth and occupy his affection for the next dozen years—his interest in villagers.

"Living in villages initially was an escape for me," he explains. "The war, we were told, was for the hearts and minds of the people. Well, what people? You didn't know. So I went into the fields and interviewed the Vietnamese with the help of a marvelous interpreter who turned out to be a Vietcong. And after it was over, I went to Mauritius and then India, Indonesia, Iran, Egypt, and so on. Living in the villages was like a resurrection. It was a kind of Tolstoyan experience. Life was reduced to the basics and very simple. You got up in the morning and you knew almost nothing was going to happen. And it was healthy and you were out-of-doors. I used to smoke like mad. And I lived on ten thousand dollars a year, which is amazing, but I had *plenty* of money. You didn't need it. It was great. It was wonderful. It was a sense of being *alive*."

Focusing on the lives of ordinary people, Critchfield embarked on a long, peripatetic migration through Asia, Africa, the Middle East, and Latin America, living in villages for anywhere from three months to a year or more, acquiring conversational fluency in such tongues as Russian, French, German, Portuguese, Hindustani, Arabic, and Urdu. While another writer might have wired home stories about wretched miserable souls caught up in the hopelessness of poverty, of drought, of famine, of war, Critchfield captured the dignity of the people he bunked with, the humor and the irony that lightened their way. The theme that threads through all his books, he explains, is the response of a culture to change, which he examines through a look at family, property, and the advent of a technology.

His subjects have included a Moroccan gangster now in a French jail, a Nubian witch doctor, Mauritian fishermen, farmers in India, Africa, Mexico, and Java, and a young Egyptian girl condemned for extramarital relations. His characters—aptly called, because though his works are nonfiction they read as smoothly as well-crafted novels—have names we are unlikely to have heard of: Mustafa, Barek, Hadj, Kuwa, Ngodup, Tonio, Saroop, Catalino, Buldev, Pala, Dhakel, Tjasidi, Ommohammed, and the devilish Shahhat. They are all inhabitants of the Third World, all people with whom he has lived, and worked, and drunk, and even, when demanded by the circumstances, brawled. They are friends who sat with him cross-legged under the banyan tree, smoking endless cigarettes and arguing village politics from nightfall to the luminescence of dawn. He knows them well, and, in the end, so do we.

A wandering man, Critchfield has traveled extensively in more than sixty countries, revisiting a sizable number of his beloved villages two, three, and four times. His travels and his work are inextricably intertwined—his journeys affecting his work, his work affecting his journeys. Every place he stops, he fills notebooks with the raw material from which he will explicate the broad themes of cultural change that interest him. A dense, full-bodied specificity of detail is the essence of his narrative voice. But it's too simple a sweep to conclude that the effect of his travels on his creativity is that it provides him with the virgin material from which his books and articles emerge. It's more than that, he explains. It's that the variety and intensity of his experiences have enriched him with career-shaping styles of thinking and working. Through his exposure to these ancient cultures just at the point when they are vanishing from the earth, he has become more curious, more attentive to nuances, more concerned for the world, less complacent, more alert, more perceptive—all attributes of a fertile imagination.

He is relentlessly on the move, constantly stimulated; the thoughtless habits and stale eye that may cramp another person's creativity are simply not an issue for him. His is a mind-expanding existence, and with his unquenchable thirst for detail he soaks up and meticulously recounts every aspect of the landscape, from the earthworm wriggling in the field to the tribal leader contemplating the stars. One reviewer, trying to come to grips with Critchfield's style, called a book of his "a rambling, idiosyncratic tour de force." The same might be said of the author: a compact, solidly built, gentle man who could outtalk a Sunday preacher, riding the rhythm of a tribal storyteller, hardly ever finishing a sentence or staying put in a chair.

". . . anyway, the fortune-teller at the state fair convinced me to drop the idea of law school in order to write, so I switched to journalism school, but after that I didn't have any money left or anything. Then, luckily, an uncle sent me a check for a thousand dollars. He was in his eighties and had no children, but he had fifty-six nieces and nephews and he wanted to escape inheritance taxes, so he sent them all various amounts of money. One thousand was the lowest, but that was okay. And he did it twice. The second time he didn't include me because I spent the thousand going around the world and Uncle thought it should have gone into the bank, you see. He couldn't understand that. I got as far as Hong Kong and then I had to write him to borrow three hundred more to get home. He *really* didn't like that. . . . A peripatetic life? Well, you know why that is, don't you? You have only one life and you want to sort of pack everything in."

Adrift in the undefined vastness of the world, intent on his quiet pondering of the great human tumult, he wouldn't have it any other way.

■ 3 ■

"WHY DO I LOVE to travel?" echoes Brad Leithauser, a young poet and novelist who lived in Kyoto (the setting for his first novel) and later in Rome, in London, and now in Iceland. "Partly, I suppose, it's a response to the blandness of my own upbringing. I can't think of anything more bland than the Midwest, and not having any particularly interesting ethnic origins, and being raised Protestant Presbyterian. It's bland— the whole environment is so bland.

"But it's also true that one of the things that happen when you go and live for three years in Japan," he continues, "is that you don't catch a glimpse the whole time that you're over there of *The Paris Review*, say, or *The New York Times Book Review*, or the *New Criterion*, or whatever. It gets very hard, then, to come back and feel that New York is the center of the world, because for three years it vanished but you survived. That's one of the main reasons I like living overseas. You deal with Japanese people in Kyoto, say, and for them Tokyo is the center of the world. Go to Iceland and Reykjavík is the center of the world. One needs to be constantly reminded that there is no center of the world. And there is a certain amount of clarification that comes with that."

The kind of clarification he's thinking of is the break from habit. It's not that habit is *all* bad. The usefulness of it is that it allows us to rely on routines and structures we've already thought through and have no need to think through again in order to live.

But by its very nature, creative thinking requires a break from habit that is, really, a kind of wooden thoughtlessness. Travel is one way, and apparently a common way, that creative people make the familiar strange again. Trying to get around in a strange culture, to feed yourself, to make sense of the news, to buy toothpaste, to manage a local bus, to express discontent, to profess love, to operate a vending machine or a telephone—all are familiar gestures made highly peculiar again, as they were when you were a child. In addition to all the personal and professional reasons to venture forth, leaving home is a way of retaining a kind of plasticity of response that keeps the eye unveiled, the mind sharp.

"My own sense is that if you have any realistic perception of yourself, you're acutely aware that the aperture through which you view the world is so tiny and so limited. I mean, here we are, in Yeats's phrase 'fastened to a dying animal.' From year to year you're stuck in your gender, in your up-bringing, in your language, in your own very, very limited mastery of anything. If you realize this, a kind of desperation sets in. There is nothing you can do about it except to widen your interests a bit. Change your horizon."

Leithauser breaks off for a moment with a short, pleading discourse on how he aches to live for a time in the frozen North Atlantic countries. He likes to be the foreigner, he insists, a dreamy, plaintive lilt to his voice. It confirms for him what he always suspected was true; that he doesn't fit in, that he is different, that he is a loner justified in complaining, only partly in jest, that his friends don't write him often enough. Just to be abroad for him has a tremendously liberating effect on his imagination and encourages new ideas, fresh perspectives, and a kind of hopefulness.

"I think I carry around with me an unrealistic, even silly, but absolutely irrepressible sense of the salvation of geography," he summarizes, sighing romantically. "Wouldn't I create fantastic poems—I say to myself—if I could only work on them under the aurora borealis?"

■ **4** ■

THEATER DIRECTOR Peter Sellars had not been easy to track down. To find him, I sent letters to his sister in Boston, his mother in Vienna, his old office in Washington, D.C., his new office in Los Angeles, a production group in Brooklyn, and a theater in upstate New York. No reply. As the months passed, I grew more and more desperate:

Dear Peter,

I think I've managed to alienate someone named Elsa at the Brooklyn Academy of Music who assures me that she is NOT your secretary. And various people at Lewis Allen Productions would be very happy never to take another message from me. But for all my efforts, I still haven't spoken with you about when and where we might meet. . . .

Dear Peter,

With over 200 MacArthur people from whom to select forty, why don't I give up trying to find you? Because Fred Wiseman tells me that you have a sense of humor which I could use right about now. Also, I liked the sound of your voice on my answering machine. You remember, don't you, that message which said, "No problem. I'm game. I'm in L.A. this weekend but after that. Okay? Let's talk . . ."—and then you hung up without leaving me a contact number. . . .

Say Peter,

The word is, you travel a lot. Here are some options. . . .

I offered to meet him in all the places I had heard he might be and that I thought I could get to, a list confined to a mere handful of the several continents he intended to visit within the next six months. When at last we came face-to-face, I asked him what it was that he got out of traveling and whether he thought it affected his creativity in any way. He answered by telling me about his mother.

"She is really great, quite amazing. I mean, she just ups and decides that it's time to live in Paris, where I was before going to Harvard, or Japan, which she did for four years. Now she's in Vienna. And she called and said, 'Well, let's go to Egypt for Christmas,' which is what my sister and I did. It's not that my family has any money, it's just that my mother decides it's time to do this. So we do it.

"These trips have, actually, a very great effect on my work. What I do is to spend a lot of time in museums and a lot of time looking at art not just because it is genuinely mind-expanding but because it makes you reconsider certain problems and I'm always interested in someone else's solutions. It's reassuring that you're not the first person to think about this but that this was also an issue for Rembrandt. And you can say to yourself, Okay, now how did Rembrandt think about this? It's very reassuring to see that Titian has treated this, or that Jackson Pollock has been on the problem. And, too, there's the exposure to all this specificity of firsthand detail. In theater, and probably in any kind of work, what gives it interest is specificity. What matters is to concentrate on something which provides you with an angle into the work. It's just a way in."

The way Sellars often gets "a way in" to a theater piece is to look around him for models, similar events, metaphors, analogies, and then add to that from his own observation. To accomplish this, he turns his intense focus on the play or opera, staring at it until a fragment of it suggests some image from contemporary life that an audience would recognize and that could serve as a guide to the meaning of the play. Sellars then twists that image into a prop, or costume, or character interpretation, or joke, or setting for the play. These images come from a fertile life of stimulation—much of it foreign-derived.

"For example, I'm staging *Julius Caesar* once again, an eighteenth-century opera by Handel sung in Italian, but I've made it a situation where it's the taking of hostages in the Middle East. I've set it up this way both because it's a situation that we know about, which has resonance for Americans who are going to watch this show, and because it's a genuine problem in the world which we should think about. So, okay. There's a scene at the end of the first act where an American woman and her son are taken hostage. The scene closes with a very beautiful lament that they sing, '*Sono nato per piangere*,' 'I was born to weep.' "

He pauses, lost for a moment in the tug of the scene's emotion and in the remembrance of all the trouble he had staging it to full effect.

"I knew it could be a very powerful, very moving thing if I could figure out how to stage it properly, but I was having problems with it. And then I went to Egypt over Christmas with my mother and, among other things, saw the tomb paintings of mourners at an Egyptian funeral. It was a series of weeping women, which is one of the most beautiful of the Egyptian tomb paintings. There it was: the answer."

What Sellars ended up doing was posing the figures in the Handel opera exactly the same way as on the tomb. His audience, of course, had no idea that the assembly of characters was based on an Egyptian tomb painting; all they knew was that the scene was very powerful, very moving.

"A hostage situation is, for most of us, only a newspaper headline or thirty seconds on the news. But the way I've filled it out, using Handel, using Egypt, using a Republican woman and her preppy son, it takes on another dimensionality which is more than just sensational and is more than just shock, but conveys a *grief*, something *lasting*."

If he hadn't seen the tomb paintings, he wouldn't have resolved the scene in precisely this manner. Yet Sellars is quick to point out that it's not just the begging and borrowing of foreign influences he derives from travel, but something larger than that. The value of his far-flung travels to his creativity goes to the very core of art itself—what it is, where it fits, why we care about it at all.

"What pleases me, what I keep looking for in American theater, is that moment when art takes on a civic importance. Take Japan, for example. The average Japanese village has a *matsuri*, an annual festival which to us looks like a performance, a Shinto art event. To them it's life. Or when we bring over a village dance from southern India. To us it's art. To them it's life, it's what they do every March.

"In America, there's this giant gulf between art and life. It's not part of the ongoing texture of things, something we encounter when we go to the supermarket. Instead, art is this bizarre thing with people wearing costumes in Lincoln Center. It's all these people watching while all these other people are doing. It's this imperialistic conductor at the head of a symphony orchestra. When you travel and look around, you see it's not like that in other places, the Pacific rim, for example. Art there is participatory and based on a collective village experience. Its exists without Herbert von Karajan. It doesn't happen in a hall where a proscenium arch separates the doers from the watchers. It happens in locations that have some significance to local geography, to the shape of the village, to shared history. Right now, what happens on an average Tuesday night at the Metropolitan Opera has nothing to do with shared history."

Sellars's next major project is to embark on a program of bringing ethnic and Third World work to America. He'll be traveling to Thailand, to Burma, to Tibet, to Chile . . . and everywhere he stops, he will be flooding his mind with stimulating detail, new ideas, and fresh perspectives.

"What interests me is the year 2000," he says, his rubbery face stretched wide with enthusiasm. "The way I see it, the first two hundred years of American culture were made by Europeans coming to New York, living on the Lower East Side, slugging it out, eventually moving uptown, building

Carnegie Hall, and that's culture in America. If something happened elsewhere in the land, it had to first go to New York and get the seal of American culture stamped across its forehead and then it was sent back to where it came from. I think the next two hundred years of American culture are going to be shaped by *another* set of immigrants—Asians and Hispanics—who are going to create *another* set of vocabulary with its own sense of moral values, and the distribution center will be Los Angeles."

◼ **5** ◼

SO WHAT can we learn from Richard Critchfield, squatting in the dust under an unforgiving Persian sun, or from Brad Leithauser, roaming the icebound upper reaches of the globe, or from Peter Sellars, who seems genetically incapable of spending a full week in one spot, or from our own travels, no matter whether across the state line or across the equator? It's this: expanding our horizons expands the reach of our own creativity. It's a principle that calls to mind the cry of the German poet Rainer Maria Rilke: "Whoever you are, go out into the evening, leaving your room of which you know every bit; your house is the last before the infinite, whoever you are."

■

SUSTAINING CONCENTRATION

AND DRIVE

FRESHLY CONCEIVED, innocent, and untested ideas, no matter one's field, hold certain characteristics in common. They are, for the most part, ephemeral in nature—which is to say, timid, indecisive, fluid, and unstable. When we first think of them we experience the held breath of anticipation, and when we talk about them, the hot flush of uncertain promise. These are characteristics that will endure until an assault has taken place in an effort to claim dominion. Without the attack, a new idea is nothing but fragile potential. Owning it is something else again. In the cold, hard business of giving it form and setting the parameters and running it through its proofs, what was once lively and airborne turns as heavy and as obstinate as dour stone—this is where drive and concentration figure into the creative process.

Consider, for example, psychologist Howard Gardner, a genial man long interested in the mechanics of the mind. In the spring of 1987 he visited China—his fourth and longest trip since 1980—to take a look at creativity and arts education. Upon his return, and during the space of a scant six days punctuated with the responsibilities of running a bustling research institution, he sat at his typewriter and wrote a four-hundred-page book on the subject—single-spaced. On the seventh day, like all ambitious creators, he rested.

Or consider writer-filmmaker John Sayles. In order to finance his own films, he accepts freelance scriptwriting assignments. Once he had to hole up in a Los Angeles hotel room to write—on incredibly short notice—an entire screenplay, popping in and out of the swimming pool and setting alarm clocks at half-hour intervals to be sure his attention didn't fade. But he did it: one hundred and twenty inspired pages of scene, action, plot, and dialogue in the space of three days.

Or, too, there is Shirley Brice Heath, a tall slice of a woman with a silvery, tinkling laugh and an endlessly elegant bearing. From the first warm handshake it is at once apparent that she is of gentle blood and good bone. Never for a moment would her cultivated manner, her articulate speech, and her intellectual dominance cause one to suspect that she came of age in the backwoods of the Deep South, with farm animals for companions and the Bible the only reading material within miles. In the early years, Daddy was a traveling salesman, Mother was a dime-store clerk, and Shirley was sixteen before she learned the difference between cabbage and this thing called lettuce that you're supposed to tear, not cut. That she is now a full professor in the social sciences and humanities at Stanford University is, in a word, extraordinary.

Are there any tricks involved? any fancy footsteps? any miracles? I don't think so. I think what we're talking about here is sustained concentration and drive. Those are fairly mundane concepts, straightforward and available to any of us. What we're talking about is plain, purposeful hard work.

■ **2** ■

"AS AN ONLY CHILD I grew up essentially alone," Shirley Brice Heath explains. "Our home was in southwestern Virginia, dusty rural tobacco country, fifty miles from the nearest town. My grandmother was around a good bit, but she wasn't educated. My father would show up occasionally, but then he'd be gone. My mother wasn't happy on the farm, so she would also take off. Other than my grandmother's Bible, there were no books in my household. I never remember seeing either of my parents read, and the extent of their writing was maybe a check or a list."

Shirley Brice Heath sits with an erect carriage in the lounge of Mariposa House, the sun-bleached, whitewashed home of Stanford University's humanities department. Her deportment is that of a woman of privileged breeding: mint tea sipped from a china cup, the smart looks of classically cut clothing, crisp speech, a certain refinement of spirit, idle hands folded neatly in the lap. There is a gentleness about her—and there is nothing stronger in the world than gentleness.

"I think the first time I was really conscious that there was more to life was when I lived with a foster family for a period when in grade school and also when at sixteen I spent a summer with an aunt and uncle. These relatives were educated people living in a northern college town. They told stories of their experiences and the stories were exciting. My cousins had books around them, they had seen plays, they had done all these things, and I thought, My gosh, there is all of *this* out there? I suddenly realized that I had to work hard and fast to find out all about it."

One of the most neglected areas of the study of creativity is that of drive and intentionality. Habit is so much easier to manage than will. Routine is far kinder to the mind and body than the effort required to animate the heavy, cold stones of something new. The blueprint for Heath's life had long been established: when she came of age, she would quit high school and marry the boy up the road, a fine, hardworking boy, everybody said, with an eighth-grade education, plenty of solid know-how for one household. After marriage she would settle down to farm chores, child rearing, home tending, and, in the fullness of time, be buried in the town lot. Here lies Shirley: earth to earth, ashes to ashes, dust to dust.

"It was when I was living with my cousins that I suddenly woke up to the fact that if I accepted *anybody's* definition of what there was in the world, I would be limited. It was an enormously powerful realization, which caused me to become very cautious of abiding by anyone's assessment of what the limits were. From that moment on I never let *anyone* tell me what was and was not possible."

Through the sheer power of will, backed by the encouragement of her northern kin, Heath insisted on finishing high school, the first to graduate in the history of the entire region and for the next ten years thereafter.

The struggle to get to college was even more monumental, but in the end she enrolled in a fundamentalist Baptist college. After a year of that she ran away, first to Gulfport, Mississippi, where she took correspondence courses, then to southern California, where she taught three days a week to earn the money to continue her education. A detour to New York, two marriages, two children, and a doctorate later, she assumed an enviable position at Stanford. Here towers Shirley: a distinguished scholar, and a woman for whom the crest of life is still rising.

"If there is a key to my progression, I think it is in the fact that I never accepted any sort of constraint but immediately moved out beyond it. For me 'can't' simply isn't acceptable, and I urge my students to get it out of their vocabulary. I want them to kick against any boundaries that are set up and to figure out how they can shift resources to move beyond them. It takes imagination and hard work because, as far as I'm concerned, there have been no good solutions to problems that haven't demanded a lot of hard work."

Drive and discipline form the undercarriage of her existence. Not only does determination account for her ability to have transcended the boundaries of her childhood years, but it also enabled her to sustain decade-long research projects delving deep into anthropology, sociology, ethnography, and linguistics. Her first book is a definitive work on the evolution of language in Mexico. Her second explores how black and white children in rural and suburban communities learn and use language in family and school systems. Her third one, the one she's wrestling with now, will be a social history and ethnography of major American writers, her most ambitious work to date. All her writing is careful, exact, as finely tuned to language as harp strings that sound with the passing breeze. When she's in need of a model of elegance, she tells me, she reads not literature but hard science, preferably physics.

One book every ten years is the creeping pace of a very serious, very devout scholar. Heath possesses the seriousness to sustain these long periods of intense concentration and the devotion to insist upon the kind of thoroughness that would make it difficult for her to pass on a recipe for apple pie, for instance, without first examining all the literature concerning apples starting with the Garden of Eden.

Apart from establishing her reputation in academic circles, her drive has also sustained her through some shattering personal experiences, prime among them an accident suffered by her daughter which resulted in extensive brain damage. It is tragedy of a magnitude that anesthetizes the mind and ices over the heart. There is nothing anybody can do, she was told, but she rejected that assessment, marshaled her resources, and went to work. As a result of her efforts, her daughter is much improved.

"People are always saying to me, your story would make such a wonderful story for people who have brain-damaged children, why don't you write it up? My answer is that I don't know if one could sanely recommend the kind of hard work that it takes to identify resources and shift them to best advantage. Luckily, I had resources: I had colleagues in high intellectual positions who knew my daughter before the accident and who were able to come to dinner once a week, even when she wasn't supposed to be seeing anyone, and pull her into the conversation and act as though she were behaving normally. I had the energy to meet my responsibilities here on campus and also to be a mother and a half on call with her. I had access to medical information; I went to the medical library and read everything I could get my hands on. I had the belief that if she would just come out of the coma, if I just had *something* to work with, I could go on."

In the same week her daughter was to be released from intensive care, her husband was whisked into the emergency room with a stroke. Again, Heath handled it by the same three rules that have governed her adult life. She quietly ticks them off for me, one, two, three: *never* accept that it can't be solved; understand that in order to solve it you're going to have to break down some structural barriers; and don't *ever* think the solution is going to be easy.

"I take a perverse approach to anything that is offered as simplistic or finished or universal," she explains. "My tendency to any of that is to turn it upside down. Or go at it sideways. Or break it apart. I'm very leery of anything which is presented as being simple, neat, and finished. I have strong doubts about any of those things. The human condition defies simple, neat, finished. I think part of our destiny as humans is to prove that those three things are not productive, are not appropriate for creative growth."

When she reflects on this period, her voice slides up a tiny bit in pitch and her thin, graceful hands flutter like the restless wings of a butterfly. These minor signs of angst notwithstanding, there is a deeply rooted, palpable strength about her and the appearance of stature. Determination makes one taller. Certainly she is lucky to have been born into this world made of such durable fiber.

"Luck has nothing to do with it," she assures me, "and I've seen very few examples in which that wasn't the case. I really *believe* that if you're willing to work hard enough, and if you're shrewd enough, and if you learn from other people, and by sizing up situations—you can do absolutely anything. There are no secrets, no inside easy steps that everybody hopes for. We all want to find the secrets, but they just don't exist."

The point, of course, is to commit yourself to the task, to stay focused, to stay concentrated, but there's a subtlety here that shouldn't be missed: too often, we mistake the idea of drive with staying rigidly and irrevocably focused on a goal. Accordingly, we act aggressively and urgently, we take the offensive, and we propel ourselves forward. The misconception here is that often we do not possess the means to get what we want—either we don't have enough knowledge, or we exhaust ourselves, or we make an error, or we haven't assembled all the tools, or we are unlucky—and so simply driving hard toward a desired outcome is likely to result in nothing more than a waste of precious energies.

Shirley Brice Heath, by contrast, is driven, but she understands the all-important notion of remaining flexible in that push. Through that flexibility she broadens the means available to her to solve the problem she's working on. If it's not going well she calls upon other resources, or she shifts her priorities, or she goes to the library and educates herself on the options—this is willful driven behavior but it's not rigid. If one refuses to hold firmly to a single approach, it becomes possible to make one's way along one or another of the bypaths that open up to all sides. It is this sort of flexible drive and flexible hard work that make the difference between innovative progress and something less satisfying.

■ 3 ■

JOHN SAYLES WAS thirty-three when he was awarded his MacArthur Fellowship, the age at which geniuses once died. But turning out a steady progression of books, plays, films, short stories, and scripts, he lives as if one never died.

Sayles's first adult taste of artistic success came in response to a fifty-page short story he sent blind to Atlantic Monthly Press. Peggy Yntema, an editor, read it and immediately shot back a quick note asking: "Who *are* you?" He's John Sayles. He's always been John Sayles. But if she was asking, Are you a professional writer? Are you published? Have I seen your work someplace else before? the answers were no, no, and no.

At the time he was working as a meat-packer in a sausage factory. To Sayles it was just another job in a succession of the sort of jobs an able-bodied person took on to cover the bills: hospital orderly, ditchdigger, factory worker, seller of his own blood. On occasion he was the only white man in the factory; at times, the only one who spoke English.

The story he had written featured a dwarf private detective who dressed in drag to play baseball in a traveling freak show. This from a man who stands a lanky six feet four inches tall, is muscular, big-boned, and strung together with the rangy looseness of a guy who likes to shoot baskets at the neighborhood lot.

He was encouraged to turn the story into a book, and six months later finished *Pride of the Bimbos,* his first novel, which sent an electric shock through blasé literary circles. Less than a decade later, he could write a résumé more suited to a man twice his age: a second novel, *Union Dues,* nominated for both the National Book Critics Circle Award and the National Book Award, a couple of O. Henrys for his short stories, an anthology of his shorter pieces (*The Anarchists' Convention*), a stage play, over two dozen screenplays, six of his own films, a couple of rock videos for Bruce Springsteen, and a third novel (*Los Gusanos*) in progress, which he says has been "trailing after me like a tin can on a string."

How is such a sizable creative overflow possible? The answer, at least in part, had to do with drive. And in Sayles's case, the drive comes from an abiding desire to make his own movies.

"I realized that for me to exist as a director, I have to put my own money into things, so I've been consciously trying to build money up. It's not that I would ordinarily be that prolific, it's that to make movies you need a skill or a scam to support the work. I'm lucky I can write and that I like to write."

The quickest way for Sayles to accumulate cash has been to churn out screenplays on commission for other directors and producers. It was a line of work he fell into when Roger

Corman, master of the grade-B movie, offered him a job re-writing the script for the film *Piranha*. Sayles dashed it off quickly and effectively, bringing as much resonance as he could to the characters, seriously trying to figure out how people would really act and talk if a carnivorous, life-threatening fish were intent upon eating its way through various socioeconomic classes. The script was so successful, Sayles became a regular in the stable of freelancers called upon to write about giant alligators, gangsters, cave dwellers, werewolves, and other science-fiction and horror subjects equally far removed from his own work.

His own films—about lesbianism (*Lianna*), the reunion of college radicals ten years after their glory days (*Return of the Secaucus Seven*), the radical and economic strains that splinter a high-school romance (*Baby, It's You*), urban alienation (*The Brother from Another Planet*), the struggles of a coal-mining town when a union organizer shows up (*Matewan*), the Chicago Black Sox scandal of 1919 (*Eight Men Out*)—are hardly the kind of material Hollywood snaps up. Additionally, Sayles insists on keeping artistic control. As a result it's often been hard for him to find funding, which, in turn, means that most of his movies are not produced in the sequence in which they were written.

Take the film *Matewan*, for example, the story of a 1920s gritty union fight in West Virginia. It was a story idea that came to him during his post-college years, hitching around the country working odd jobs and listening to the yarns of truck drivers and factory workers. Sayles wrote the script, but at once recognized that to do it properly would be expensive. Accordingly, it languished for seven years on the shelf while he tried to raise the money. When at last the time came to gear up for preproduction, the money fell through again.

Time to give up, to recognize a failure?

Heck no, says Sayles, his lupine eyes registering surprise. Instead, he just kept working. Uninterested in the distractions of drugs or liquor, or the high life of Broadway, or the carnival of Hollywood, Sayles plugs on, turning it out, page after page, film after film. *Matewan* would get made eventually, he was sure (and he was right), but in the meantime it made more sense to him to focus not on the loss but on what he might do in its place.

"And so, we decided to do *Brother from Another Planet*, but in order to finish filming it before snow fell we had to do it right away, which meant that I had to write it right away. But I was working for somebody else at the time on a rewrite of a script. A lot of movies I write for other people have been rewrites in which they have an absolute start date for filming, so I have to produce the new script quickly, throwing out everything the guy before me wrote, and starting over. So, very often, I have only a couple of weeks to produce and my own work gets sandwiched in where I can."

Brother from Another Planet is a strange, evocative little film about a mute black man from outer space who lands in Harlem and can't explain why or how he got there. The main character is ideal for portraying alienation: he is a jobless, homeless, speechless, helpless, hopeless, unloved minority figure in a nasty part of town, and an alien, figuratively as well as literally.

The idea for the film took shape from a series of four dreams, disjointed and full of odd and wild images—the way dreams can be. Sayles quite clearly remembers the imagery that shuffled through his sleep: menacing street corners, a crazy title appearing in three dimensions on a screen, a bigfoot character running around a black neighborhood, a growling cop, and a lot of saxophone music filling up dark, gloomy alleys.

Does it seem incredible that a jumble of incoherent dreams could give rise to a movie?

How the brain, in our dreams, selects and distorts certain images from the thousands of pictures we are bombarded with each day is still very much a mystery, but it's not unusual for creative, hard-driving people to generate good ideas when they sleep. Examples of creative dreaming fill the literature: Giuseppe Tartini, the eighteenth-century violinist and composer, dreamed about the devil, which gave rise to his sonata *Trillo del Diavolo*, or "The Devil's Trill"; William Blake learned of a copper-engraving process in a dream in which he conversed with his deceased brother; Alexander the Great plotted his battles according to his dream interpretations; and contemporary artist Jasper Johns launched his star-spangled career by putting on canvas an image that haunted him nightly in his dreams—the American flag. Here, exactly, lies the value of immersion in work. Someplace between conscious striving and accident, partway between inaction and action, something somnabulistic occurs, and an idea moves from shadow to light. It's a gift from the self to the self—unexpected, yet there all the time, waiting to be recognized.

It doesn't seem unusual to Sayles that the movie came together from a series of dreams. He credits the spillover effect to working very, very hard at the time, writing five screenplays for other people that year, to say nothing of his own work. In the end, *Brother from Another Planet* got made: it was written from start to finish in six days and filmed in twenty. The beauty of drive, it seems, is that it works.

□ **4** □

HOWARD GARDNER IS INTERESTED in the kind of questions that have wandered in the minds of all thinking men throughout history: What is intelligence? How does the mind work? What does it mean to think? Where do the gifts of genius come from? What makes a Mozart? a Darwin? a Dante? When a poet asks these questions, lyrical sonnets are spun. When a scientist asks them, research institutes like Project Zero are born.

Project Zero, housed within Harvard's Longfellow Hall, was conceived in 1967 by, among others, philosopher Nelson Goodman, to study the development of artistic skills. The name comes from Goodman's quip that when it comes to studying the mind, "no one knows anything about it, so we'll call it Project Zero." Howard Gardner has been affiliated with the institute since its inception and has been codirector since 1972. Not surprisingly, then, it was within these offices that I found him, a man with a kind of round, boyish face, quick wit, and bubbling enthusiasm that belie his forty-some years.

Dr. Gardner's approach to the mind is to navigate the waters of ordinary children, child prodigies, idiots savants, artistic kids, and brain-damaged patients. Dividing his time between neuropsychological research at the Boston Veterans Administration Medical Center, writing books, teaching classes at Harvard and at the Boston University School of Medicine, and overseeing the research group at Project Zero, he has enjoyed a many-sided look at questions of creativity.

At the beginning of his multifaceted interest in human cognition and arts education, he focused his efforts on the study of symbols, drawing on Ernst Cassirer's work among others. Cassirer postulated that understanding how humans manipulate symbols provides us with a key to various forms of creativity. More recently, Gardner has been drawn to the area of intelligence. Rejecting the notion that human beings can be assessed in one flat dimension—that is, the old idea that intelligence is a gift we were either born with or not, and that it can be measured by a single I.Q. number, a score of 70 branding us "dumb" for the rest of our life while a score of 130 puts us over the top into the realm of "genius"—he has developed a far more expansive and pluralistic view of how the mind computes information. In *Frames of Mind* he identifies seven types of intelligence: linguistic, logical-mathematical, spatial, musical, kinesthetic, interpersonal, and intrapersonal. It's a theory that recognizes the need for better ways to assess the strengths of the whole child. Thanks to Gardner's work, the old question: How smart is he? is giving way to the more meaningful inquiry: How is he smart?

Such an expansive view of man's intellectual potential has cast Gardner, at least insofar as the lay world is concerned, as something of a hope-giver: it is not, for example, that your child is dim-witted but rather that he may possess the kind of gifts that are not measured by S.A.T. scores. But this is a role he never intended for himself. When asked about his contribution to the field, he sums it up neatly by saying that if he has added anything to psychology it is in getting people to pay attention to artistic ways of thinking as well as the scientific ways.

It's an assesssment of self that fits well with the dual sides of his nature: on the one hand he is a scientist rigorously committed to unraveling the mind's secrets; on the other, he is a lover of music with an uncontained passion for Mozart, whose biography he hopes one day to write. It's this same duality that makes him the perfect person to talk with on matters of creativity.

"I think if you're going to write something about creativity for the public," he advises, "one of the main points is to disabuse them of the nonsense you see advertised: 'Come for a weekend, learn to brainstorm, learn to free-associate, we'll make you a creative individual.' I mean, that just doesn't work. It's a serious business for serious people. Creative work requires, I think, being a certain kind of person, which includes being able to work on things for years, a drive not likely to come to people who paid five hundred dollars for a weekend under a tent."

What carries creative people through from the conception to the completion of a project is drive and concentration born from a sense of purpose. Purpose is what dictates the entire range of the enterprise. Through intention, goals are shaped and ideas generated to fulfill them. Through relentlessness come the cultivation of skills and the perfection of technique. Through motive come the decisions as to which projects to pursue and in what order. Through resolve, resources are marshaled and the necessary strength mustered to overcome obstacles rather than to be overcome by them. Through tenacity, friends and collaborators are selected. And through will comes the wisdom to know when to part paths with influences one has outgrown.

Creative work doesn't evolve simply from wishing or accident, or wholly from a mystical flash of inspiration. It also requires a sustained purpose and the discipline of trying over an extended period of time.

"I mean, Thomas Mann's novels got greater because he was dealing with seventy years' worth of experience and reflections upon those experiences, and not because he suddenly started to do something new," Dr. Gardner remarks.

Of course, he is right. It's effort that most often accounts for enduring works of art and invention, regardless of one's gifts, regardless of one's elevated sensibilities.

▪ 5 ▪

AT THE OFFICES of La Mama, three flights up a ramshackle brownstone on New York's Lower East Side, a tall, thin man known as Jimbo is rooting through a bank of file cabinets, pulling out wads of press clippings he thinks I ought to have. As Ellen Stewart's longtime friend and manager, he knows all the wacky stories and treats me to his version of them as he helps to stuff the clippings into a grocery sack.

"Thanks a lot, Jim," I tell him as I test the weight of the bag. "I think I've got plenty, and besides, it's hard to say if I'll even get to talk with her."

It seemed like the right thing to say. If anyone could arrange a meeting, he could. But if I was looking for assurances that I would at last come eye to eye with the doyenne of Way Off Broadway theater they weren't forthcoming from Jim. He chuckled and looked fondly at a photo of her—a determined woman dressed in safari clothes, hands solidly clamped on her hips, feet planted firmly in the middle of a dusty Moroccan bazaar. She looks pleased with herself. She should be. She just bought a pile of rugs for her castle at a giveaway price.

"Well, that's the thing about Ellen," he sighs. "I've never met anybody with so much energy, so much determination, so much purpose. Her drive is unbelievable. Incredible, really. I've alway said that if she ever dies it will be going downhill at full speed on roller skates."

■ **6** ■

"BUT THERE'S A POINT about drive that you're missing," said Ved Mehta, feeling for the window ledge so he could shut the window to keep the rain out. Mehta, a Punjabi born in Lahore, India, is totally blind from a disease he contracted at the age of three. When Ved was still a boy, he was sent to this country by his caring and well-intentioned father to attend a school for the blind. At fifteen he was completely on his own, a blind boy, a poor and tentative boy, an Indian, an exile. "I think what you need to consider is the matter of *why* a person is driven."

Why? Well, there are a thousand reasons, aren't there, but at the bottom of it all, isn't a person driven by the hope of success? Isn't the hope of victory at the core of any tremendous effort, any enormous show of will, any momentous span of endurance? Couldn't Mehta himself attest to the seductive lure of sweet success, given the numerous acclaimed volumes he has written of his family's history, his much praised work for *The New Yorker*, in whose hallowed offices we sit, his nonficton works on Gandhi, on India, and on the English?

Mehta thought about this for a minute, the rain outside the window like the beat of a wild gypsy tambourine, and then answered:

"What does it mean to succeed as a writer, if you really think about it? Sometimes I long for the kind of success—you know, a man walks into a party with a *big* voice and a *big* handshake and you know he is comfortable with himself, he is at ease with himself, he is at ease with the world. But for the writer, you could give him a Mercedes, châteaux to live in, every earthly thing, and still he wouldn't be comfortable. There's something in the nature of the craft that will always set him apart. Tolstoy. What did Tolstoy really want or need? Here was a man who denounced *War and Peace* and *Anna Karenina* as false books not worth reading. He had children. He had marriage. He had genius. It wasn't enough. Why? It's the discomfort of genius—I don't know how else to put it. A writer can never be satisfied with an idea of success. Writers may have something in common with nymphomaniacs—they have to keep going. More and more and more."

Why does a writer or any creative person feel compelled to do more—and more, and more, and more? The answer may be that tucked in the recesses of a creative person's mind is the notion of the Ideal—and there can never be any discussion of success or fulfillment or contentment but only of failure because the ideal is impossible to attain. Nonetheless, the creative person is driven to try and try again.

"All I can say," confirms Joseph Brodsky, another exile, "is that I never cared that much with what is happening with me and my work. That's one of the reasons because of which I don't consider myself a professional." (If you ask Brodsky what he does for a living, he will tell you that he is a teacher. He would rarely consider calling himself a writer and certainly not a professional writer. Writing, he says, "is a sideshow for living, for thinking, for being.")

"I'm not trying to be coquettish," Brodsky continues. "I never put much of premium on the premiums, *ja?* All I want to do, the main thing is simply the process itself of work. And that's tremendously self-rewarding. It's easier for me now to say that I don't care about success, et cetera, et cetera, et cetera. Nobody would believe it because my story up to a certain point is the story of a successful writer. But—how should I put it?—it never meant much to me and it still doesn't. And, technically speaking, if you put my success in perspective and compare either the MacArthur or the Nobel to the annual income of the New York, let's say, dentist or lawyer, *ja?*, well, you wouldn't call it success. When you get this or that sort of small, or big preferably, revelation in the process of work— and when you are capable to express or convey that revelation in a memorable fashion—that's basically what it's all about."

What, then, drives a creative man? The discomfort of genius, the process of work itself? A sense of mission, the call of duty, the need for respect? One thing is for certain: it has little to do with the hope for success, little at all to do with the rewards of victory.

ENCOURAGING LUCK

WHAT A STRANGE and contradictory idea, *encouraging* luck. Everybody knows that by definition luck is the absence of assignable cause. Which is to say: uncertain, random, fluky, chancy, stray, unforeseeable, indeterminate, accidental, unintentional, haphazard, fifty-fifty, fickle, freaky, iffy, in the stars, in the cards, the way the cookie crumbles, the world turns, the coin tosses, the wheel spins, the dice fall, the ball bounces. . . .

Language is so revealing; it is the mirror that reflects our innermost convictions. So many words and phrases to express the same sentiment amount to strong evidence that a belief in luck is deeply ingrained in our concept of how events are shaped. One has only to pronounce the word to produce good spirits. Accordingly, it comes as no surprise that there is a natural tendency to admire these MacArthur Fellows from a distance, to tally up their dazzling achievements, and to sigh from some deep and sorrowful place within when uttering the claim: Fine for them—some people have all the luck.

To the contrary, that is both a naïve view of the way things work and a convenient crutch for our disappointments. It's the defeatist who seeks to explain away creative achievement solely in terms of luck, a perspective that would have us believe the role of luck in creativity is something akin to a fortuitous flash of lightning. A more accurate assessment would be if a person went to the hardware store, bought the best lightning rod he could find, climbed to the highest point of his roof, bolted the contraption in place, and then waited patiently next to it for a storm.

There are accidents in life, but it's simplistic to believe that chance occurrences account for wholly unanticipated finds. More often a lucky break is really an accident the creator has converted to his purpose. If the accidental discovery fits the context of one's work, it's because he struggled to make it fit. "Chance," Louis Pasteur once remarked, "favors the prepared mind."

There are a thousand accidents in a week of life, but to select among them is something else again. Certainly, there is no trick involved in recognizing those dazzling moments that are decisive in shaping one's future. The profound, the audacious, the startling, and the epiphanic rarely pass without notice. But what is more difficult is to detect the subtle happenstances and to appreciate, by turns, their providential thrust. Making enough room in our lives for accidents to happen and exercising wisdom in our selection among them affords us the room to try to *encourage* our luck. There are three ways, at least, of doing this: being attentive, so you notice the nuances in daily life; being curious and inquisitive enough to follow your curiosity around a blind corner; and being able to relax and have a good time.

◦ **2** ◦

IAN GRAHAM KNOWS all about the kind of luck that comes from maintaining an air of attention and an eye that notices odd things. So does another MacArthur Fellow, David Stuart.

Graham, an Englishman, was fifty-eight at the time of his MacArthur, working away in the decrepit upper reaches of Harvard's Peabody Museum. David Stuart, an American, was eighteen and about to start college at Princeton. Given the spread of their ages, you would think that the two wouldn't have much in common, but, in fact, each is an important player in the same fairly arcane field: the story of the lost civilization of the Mayas.

David Stuart's introduction to the field came from his father, George, an archaeologist for *National Geographic*. When David was eight, George Stuart was asked to join an expedition to map the ancient Mayan city of Cobá. He accepted the opportunity, and with his wife and four children, moved from a stately block in Washington, D.C., to a thatched hut buried deep in the Yucatán, where they remained for five months. David's memories of this time are of playing in the ruins and digging up potsherds from the dirt floor of their primitive shelter.

Ian Graham's love affair with the field is less easy to trace. Originally, he was educated in England as a physicist. The shift to all things Mayan, as he tells it, had to do with "an astonishing 1957 Rolls-Royce" that he once owned and drove across America some thirty years ago, making one too many left turns, which landed him in Mexico.

Where he comes from, he says, it was perfectly normal for a young single gentleman to drift about aimlessly instead of aggressively pursuing a career. Oh, eventually he intended to sink his teeth into something, but, good heavens, what was the hurry? People of his social standing didn't see the need to be so urgent about a career the way Americans carried on. What was the rush? Why such insistence?

And so he stayed, washed up on the shores of Mexico with no plans. To amuse himself he visited museums, and took excursions to dusty towns populated with round-faced Mexicans and thin stray dogs more idle than he. He also went to lots of dinner parties—in high demand, no doubt, this charming young English gent with his handsome bow ties and his astonishing Rolls. Often, over the clinking of glasses and clattering of forks, the talk came round to the Maya. "The who?"

Graham mused, and for lack of anything more pressing, decided to find out.

The Maya flourished, the experts are fairly sure, between A.D. 250 and the Spanish conquest. At the height of their empire, the civilization stretched from the Yucatán peninsula through Guatemala, Honduras, and Belize. As might be expected from an empire so large, it was a highly sophisticated civilization. We know, for example, that they wrote books and poetry, favored heavily the use of puns, and developed what some call the most complex writing system ever practiced in the Western Hemisphere. We also know that they used a currency, studied the stars, waged war, grew crops, built elaborate drainage systems, fabricated an extensive mythology, and devised a calendar system so sophisticated that it could pinpoint the date of planetary activities thousands of years past. Then, within a very short period of time, they simply vanished, the signs of a collapsed civilization all they left behind.

There are theories, of course, but nobody knows for sure what happened to them, and that is still the primary question occupying Mayan scholars. It hasn't helped that so much time—nine hundred years—has passed from when they disappeared to when the ruins were discovered in the nineteenth century. It also hasn't helped that nearly all their books, written on flammable bark, were destroyed, presumably by emissaries of the Spanish Church, who believed they contained the word of the devil.

Ian Graham's office is at the end of a long hall with creaky wooden floors; a rabbit warren of passages, archways, and unpredictable chambers. It's a dusty space with character and high ceilings and a cranky radiator that groans loudly at the effort required to bring heat up from the basement. All around are the relics of the life of an adventurer—maps of places not immediately recognizable, books with crumbling leather spines, ancient colored bottles, stone artifacts. Strewn across large drafting tables are endless stacks of photographs and lots of drawing pencils.

The drafting tables are pushed up against the sooty windows and well lit by lamps. Ian Graham's work for the last three decades has been to record, faithfully and assiduously, the inscriptions found on Mayan artifacts. It is very precise, painstakingly meticulous work—and a lot of it. He is on volume 15 of a projected corpus of sixty.

Though Graham is physically comfortable here, content to labor away for hours at the drafting tables, Chopin playing softly on the radio, the occasional bottle of good champagne tucked away in the fridge, his spirit wanders the middle land of Central America. Graham came of age in the time of *The Boy's Own Paper*. He is a wandering man, an explorer.

His is a world of slick, pitch-black caves, the flashlight flickering on the walls, the pathways untrespassed for centuries. He has seen the vast landscapes of remnant derelict cities, only reachable by canoe, and only then if the current is with you, and if the rains haven't swollen the river over its banks. He has experienced the thrill of coming across a thick, heavy stone, facedown in the mud. That it is thick is a sign that he has beaten the looters to it, for they would have sliced away its mass to lighten the shipment to art sellers. That it is facedown increases the likelihood that the inscription hasn't been wiped clean by the insults of time. Thrashing through thick jungles in search of new sites, the screaming of monkeys and birds overhead, the rustle of a jaguar at his elbow, Graham has served variously as mapper, scout, photographer, lead man, camp cook, and lookout. Of all these, the job of lookout is the most important: a colleague died at his feet once, he says, shot by looters they had accidentally interrupted.

"It was my luck not having many academic ambitions," Graham continues, in confirmation of my long-standing suspicion that an aimless, vagabond freedom is far more conducive to the education of a high-minded youth than any amount of formal book learning. "The wind just blew me this way and that. I just drifted in. If I'm creative at all, it's in having invented the job in the first place, especially since nobody was interested in all this exploration business. It's tough to finance an expedition, but I wanted to stick to it. Doggedness, really. There was no burning passion to untangle the Maya. I just thought it would be fun. I just drifted in and doggedness accounts for the rest."

"The rest" is Graham's efforts to record pictorial inscriptions by drawing them, sure bold lines where there is no doubt as to the figure, dots, dashes, and shadings to indicate where the line might have traveled if the rest of the stone hadn't been broken off or worn away or stolen. It's work that is both representative of what is and interpretative of what's missing. The accuracy of his drawings is beyond reproach. The arresting beauty of them—underworld gods, priests ripping out beating hearts, fearsome commanders—a bonus. Good light and steady hands are essential.

Stumbling across the untrammeled slab in the first place holds an element of luck. But really looking at it, working with it, *noticing* the intricacies of it has a way of amplifying that luck, Graham says. "If you ask me, what is helpful to creativity is training the eye to *notice* things, to observe closely and precisely, being careful not to make a muddle of it." If you do that, it is likely you will discover things other people call luck, but, in fact, you've simply noticed something that has escaped the hurried man's attention. Often in creative work it is not the manipulation of high-flown theoretical abstractions that matters so much as one's ability to notice the concrete, the precise, and the particular details.

Which brings me to the second Mayanist: the young David Stuart. I found him in his dorm room at Henry Hall, the pseudo-regal architecture so inviting from the outside, so grim from within. Typical of three boys sharing a suite of rooms, the place was a comfortable collegiate mess of unmade beds and rumpled clothes. The computer in the corner was humming and blinking quietly. Near it, someone had also switched on a dull blue lava lamp, a relic from the college decor of the 1960s. That one should still exist, and not in a garage sale but here silently erupting in a college dorm room, raises it to the level of a dubious cultural artifact. Stuart adjusts his glasses, digs his sneakered toe into the carpet, and acknowledges that it's an odd thing to have, but he likes artifacts, he explains, and he has arranged his life to be around them.

David Stuart's position in the public eye comes from his talent for deciphering the meaning of the Mayan hieroglyphics. In the language of the field, he is an epigrapher, one who studies inscriptions.

You could also say that he is very lucky. Certainly, being exposed as a small boy to the still-emerging cosmology of the Maya was only the first of his many strokes of good luck. He is also lucky in having an eye for pictures and a good visual memory. He is fortunate, too, in having made the right connections and in having become involved in an aspect of Mayan work that few people understood. And there is also the luck of his personality to consider. A plain-faced, guileless, friendly young man, he is someone people like to have around. He possesses, in Yeats's phrase, a sweetness of the breast, there is nothing serpentine about him, and one suspects that he will never mutate to that most despicable of all creatures, the full-blown adult who connives and wangles and uses syntax as a weapon. For now, anyway, he is of the sort who are genuinely amazed by meanness, and still young enough not to recognize the marvel in that.

All of these things taken together have coalesced for David Stuart into opportunity. He has been invited to join expeditions, write articles, and deliver his papers to a roomful of professionals eager to hear him. These opportunities usually come at the pinnacle of one's career, but David was picking and choosing among them even before he was old enough to shave.

Call it one long chain of happy accidents? David Stuart, Fortune's child? There is no denying the role of accident in his life, but at the same time part of his luck has been of his own making. Through his willingness simply to pay attention and *notice* things, he has encouraged his good luck.

More specifically, if a Rosetta Stone for the Maya exists, it hasn't been found. Indeed, it was as late as 1960 before the experts finally agreed that the inscriptions (which are pictures, not ciphers) were, in fact, a language at all. David cracks the meaning of a glyph by exposing himself to the hundreds upon hundreds of different images, simply observing and paying attention. When he's on site, he uses the real thing. When he's back in America, he uses photographs or, better yet, the hauntingly evocative and painstakingly clear drawings of Ian Graham.

Through exposure, and with an open mind, he notices how the image of a jeweled skull, say, appears slightly different from picture to picture and wonders why that might be. He studies the trail of dots winding around the edges of another stone. A path or a trail? Drops of blood? Maybe, but then again maybe not. He remembers having noticed a similar image in another glyph and matches up the two. That gives him an amplified frame of reference, from which he makes further guesses as to the meaning.

Given enough time, he will eventually make a small discovery. With luck, it will be with respect to an image that fits into the puzzle in a few places. In this new context it may shed light on an aspect of Mayan life, the story of a battle perhaps, or maybe just an aspect of erotica. A lucky find straight from a guardian angel? Not really: it's the luck of having noticed.

■ **3** ■

NOTICING HAS A COUSIN: curiosity. You can tell they share the same bloodlines because one is usually shadowing the other. Curiosity leads, noticing follows. Or perhaps it's the other way around, noticing coming first, spotting some wrinkle and insisting on a closer look; curiosity wondering how the wrinkle affects half a dozen other things. In time, a connection is made and a revelation discovered. If you didn't know any better, you'd call it blind luck.

Tucked to one side of the University of Michigan campus is Robert Axelrod's neat, roomy office fully lined with books, except where two oil paintings hang, the works of his father, a commercial artist. Despite his youthful appearance, Dr. Axelrod is a seasoned political scientist and tenured professor. He is also the owner of a lively wit and a keen, curious mind. He's curious about a lot of things, but one question in particular has troubled him for years, and it is this: Under what conditions will cooperation emerge in a world of egoists without central authority?

Everybody knows at least one or two or twenty astoundingly egotistical people; it isn't necessary to name names. Given that all of *us* are reasonable, measured gentlefolk, cooperation with *them*, the aggressive, self-centered brutes, is impossible, isn't it? Axelrod was curious.

Brooding over the matter for some time, he seized upon a game called the Prisoner's Dilemma, which seemed like an ideal vehicle for resolving the question. In order to understand this phase of Dr. Axelrod's work, you have to know something of the way the game is played, which is well explained in his book *The Evolution of Cooperation:*

To begin, two players are faced with a series of decisions about some course of action—two sparring countries, say, trying to determine whether or not to honor a cease-fire treaty. At every junction of decision-making each player has two choices, namely to cooperate or to defect. Each must make his choice without knowing what the other will do, which is how the real world works (unless you've cheated somehow by planting a mole in the other side's operation).

Now this is a scored game because—again, as in real life—there are winners and losers. After each move the points are decided as follows:

IF BOTH COOPERATE: 3 points to each
IF ONE DEFECTS: 5 points to the traitor
   0 points to the sucker who trusted him
IF BOTH DEFECT: 1 point to each as a mutual
   punishment

The dilemma is this: If both cooperate, both do fairly well, but if both defect, both do terribly, and no matter what the other side does, defection always yields a higher payoff. The dilemma, summarizes Axelrod, comes with the realization that the very same logic also holds true for one's opponent.

Let us return, then, to his original question: What conditions in a world of egoists would promote cooperation? To answer it, Axelrod devised a computer tournament playing the Prisoner's Dilemma and invited professional and nonprofessional game theorists to submit their favorite strategy. To make a long story (full of statistical analysis and pairing and computer shoptalk) short, the bottom line was that the winning strategy was the simplest of all: tit for tat, meaning cooperate on the first move and then do whatever the other player did on the previous move.

The generous-minded, good-natured Dr. Axelrod didn't believe it—whatever happened to the Golden Rule, he wondered, the turn-the-other-cheek philosophy, the do-unto-others-as-you-would-have-them-do-unto-you approach to life? He ran the tournament again—and again the tit-for-tat strategy prevailed.

Using these results, Dr. Axelrod drew up a theory of cooperation based on the teachings of the game: avoid unnecessary conflict, respond in the case of uncalled-for provocation, forgive after that response, and be clear about your actions so that the other side knows exactly where you stand. These conditions became the basis for his discovery that cooperation can indeed emerge in a world of egoists without central authority. A remarkable conclusion, considered by some to be simply the lucky fluky outcome of a computer game.

But this was only the first of Dr. Axelrod's so-called lucky discoveries. Having a curious mind, he began wondering if the theory held true in situations other than diplomacy. Take the gritty, obscene battlefield of war, for instance: would a tit-for-tat strategy produce cooperation between enemies holding guns?

He found his answer in the "live-and-let-live" system of the trench warfare in World War I. Thanks to the static nature of trench warfare, Axelrod writes, where the same small units faced each other for extended periods of time, a tacit balance was achieved. Both sides observed the peace as long as the other side did the same—even if this required a violation of direct orders from on high.

Fascinating, thought Axelrod, but again his curiosity got the better of him and he wondered about natural selection, evolution, and the balance of nature. Did this theory of co-operation based on reciprocity operate in nature, where the so-called participants (bacteria, for example, or birds) wouldn't appreciate the consequences of their aggressive behavior? With the help of a biologist friend, Axelrod investigated the matter and once again found the theory held.

Robert Axelrod's probing curiosity is boundless. Another person might well have stopped after the first computer game, content to reap the praise of a job well done. But for Axelrod, every new finding led to a dozen fresh questions, and he is inquisitive enough to try to find the answer to them all.

◼ **4** ◼

THE THIRD COMPONENT of trying to encourage luck is actually the easiest of all. It is to play. The relationship between luck and fooling around has been explored in depth by Edward de Bono, a psychologist who has spent the better part of a lifetime investigating creativity. He writes: "If the purpose of chance in generating new ideas is to provide one with something to look at which one would not have looked for, then there may be methods of encouraging this process. Play is probably the ideal method. It must, however, be purposeless play without design and direction. Just as a carefully designed experiment is an attempt to hurry nature along the path of logical investigation, so play is an attempt to encourage the chance appearance of phenomena which would not be sought out. Playing around is an experiment with chance."

What kind of play are we talking about here?

Think back. Once upon a time you were a child and, presumably, you played—in the yard, with your toys, with your friends, with your dog—all the while pie-eyed at this wondrous world. "Let's pretend," said Alice to the White Queen, who herself practiced make-believe for half an hour a day and believed as many as six impossible things before breakfast.

When and why do children stop playing? De Bono suggests that it's when "the world changes from an unknown place in which wonderful things can happen into a familiar place in which there is an adequate explanation for everything."

But for a quizzical, curious mind that notices the nuances and discrepancies, adequate explanations are too thin to suffice and tinkering with the possibilities becomes an enticing proposition. To retain the simple playfulness of childhood through one's riper years is what opens a person up to the creative possibilities within a situation. Amusing oneself is an effective way of encouraging that good fortune.

Among the MacArthur Fellows interviewed, the favorite forms of extracurricular diversions I heard mentioned were listening to music, looking at art, reading, dancing, playing with one's children, traveling, seeing friends, and shooting baskets with the neighborhood guys who don't care what you do for a living and have never heard of the MacArthur Prize.

But there is also playfulness within work: an artist plays with materials, a political scientist monkeys around with game theories, a theater director toys with sets, characters, and interpretations, a writer fiddles with words, an activist experiments with strategy . . . and then there's MacArthur

Fellow Bill Irwin. He's a master of the playful, but then again he should be: he was trained as a clown.

■ 5 ■

WATCHING BILL IRWIN TEACH a studio workshop is an education in play. An hour before class was to begin, he was already at work, a solitary figure dressed in his trademark baggy pants, hitched up with suspenders over an enormous white starched shirt. This morning he had chosen a soft gray bowler from his hat collection, which for years hung high up on hooks running like a halo all the way around his ceiling. Top hats, bowlers, a Turkish fez, smashed flea market specials—a hat for every mood. Space is a problem in New York, especially for a young performance artist whose closets tended to fill up raidly with scrawny rubber chickens, giant shoes, assorted fake noses, collapsible chairs, fright wigs, and miles of plastic spaghetti.

The only sound in the studio was the soft shuffle of his shoes across the worn wooden floor and the whisper of a count as he tried to work out a new step: "Five, six, seven, eight, and *hop!*, two, three, four . . ." He adds a gesture, takes two away, fiddles with the swing of his arms, his reflection repeated in mirrors all around, a hundred dancing clowns determined to get it right. Playing around, first he makes his knees bend out into a wishbone, next he grows considerably taller, and then he shrinks to half his normal six-foot size. He practices a trip, but catches himself before he falls. Then he tries going completely limp in a dead faint.

In time, the first students arrive and from a distance try to copy his motions. They fail miserably. Irwin's too good to be casually imitated. Every inch of him understands movement and exactly how much can fit in the space of a split second. His gestures are lean, tight, targeted, spare. He wastes nothing. His concepts are neat, not epic. And when you're not laughing at his antic behavior, you are dazzled by its elegance.

Humor is a large part of Bill's work. He experiments with it incessantly. In fact, it was his love of the lighthearted that caused him to leave traditional acting in the first place, and enroll in the Ringling Brothers and Barnum & Bailey Clown College. It was there that he learned how to make slap shoes *thwack!* and how to lean forty-five degrees without falling, and how to pretend that he was being sucked offstage by an invisible vacuum, or chased by an invisible demon. It was there that he learned how to bounce on the trampoline, fly through the air, juggle, spin a plate, ride an elephant, and eat fire. He is still fairly proficient at all of these talents, though elephants aren't too common in Manhattan, and fire-eating, which once sent his face up in flames, is something he tries very hard to avoid.

After clown college Bill turned down several offers to join the circus in order to go it alone, "a move akin to going to West Point and then resigning your commission to be a freelance soldier," remarked theater critic Mel Gussow. In time, though, playing around with the various techniques of clowning and acting, he co-wrote, directed, and starred in a collaborative work called *The Regard of Flight*, which ran in several of the country's most respected theaters and was shown on educational television. It was the piece that established his reputation.

In it, Irwin sowed the seeds for a kind of character that he would continue to refine in subsequent performance works: a kind of Everyman at odds with the world around him, a bit inept, honest, struggling to understand, to cope, to get it right, but continually caught in a moment of unexpected awkwardness, relentlessly the victim of some embarrassing human foible. The Everyman label came from a critic, not Bill. His vocabulary is movement, and he thinks movement works better if you don't try to put it into words: "The only way to make something completely your own is not to name it—you may not even be able to name it—but to let your body control it. Feel the ease of the meter. Play with it. That's what will give it power to the eye and the pleasure to perform. That's what pulls it along," he says.

At precisely eleven o'clock Bill saunters in an exaggerated penquin walk over to the record player and puts on a lively jig, eight beats to the bar. "All righty," he announces, and twenty eager faces assemble around him. For the next two hours he puts them through the paces, teaching them the rudiments of his special vaudevillian strain of performance art while at the same time working out material for his next production. It's a couple of months until the curtain goes up, so he's not yet feeling the intense strain of figuring everything out. At the moment he's playing with various ideas, stringing together a few skits, changing them, trying them again. In this playful mode he may get lucky with an idea or two.

To the onlooker, the accidental way a skit comes together may look like a streak of lightning out of the blue, but that is an illusion. As the Harvard scholar D. N. Perkins has pointed out, it is naïve to think that accidents account for the dramatic opening up of wholly new paths leading to wholly new consequences. More accurately, accidents "deflect, enlarge, sharpen, and simplify." The accidents Irwin stumbles across are largely because he has put himself in a position to stumble, and is wise enough and focused enough on his own goals to recognize a stumble of potential artistic value.

It helps that he is sensitive to movement, to form, and to structure. Prowling the streets of New York he *notices* the way a bag lady shuffles up the street, how a crowd presses around a card hustler, or the look on a waiter's face when he trips over a chair. These are all motions he stores in some remote but active corner of his mind. At home he fools around with the gestures he has picked up in his sauntering. He practices a limp up and down his hallway and makes faces in the morning mirror. In the studio, he scales up his ideas to see how they look when a whole troupe performs a trip, a stumble, a dead faint.

The piece he's working on today, he says at the break, got its start from a hazy, ill-formed notion of what it is he thinks he might like to do, maybe, possibly, if it works, if he can pull it all together before the curtain call, if the budget is there, if the stage is the right shape, if it says something in the end, if it has an idea or set of ideas, and is funny, that is maybe. It can be expressed in one skinny line: "I thought it might be fun to do a rumination on videos and how videos have sort of taken over our lives and what that means and how that plays out." That's it: the entire inspiration for a feature-length performance piece. The rest of the piece is filled in through his experimentation. When *Largely/New York* opened at City Center two months later, the idea had taken shape, was polished, and made a statement while at the same time sending staccato bursts of laughter through the audience.

▪ 6 ▪

MEANWHILE, axiomatic within our effort to identify some of the attitudes worth cultivating in order to encourage one's luck is the presumption that luck is a welcome thing.

"But let me tell you something about luck," warns Mac-Arthur recipient and journalist Tina Rosenberg. "A so-called lucky break may not always be what the world at large thinks it is."

Tina was twenty-seven when she received her award, and the author of many good solid features for respected magazines, including *The Atlantic* and *The Washington Monthly*. Immediately, her age caused some onlookers to lament that such a high honor would disrupt her natural progression as a writer. Which is to say, editors would expect so much from her and, thrust into the limelight, she wouldn't be given the luxury afforded other young writers to make mistakes, to experiment in the relative safety of anonymity, to define her turf and find her voice. Tina is delighted to have received her award, but savvy enough to recognize some of the realities of the ripple effect.

The same is true of Bill Irwin, only thirty-four at the time of his award and a member of the very first class of recipients. His young age, his appealing choice of profession, and the trumpets associated with the news of this glamorous new fellowship caused the press to swarm to him like mosquitoes to a bare ankle. Bill wonders about the long-range effects of his loss of anonymity. He worries about being trapped in conversations at cocktail parties that he doesn't want to have, and being beset by calls from managers "who want to *handle* me, and *handle* the things that nobody can do for me except me, and make me *big*, and *arrange* my affairs in such a way that I'd have to give up subways and exist on limo-juice."

And, too, there's the touch of guilt that shows when he has to address a performance troupe and explain how little they will be paid and how thin the budget is for his upcoming production. The MacArthur largesse, for a young and less-than-well-established actor, is, indeed, a lot of money. But as a result, Bill laments, "Everybody always expects you to pick up lunch."

Apart from the various shades of guilt some of the younger Fellows experience at their sudden financial well-being, however, even those who are considerably older and more established in their careers feel a range of pressures. These are self-induced pressures, to be sure, as the Foundation asks absolutely nothing of the recipients and never even meets them unless they choose to attend the all-expense-paid reunion weekends, but pressures all the same—to produce, to be brilliant, to do something worthwhile, to spend the money wisely, to justify the confidence placed in them, to smooth over relations with colleagues with whom one has collaborated for some time.

The day you win a MacArthur is a day you open champagne, Tina Rosenberg says. "But the next day, trying to get any work done is a lot like typing on the top of a fresh piece of paper: 'This is the next brilliant article by the newest recipient of the MacArthur Award.' What do you think will follow? Nothing."

Her observations about the odd spin of luck explained an ironic refrain that has been circulating within the MacArthur community: "Hey, Joe, I'm just calling to say congratulations on your MacArthur—and don't let it get you down."

■

THE HARMONY OF INSTINCT
AND JUDGMENT

■ 1 ■

IN THE HEAT OF CREATION how are decisions made?

On the one hand there is instinct, that delicate, vulnerable, fumbling sense that allows a creator to operate in the dark, blindly groping, nose cocked to the wind, radically trusting in some unfathomable radar, storing faith in the hope that the ineffable will not fail him.

("But come on, Ralph, you're not answering my question. *How* do you bring these great big symphonies of yours to life? *How* do you manage these 'architectural structures in sound,' as you prefer to call them?")

Composer Ralph Shapey cackled wildly, his flyaway mane of starchy white hair flashing brilliantly in the increasing afternoon sun: "My dear, let me tell you something. You can believe it or not as you choose, but it's true: I have had all my life a series of strange, indefinable, instinctive feelings and visitations that bypass logic and make no sense. Call it intuition. I don't give a damn what you call it. I think of these moments as something instinctive at work.")

And on the other hand, there is judgment, which is a logical, deductive, rational process, understandable and linear, rigorously sequential, and above all, defensible.

("But, Derek, I appreciate that inspiration can come from anything at any time, but how do you *know* which of these hundreds of sounds you hear in your head, which of the countless images you store in your mind will be worthwhile to you when you sit at your desk to write?"

The Caribbean-born poet, playwright, and watercolorist Derek Walcott sucked hard on his cigarette, one eye squinched against the curl of smoke. There is a solidity and massiveness to this man that derive less from his build than from the sureness of his ideas. He answered firmly and without hesitation: "Look, it's this way. A professional knows what is good and what is not good. You know, you judge. You look at a poem or a play and you decide: this is good, this is not, I tried this but it didn't work. If it's lousy you throw it out. Only an amateur tries to save it and defend it. A professional knows better. He uses his judgment.")

Within a thinking man's mind a war rages, each side rattling a saber at the other. The cry of instinct is urgent, philosophical, even faintly spiritual: "Come this way, this is good, don't listen to the naysayers, turn your back on prophets of doom with their undernourished imaginations, trust *me*, I am with you always, only I abide." But then judgment speaks: "Forget it, get wise, those who tell you to abandon this foolishness know what they're talking about, and besides, look at the evidence, it doesn't make sense, it's not logical, it won't work and you'll be ashamed and humiliated if you try, stop now, why risk everything, ruin will surely follow."

In the heat of creation, which voice do you follow—the elusive unsupportable cry of instinct or careful reasoned advice of judgment? The answer is not to choose between them but to harmonize the competing tensions, because each is valuable, each a version of the truth. Creativity, indeed survival itself, depends upon the ability to perceive the synergy of opposites and harmonize the extremes.

This is a principle that Dr. Robert Coles well understands, but then his has been a life of balancing his instincts with his judgment, weighing his gut against his reason.

▪ **2** ▪

ROBERT COLES IS a child psychiatrist, but more than that, he is a storyteller possessed with as fine a sense of the poetic narrative and of character as any of the dozens of writers whose works line his office shelves, among them Walker Percy, James Agee, Flannery O'Connor, Leo Tolstoy, Raymond Chandler, and his mentor, William Carlos Williams. His own books, well over forty now, including the five-volume *Children of Crisis* series for which he was awarded a Pulitzer Prize in 1973, are piled out of sight in the closets. The most recent listing of his publications required forty-three pages and ended with entry number 1001, a review for *The New Republic* of MacArthur Fellow Fred Wiseman's latest film, *Deaf, Blind* . . . The world gets smaller when success finally finds you. In the beginning, though, long before recognition and the hybrid career he fashioned from literature and medicine, the battle between the pull of his heart and the push of his mind was fierce.

Born to hardworking parents, Coles enjoyed a comfortable New England childhood, graduated from Harvard, and went on to medical school at Columbia University. Then a call to arms intervened and he was drafted into the service. He had hoped to be stationed in London or even San Francisco or Los Angeles, where he stood the chance of doing some interesting medicine, but fate had a different plan: he was sent to Mississippi in the early 1960s, a time of bitter violence and grave civil unrest.

One day, quite by chance as he tells it, he stumbled across a young black child named Ruby Bridges who was to have a profound influence on the course of his life. Coles was in his early thirties, unsure of his talents and feeling constrained by the orthodox teachings of psychiatry, yet thinking that perhaps he ought to succumb to the pressures of his traditional medical training. Ruby was only six and battling intense hostility in her effort to attend an all-white public school in New Orleans. They became friends, and she trusted him with her worries and hopes that, in time, he recorded in *The Moral Life of Children*:

"I knew I was just Ruby, just Ruby trying to go to school, and worrying that I couldn't be helping my momma with the kids younger than me, like I did on the weekends and in the summer. But I guess I also knew I was the Ruby who had to do it—to go into that school and stay there, no matter what those people said, standing outside. And besides, the minister reminded me that God chooses us to do His will, and so I had to be His Ruby, if that's what He wanted. And then that white lady wrote and told me she was going to stop shouting at me, because she'd decided I wasn't bad, even if *integration* was bad, then my momma said I'd become 'her Ruby,' that lady's, just as she said in her letter, and I was glad; and I was glad I got all the nice letters from people who said I was standing up for them, and I was walking for them, and they were thinking of me, and they were with me, and I was their Ruby, too, they said."

These are the self-observations of a child under stress as recounted by a man who knows how to listen. Children are not an assembly of citizens we adults are accustomed to listening to—but instinctively Coles was drawn to her, impressed with the strength of this young warrior child, stunned by the complexity of the emotions she faced. Instinctively, he knew he had found his life's work. It was a decision based on the sort of inkling that would hold no meaning for a mere logician. But Coles knew, deep down, that the decision was right, and so he continued to talk with Ruby, in time branching out to listen to other black neighbor children, as well as to the white children of Ku Klux Klan members, all the while making notes, utterly fascinated with the muddy river culture and mannerisms of the Deep South.

Though a doctor, Coles wasn't "treating" these children for the symptoms of their psychic distress. What he was doing, he explains in his writings, was trying to work out "a version of documentary child psychiatry: to record how a historical crisis (school integration), or a social and economic crisis (the trials of Appalachia's mountain families and of migrant farm families), or a long-standing racial impasse (the conditions of Indians in, say, the Southwest, or of Eskimos in coastal Alaska) bears upon the mental life of young people. I tried to uncover a psychology of everyday life; a psychology of turmoil and response to turmoil; a psychology of hope against hope with plenty of interludes of doubt and fear."

It was a mission and style of working that would characterize the next thirty years of research. At first, he confined his efforts to the troubled rural South—Mississippi, Louisiana, Georgia, New Mexico, and the untrammeled hills of Appalachia. There he entered the lives of migrant children and sharecroppers, mountain boys and Indians. He took an interest in their stories and told them his, which was in keeping with his belief that only through an exchange of stories can one person know and trust another.

Later, expanding his horizons, he went to South Africa, Northern Ireland, Northern Canada, Brazil, Nicaragua, Poland, and Southeast Asia. Wherever there were children in trouble struggling with ethical, moral, economic, and political questions, Coles settled in for a while and listened. He didn't think of these children or their parents as "patients" or "cases" but as people with serious problems on their minds, caught, through no fault of their own, in the backwash of poverty and ignorance. He didn't think of the information he was collecting as "material" or "data" but as chronicles and narratives. And he never went around asking a lot of big-shot questions.

"In the beginning just about everyone thought I was absolutely crazy to be doing this," he reflects in the long, reedy sounds that mark, unmistakably, the speech of a Bostonian. Dr. Coles speaks so softly that the listener has to lean forward to catch his roughly hewn voice. We are in his offices at Harvard University, the very same quarters occupied by F.D.R. as an undergraduate. Thrown back on his thoughts in remembrance of these early years, Coles tries hard to reconstruct the competing instincts and judgments from which he fashioned his life's work. "On the one hand, it felt like the right thing to do. On the other hand, everyone thought I was insane. My teachers thought I was wasting my education. My friends didn't understand what I was doing. Even my father, who had no use whatsoever for psychiatry and saw no value in it at all, finally, at wit's end, urged that I get into analysis. I got the same advice from people here at Harvard: get into analysis."

In fairness, he was leading a very odd life. Most newly minted doctors, freshly married, would have settled squarely down to the serious business of making money, especially with a first child on the way. Coles did no such thing. Putting their household things in storage, he and his wife, Jane, loaded up their station wagon (appropriately, a Lark from the old Studebaker line) and wandered from one unsavory corner of the earth to the next, the migrant literate doctor heeding the lowly and the exiled.

The first of his three sons was born, and still he kept on, living as inexpensively as possible. In time, his other sons were born, but stopping this global wandering was out of the question. More years passed and he was offered a very secure, fairly prestigious position in mainline Boston medicine, but still he preferred his self-fashioned research, a cross between doctor, poet, and documentarian, his findings woven together with a spellbinding narrative power. Even his classes at Harvard are hybrid and story-oriented: his law students are instructed to read Dickens; his divinity students discuss Flannery O'Connor's tales of spiritual grace; his business students graze on sagas of greed; and his medical students are immersed in the works of Chekhov, Sylvia Plath, Thomas Mann, and Coles's own great friend, William Carlos Williams.

In retrospect, it is perhaps not so difficult to see how Robert Coles's life evolved into such a fruitful and highly creative amalgam of medicine and literature welded together with his sense of social responsibility. Hindsight makes everything seem effortless, and every one of us a genius. In the beginning, though, his instincts were telling him one thing and the cold hard edge of judgment dictating another.

"But, Dr. Coles," I urged, "how did you know, especially with everyone telling you that you were over the edge, that you had found your life's work?"

He took his time and answered carefully: "I just knew it. I knew it inside. I trusted my instincts. I knew how to go to these neighborhoods. I knew how to talk to these children and how to draw pictures with them. I knew how to talk with their parents and how to drink and eat with them. I was stunned at the things I was learning. I was fascinated. And here's pride coming in, but I'll just say it: I had a sense of competence and that I've learned how to do this work and that I *loved* this work."

"How did you justify such a departure from traditional medicine?" I continued. "How could you be sure that this wayward life would amount to anything? What made you think you could turn these rambling narratives of children to good purpose?"

At this he smiled: "I didn't listen to the criticism nor to the people who were trying to classify me as a sociologist or an anthropologist or something other than a doctor. I exercised my own judgment. I rejected some of the teachings of my training, especially all that awful reductionist rhetoric and those neat labels that medicine clings to and forces on students. But I kept the aspects of my education that fit the task, and I developed the other skills necessary to do this work. I believe in this work and I judged it to be important, something that could never even be completed in my lifetime."

What intuition provides is an inkling, an itch, a yearning, a mist of possibilities. What judgment provides is structure, assessment, form, purpose. Blend them together—and, in the example of Robert Coles, season this marriage with a strong dose of moral imagination—and you will begin to recognize the tiny, pert buds of opportunity, that, if pursued, may well lead to a dramatic flowering of the most creative work of your career.

□ **3** □

THOUGH ROBERT COLES HAS a remarkable facility for harmonizing the competing tensions of his nature, he is not alone in this ability. Within the MacArthur population examples abound:

Instinct tells filmmaker Fred Wiseman to film this, film that, and then go over there and film some more. Judgment is how he edits ninety hours of film into two.

Instinct is what might cause Kirk Varnedoe to pay attention to an artist's work. Judgment is what dictates his interpretation of it, and whether or not he believes the museum should acquire it, and, if so, how to assemble an exhibition to show it off in the best and most meaningful light.

Instinct is what caused self-taught art historian Henry Kraus to doubt the prevailing scholarly wisdom about the correct interpretation of a panel in Notre Dame. Judgment is how he assembled the evidence to prove he was right.

Instinct presents the creator with a range of possibilities; judgment is how he selects among them, keeping what is useful and turning aside that which clutters, distracts, and causes static in the mind.

But how does the creative person manage this ebb and flow? What devices does he use to manage the inconsistencies, the tussle between the two sides of his nature?

With respect to instinct, the best advice culled from the MacArthur Fellows is to learn to recognize it and to trust it even though it can't be explained in nice, neat, tidy terms. If something more useful could be said to facilitate this effort, it would be in the area of recognizing that the cultivation of instinct is a lifelong process and is rooted in a firm knowledge of one's field—and in trial and error, however tiresome that can be.

With respect to judgment, however, the advice is more specific and turns on the question of timing. Judge too soon and a new, imperfect, and fragile thought born from instinct or from some even hazier impetus may be cut off before it has a chance to mature and withstand scrutiny.

It's sound advice, but the trouble in following it is that Western culture deeply prizes the ability to judge. As parents, right and wrong dictate much of what we drill into our children. In the workplace, unshakable leadership is a much rewarded trait. As members of our communities, and citizens of our country, we are constantly required to vote "a" or "b," pro or con, yes or no—it can't be both. Time spent wavering in the middle is interpreted as weakness. Indecisiveness is not valued.

It is hard to know when the time has come to judge the merits and possibilities of one's work. Still, there is one small way of easing this difficulty, which came to light during the course of conversations with the Fellows. It is to think about one's effort as a "work-in-progress," that is, a temporary resting place in a continuous creative process.

The magic of this hospitable phrase is that it provides a warming sense of liberation. If you think of each project as part of a continuum of work, it then becomes much easier to make decisions and to close it down and call it finished and move on. It's as if the creator says to himself, "Well, I would like to take the next several months and do more work on this project to make it perfect, but instead I am going to think of this one as a work-in-progress and continue on to the next thing, which will build on this and be so much better and be so much closer to what I had in mind when I first set out."

The work-in-progress refrain surfaced a number of times throughout my conversations, in a variety of contexts. Bill Irwin, the clown, calls each of his original performance works a work-in-progress, as is often stated, no less, in his program notes. Even the names of his pieces suggest their incomplete nature: "At the Very Least," "Still Not Quite," "Not Quite/ New York," "In Some Regard," and "Largely/New York." Others in the arts, among them poet/playwright Derek Walcott, poet/novelist Brad Leithauser, and theater director Peter

Sellars, commented on the feeling of settling for something less than they perhaps had imagined, of making do with this particular work, and hoping that in the next try they will be able to narrow the gap between what was dimly envisioned at the start of the project and what was produced in the end. The same holds just as true in the sciences, where "fact" is regarded merely as a temporary resting ground until the next discovery, the next clarification. Whether in science or in art, then, the ability to judge that a work is finished is more an act of commitment to the continuousness of the creative process than it is a sign of having expressed the last word.

■　　■　　■

THE HARMONY OF INSTINCT AND JUDGMENT

More loose ends . . .

Coasting to the close of Part Two, a natural resting place and an appropriate time for a moment of looking back, I am astonished to note how many open-ended questions are still loose and roaming wild on the landscape. What, for example, is the relationship between technology and creativity, especially at this moment, as we enter the twilight of the twentieth century? Why were five Fellows, out of these casually chosen forty, renegade lawyers? Did women bring something special to the creative impulse that was absent in the experiences of men? Why didn't anybody touch on Maslow's hierarchy of needs? Why did Dante come up in conversation so often? And the knottiest loose end of all: Shouldn't something be said about God if we are to understand the creative process?

When we spoke, Derek Walcott pointed out that agnosticism is a condition of poetry because if the agnostic is sincere, "it means bewilderment, bafflement, humility, devastation." No, that's not exactly what he said. What he said was this: agnosticism is a condition of poetry because if the agnostic is sincere, "it means bewilderMENT, baffleMENT, humiliTY, DE-vah-stay-TION!" Thus Derek Walcott, and when he talks I hear the dry rustle of St. Lucia palms and the rum-soaked syncopated ping of steel drums in the moonlight.

Agnosticism? A condition of poetry? Understand this: Derek Walcott is not given to leisurely derived philosophy. He is not a man lightly realized; the pitch of his voice and the sway of his ideas, not soon forgotten. In person, he is as powerful as he appears on the page. There is nothing thin-blooded about him. If he says agnosticism is a condition of poetry, there is something there worth looking at. But at what price?

To pursue this thread would have required some conversation about prayer—a difficult subject even for the devout, let alone for those of us who swing between believing and not. For those who vacillate, prayer is an especially complicated question. In one moment, the scornful side of our nature takes charge, the heretic within, roundly and soundly denying the existence of some higher authority. In the next, there is repentance, and a crashing to knees, head bowed, palms pressed hard together in a desperate plea to be blessed with inspiration: "Lord in Heaven, King on High, choose me to celebrate your glory through my art and in exchange I offer you my devotion, my sincerity, my humility every hour of my life."

No, I decided to leave God and the agnostics out of this book. Had I decided otherwise, sooner or later I would have tripped into the quicksand of superstition, black magic, ritual. Is there a creative soul who doesn't bow in the direction of ritual, whether or not he will admit to such a thing? Hot coffee, endless filterless cigarettes, a cheap bottle of whiskey, a fistful of sharpened pencils, a desk positioned just so . . . In polite company it is far better to speak of such things as "setting up the conditions" for creative work—but I wonder if it isn't a more primitive matter of assembling the talismans, the fetishes, the charms, and the amulets. I wonder, are we talking about the sacred here or the profane? I couldn't be sure. So, given my objective of shedding some light on the inner workings of how and when creative inspiration strikes, I had to leave aside the tangled issue of divine participation.

And, if the whole story be told, I felt similarly queasy about the inviting but tricky question of the relationship between creativity in the sciences and creativity in the arts. Simple, you think? Hardly.

True, Ved Mehta had an answer to this, but it turned on his favored but hard-to-hold-onto conception of irony. "What a good writer shares with a good scientist," he explained, "is a sense of the ironic, an ability to look at the same thing everybody else is seeing and see something different, something surprising, something fresh. In that way the good scientist and the good writer are both skeptics, and both have a capacity for wonder."

Derek Walcott also had an answer, but it led right back around to God: "Well, are you asking me, 'Are scientists poets and are poets scientists?' I mean, it does come down to the same large question: What is the meaning of existence?" It's a question I wouldn't begin to touch but one from which he wouldn't consider shying away. Settling in, he explains:

"I had an utterly fas-ci-NA-ting conversation with one of the MacArthur people at the last reunion which touches this. It was this guy who was doing dinosaurs and he wanted to know, 'Are dinosaurs *warm-blooded creatures?' Now, okay, the first thing you're likely to hear is, big deal, you know, who cares whether they were warm-blooded or cold-blooded or whatever. And then you realize that the process is the same!*

"What this man is doing," he continues, the small dark marbles of his eyes narrowing in concentration, "is a poetic idea, not a scientific one. It is an immense idea which then affects an idea of time, right? Someone asked him, 'Can you conceive of millions of years?' And he answered, 'Of course not. The furthest I could possibly think would be about a thousand, maybe two thousand years.' Now does that man as a scientist who has to deal with millions and billions of years have a superior sense of time than I do as a writer? He says he doesn't; he says he has the same difficulties that I have. Well, from that moment on, he's entered a world we share: the idea of temporality, the idea of human time, how we measure time, the absurdity and the vanity of our measure of time, and the question of infinity and of existence, which is, in a sense, the core of great poetry.

"What is the ultimate revelation of science?" he pushes on, hardly pausing to suck on his cigarette, the gait of his rocker matching the speed of his mind. "The ultimate revelation of science is the existence of God. I asked the dinosaur man, are you a believer? And he said, 'No, I'm an agnostic.' THAT I could understand because in the same way that agnosticism is a condition of poetry, it is a condition of science. It's a sense of awe, the astonishment of the soul. Good science and good art are always about a condition of awe. This may seem to you like a large theme, but the best science and poetry at its greatest are not smaller than that. I don't think there is any other function for the poet or the scientist in the human tribe but the astonishment of the soul . . ."

And so, there I was again, back at the beginning, squarely caught in the fat tangled knot of the meaning of existence, the purpose of poetry, the questions of if and how divine intervention fits with the creative process. It is with reluctance that I leave aside these issues— even knowing that I'll probably return to them again, in the next book I write, or the one after that—for surely the answers, if answers can be found, would be of critical importance to daily life.

THE HARMONY OF INSTINCT AND JUDGMENT

Brad Leithauser understands. In a thin, mournful, faintly desperate voice, this is what he said of his own work, but he might just as well have been lamenting the losses of mine: "One always feels that one is fighting a running and losing battle when it comes to the creative use of one's life. It's that thing of trying to put a finger in the dike, and there are so many holes that you don't have enough fingers. It's all leaking away. At some level one is deeply despairing. Most of what is interesting and lively and potentially enduring passes you by, and if you take such things seriously (as you should) you are always doing a rather desperate rescue operation. . . ."

That's it, exactly.

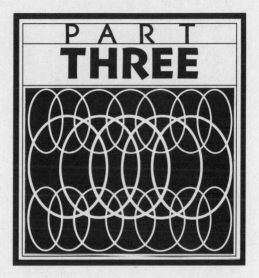

PART
THREE

DESPAIR AND ISOLATION,
MADNESS AND MEANNESS

EDGAR ALLAN POE WAS a drug addict. Sir Isaac Newton and Ezra Pound were schizophrenics. Van Gogh was psychotic. Is there a connection between creativity and madness? Surely no other question has been as widely or as emotionally debated in the far-flung study of creativity as this one.

T. S. Eliot suffered a nervous breakdown. So did the young Albert Einstein, who recovered but was still considered distant and unknowable as an adult. Darwin ailed from a manic-depressive illness, as did Jack London, who committed suicide by narcotic overdose at the difficult age of forty. How convenient it would be to take refuge in the deep creases of the idea that the creative impulse stems at least in part from the darker forces of the universe, the shadow side of the psyche. Such a belief would offer sanctuary, solace, excuse, redemption.

Robert Frost and Mark Twain were both melancholic. Virginia Woolf took her own life. Beethoven cheated his publishers and, like Byron, was promiscuous. Wagner was a self-centered anti-Semite.

Arrogance, snappishness, ruthlessness, greed, nastiness—it would be so easy to dismiss, through the claim of creative genius, the harm sown from such behavior.

Haydn wrote his girlfriend of how happy he would be on the day his wife finally died. Picasso, it's been claimed, abused women; Freud, men. Tchaikovsky and James Agee were self-effacing and self-lacerating to the end.

"*Mea culpa,*" our genius is quick to say, "but you know I can't help my inner demons." And if further proof is needed, he has but to rattle off the long roster of disturbed ghosts in whose company he wanders.

The idea that madness and creativity are linked has long enjoyed a certain vogue, which may be attributed in part to the fact that each of us, at one moment or another, has suspected the madman within. It's a notion that has existed at least since the Greeks, who took it one step further by believing that creativity was inspired by divine forces. Tricky business, divine inspiration: just enough and a man teeters on the brink of sanity, suspended in an exalted state of agitated inspiration; too much of the divine touch and he's pushed over the edge into the abyss of madness.

Today the cognitive scientists have taken up the issue of creativity and madness and publish one study after the next, attempting to put the question to rest, but the results are contradictory. Just recently, the report of a fifteen-year study, discussed in the April 1987 issue of *Psychology Today*, concluded that there was definitely a link and that "the tendency toward manic depression may facilitate access in creative people to a richness and intensity of experience that is not shared by the rest of us." The summary went on to note that the data were in line with the findings of an earlier, 1983 study conducted by English psychologist Kay R. Jamison, who surveyed forty-seven of the top British artists and writers and found that roughly thirty-eight percent had sought treatment for mood disorders—a rate about thirty times that of the general population.

More recently, though, *The New York Times* noted a study made available in September 1988, which argued that the relationship between madness and creativity is not that the genius himself is disturbed but rather that his *siblings* tended to suffer various types of psychological disorders.

It's hard to know what to believe. It's a debate that some suggest will boil down to no more of a link than that both the madman and the creative man favor unconventional thinking, and that both often feel a keen sense of despair and isolation. It's an observation that doesn't take us very far, yet one that is made to represent so much.

To be creative must a man welcome hardship and expect a life of suffering? Was Dryden right with his pronouncement: "Great wits are sure to madness near allied"? The evidence is not in yet, but this much is certain: the MacArthur population is bursting with creative minds and great ideas and clever thinking, yet none of them (at least not one of the forty Fellows with whom I spoke) would have trouble supplying proof of their sanity. At the same time, however, it would be incorrect to leave you with the impression that creative people *necessarily* live calm, cheerful, emotionally stable, and uncomplicated lives; far from it. Take a look at Ralph Shapey, for example, the misanthrope of the Midwest.

■ 2 ■

MacArthur Fellow Ralph Shapey lives in Chicago, an odd choice for a composer. New York, London, Vienna, Los Angeles, Boston—any of these cities would have made better sense, but for Shapey, Chicago is the safe haven from the storm that he manages to whip up when moving in the high-powered circles of the musical elite.

In the foyer of his apartment, eighteen floors above the shores of Lake Michigan, hangs an almost life-sized portrait of him done by one of his past wives, the painter Vera Klement. Hardly a large man to begin with, Shapey is slouched even smaller in the painting, his eyes lost in an angry knit of brows, a jagged black hole for a mouth opened in a silent roar, hands thrust defiantly in his pockets. Shapey calls it his "fuck-you pose." One look at the painting and Chicago makes more sense: he is the ignored master, the misunderstood maestro, the outraged outcast. In any of the more populated, more prestigious cities, composers vie for the top slots. In Chicago, there is only Ralph, the determined outsider.

Vera Klement was wife number two for Shapey. Before her came the sickly Sylvia. After Vera, in 1985, came his present wife, the lovely blond Elsa Charlston, a lithe soprano who sings the solo in a few of Shapey's many recordings, the smiling figure who counts out the great big handfuls of Ralph's vitamins at breakfast, the woman who keeps him on time, soothes his angst, quietly runs an errand to replenish the batteries in his hearing aid, and all that before she sweeps out the door herself to face a busy schedule of teaching and rehearsals.

He tries the new batteries out but they don't work. "Another goddamned problem, now that's just life, isn't it?" he cusses in a voice full of gravel, and tosses the thing aside.

Ralph teaches, too, at the University of Chicago, a comfortable roost he found for himself upon leaving New York several decades ago. In the classroom all eyes are on him. His looks alone attract attention: white hair wildly swept back and curled at the nape in the manner of European composers immortalized by bronze busts, a long, grizzled beard, a face set hard in youth and deeply etched in a permanent scowl, his teeth solidly clamped down on a smelly cigar. He plants himself in the front of the room and launches into a formidable discourse, which is a mixture of deep insights into music composition, performance, politics, and much oversalted ranting and raving added for spice. He is famous for his never-ending series of exercises. He has been known to whip assignments out of the hands of his students and jump up and down on them in disgust at their shallow efforts. Nearly seventy now, he is not as strong as he might like, but he roosters about on bandy legs with the purposefulness of a man half his age and twice his build.

Apart from absorbing the considerable knowledge he has to impart, his students tend to admire his eccentric style, his allegiance to few, his proficient profanity, and his exuberant, existential outrage. They all have Shapey stories to tell, each turning on some peculiar act or exaggerated statement, but told with an unmistakable affection for the man. He, in turn, is fiercely loyal to them, and is available personally and professionally, with all the help he can muster.

"But," he insists in a rasped, cracked, abused voice, "when they come to me complaining of the hard lot of a composer-to-be, I tell them, 'Get the hell out of here! What the hell do you know about being *poor*, about *problems*, about not getting the *breaks*? I know more about it than you'll ever know, so get the hell out of my office.' "

This is true: he does know a lot about isolation and despair, and it has made him everlastingly angry, and even, some suspect, dimly mad. The problem is that Shapey has spent a lifetime moving at crosscurrents with the mainstream of his field. For one thing, he champions the little-played works of twentieth-century composers, which has earned him their undying gratitude, audience restlessness notwithstanding. For another, he himself writes very difficult modern music. It's not that he tries to be difficult; it's that a plain, simple, straight-forward melody doesn't interest him because it sings the comprehensible, and what Shapey hopes to do is to move beyond that, transcend the moment, and express the as-yet-incomprehensible. That is the difficult bargain that art makes.

For Shapey, his music is his world of beauty, his place of truth, his moment of peace. It is an intensely personal vision born from a ferocious intellectual power and immune to changing fashion. When he is working, the umbilical cord with Mother Earth is cut and he floats away from the ugliness, making his escape into a dimension that offers perfect sense, utter serenity, the sanity of logic, angelic joy. That's how Shapey hears his own music. Unfortunately, many others don't hear it quite that way.

Curl up on the couch to listen to a Shapey composition and you are met with stony, jagged, at times accentless, at other times hammered, chiseled sounds, harsh and wintry, chaotic or ecstatic, depending on your sensibilities, stringent, strident, rigorous, accusing, unforgiving, enigmatic, unyielding . . . only now and again relieved with a passage of lyricism, a refrain of the romantic, a passing moment of the euphonious. The first reaction of a listener is exclusion, a feeling of being deprived of so much as a common felicitous melody he or she could walk away humming. But the second reaction is that for all its rugged, combative atonality, Shapey's music is expressive of a certain indefinable human desperation and an epic lust after the ineffable.

This almost tangible form of his music is intentional. Shapey himself likes to refer to his work as "graven images"—by which he means music so structured and concretely conceived as to take on "an architectural form." "It's like this, my dear," he explains. "Ba-ba-ba-BAMMMMMMMMM. Do you know what that is? You *better* know what that is! If you don't, I'm sorry for you. Pretty good work, don't you think? But what is it? It's so simple anybody could have written it, don't you think? So what's the secret of the power? I'll tell you: It's carved in stone. It's a graven image. After all, what is music but an abstraction that a genius must ground and make concrete, so *concrete* that I can hold it in my hand. The masters understood that. I studied the masters and now I understand it. So all right, I told myself, I'll make graven images."

Shapey is a born storyteller. He loves to recount how his artist friends used to drift away from the electrically charged living room of his New York parties and how he'd find them in his study poring over his manuscripts and admiring the sheer physical beauty of the architectural shape his notes took on the page. It's a story that comes from his early days in New York (1945 through 1964) when he and Vera ran with the abstract expressionist crowd, de Kooning, Kline, Motherwell, Tworkov. Rich, fertile times, Shapey's artistic coming-of-age. New York: the home of his best friends and best enemies.

After twenty years in the Midwest, in 1985 he was lured back to accept a position as the Distinguished Professor of

Music at the Aaron Copland School of Music in Queens College. He couldn't resist the shot at trying once again to make New York work for him. The job lasted a year and then he hurried back to Chicago. For Shapey, even life's small successes hold the unsavory flavor of scraps to the dog. "Distinguished professor, shit! I don't even have one lousy degree to my name." Well, not quite true: he did, with considerable effort, graduate from high school.

Back in Chicago he continued to compose his graven images, but the difficult idiom of his music is only a small part of the numerous factors that contribute to his perplexity of spirit, his difficult existence. In fact, you could easily argue that the single biggest contributing factor to his life of discomfort is that Shapey is a failure as a social climber, unwilling and essentially unable to pander to the dictates of modern taste, incapable of bowing, scraping, even winking in the direction of the powerful figures who rule the music world.

That's how I put it. He puts it this way: "The whole goddamn music world. Faggots most of them. I go to bed with women. I'm not interested in tickling *their* rear ends. And cheap? You want to talk about creativity—let me ask you something: Do you think Lenny is a *good* composer, a *brilliant* composer? Tell me, do you? No! I didn't think so. And he's not the only one to mention. Well, okay, maybe we shouldn't name names. Aaron is already in his eighties, you know."

Sputtering in a staccato rat-tat-tat against the entire musical establishment, Shapey names one ancient crony after the next, all big names, all friends of a sort, all puffed-up people who toast each other at the party and knife each other in the cloakroom. One by one he mentions them, each in his turn, and then condemns them with the single verdict: "I dance on his grave."

Dense, brittle, astringent music, the inability to be at least reasonably politic, the failure to grant even some token gesture in the direction of avoiding offense—the froth of social meringue doesn't interest him in the slightest. The result has been an unhappy succession of events: conductors complaining that his works are physically impossible to perform, canceled performances, the hardship of finding a publisher, and when he finally secured one, having his work primarily photocopied instead of properly printed. The slights eat at him: nonperformance of his works by orchestras season after season, conductors who represent for him the anti-Christ, little recognition, few grants, no Pulitzer, and serious problems in cultivating a following despite the fact that he has written over one hundred compositions for symphony orchestra, chamber ensembles, voice, and solo instrument.

These things have made him swollen with anger. If you weren't close enough to the man to experience his honesty, his passion for his work, and his frustration with the human condition, it would be easy to call him mean, even off-balance. Irritable, irascible Ralph Shapey: if you didn't know better, it's a short hop in reasoning to conclude that at least his creativity stems from a kind of demented fervor.

Storming about his apartment in slippered feet, thick cigar smoke wafting behind him, Shapey delights in telling of the insults, especially those that have resulted in scandal. In particular, he tells the story of being passed over for a much coveted Guggenheim Fellowship. It's an award he had applied for time and again, and time and again he was refused, all the while watching bitterly from the sidelines for some fifteen years as many of his colleagues succeeded.

Every now and again a student of his who has been awarded a Guggenheim will nominate him for the prestigious award, which prompts the foundation to send him a fresh application with a standard, woodenly worded form letter saying that they had heard he was interested in receiving a grant. Once he wrote "Fuck You" all over it and sent it back. Another time he made a list of all the great composers and performers who never got one and sent it on to the foundation with a note thanking them for adding him to such distinguished company. A third time he Xeroxed and sent a Béla Bartók quote he has stitched in a sampler: "Competitions are for horses, not artists."

"There," he spits in a constant refrain, "am I crazy? I must be!"

Ralph Shapey: a difficult child prodigy who grew into an acidy but honest and endearing old man with very little in the middle. Old age comes. For most of us it is a long, reluctant slide into decay. For Shapey it was a tormented, exhausting climb straight up in heavy boots. On the door to his office, which (like his brain) he calls his womb, hangs a sign reading GOD. It came from a play his students put on. We'll assign you an easy role, they joked, just play yourself.

Inside his study is the chaotic mess of a creator at work, a lifetime of paperwork and memorabilia oozing and creeping over every surface like some menacing disease. An old black upright piano stands against one wall. It is not a thing of beauty: many of the ivories are missing and the exposed wooden slats offend like a mouthful of randomly missing teeth. What happened to the keys? It's not hard to imagine that Ralph pounded them off long ago in a fit of compositional fury.

By 1969 Shapey had had enough of what he perceived to be abuse from the music world, and in the most dramatic, tortured gesture of an already highly inflamed style, he renounced the official music establishment and removed his work from the world, forbidding anyone to play his pieces. It was a withdrawal into resentment and wounded pride. It was a cry of protest. "It was this," he says. "I went out on strike."

How long can a composer endure without the performance of his works, especially where the composer believes, as Shapey does, that the true birth of a piece of music is in the performance, not the composition? A month? two months? a year? Which is to ask, what is a piece of music worth if it is never heard, if it is kept hermetically sealed, sterile in silence, not reaching out to stir the soul or even to fuel the ire of an audience? How long can a brilliant composer endure the trial of watching himself grow extinct, his music fainter and fainter?

Shapey, with his enormous reserves of anger and turbulent

righteousness, continued his moratorium for *seven long years*, privately composing but never letting any of his works be performed during this time. The end finally came in 1976, when the patron saint of twentieth-century music and Shapey's very good friend, the late Chicago wine merchant Paul Fromm, of the Fromm Foundation, coaxed him back out into the public forum. "We need you, Ralph," Fromm said. Magic, healing words.

□ **3** □

SHAPEY'S STORY OF DESPAIR and isolation is perhaps the most dramatic of the forty MacArthur Fellows with whom I spoke but by no means the only such story in the crowd.

We have already heard about how the artist Robert Irwin spun off into a metaphysical isolation that produced his ten line paintings. As it happened, though, that was not his first period of self-imposed isolation. Earlier, long before it was fashionable to do so, he lived on the Mediterranean island of Ibiza in a rented cabin with neither heat nor hot water and didn't speak to another soul for eight long winter months.

In typical intellectualizing Irwin style, he looks back on the experience as a lesson to himself to strip away the temptations of modern culture every time he got bored: TV, movies, books, the idle chitchat of superficial social banter. And so he lived alone, not communicating with so much as a fisherman, not seeking any stimulation, content with only the company of his own keen mind.

Like Shapey, I believe Robert Irwin has also had his share of despair and hostility, his fill of being grossly misunderstood. There was the time, for example, when he set up an exhibit in New York's Museum of Modern Art, and a good ninety percent of the people who saw it—a carefully lit, essentially empty room, containing some translucent scrim and a line of wire, the entrance half blocked off, no curator's tag announcing it as art—didn't know that it was an exhibit at all. They walked on by, to look at the real art. The few who did notice it remarked that in Irwin's act of creation, he left everything out.

There was also the time that he worked three years to create a series of ten dot paintings he then shipped off to an exhibition in São Paulo only to learn that they were spit at, slashed with knives, and splattered with Coke. It seems that Irwin, in his effort to strip away the superficial and penetrate deeply into the heart of the matter, had gotten too minimalist for the public's taste. The works were perceived as an attack on the very foundation of the universe, a repudiation of both art and life, and that was a deeply threatening idea.

Often, Irwin is alone—even when he is in a crowd.

Robert Irwin, by the way, is divorced. So were nine others, twenty-five percent of the casually chosen forty Fellows. Some remarried, two and three times. Robert Irwin remarried the same woman he divorced, and then the couple divorced again. It's not easy to live with anyone, but the collective suggestion is that it's particularly difficult to live with a person who arranges his or her affairs in such a way as to reach a succession of cathartic, ecstatic moments. For one thing, the long buildup of angst to get there is hardly an endearing quality. For another thing, usually, breakthrough moments are solitary events—no room for anyone else except in the audience, dutifully applauding. And finally, there is the jump in awareness that accompanies such an event, with the lamentable result of one partner's outgrowing the other.

■ **4** ■

ISOLATION AND DESPAIR, work not understood, being ahead of one's time, being perceived as mad or ruthless, experiencing a succession of restless and unconvincing marriages—are these things the necessary by-products of a creative effort? Are they prerequisites?

Romanticized, conventional lore would have us recite the long roster of disturbed geniuses and answer yes, yes to both questions—but there is no proof other than circumstantial evidence, and not even enough of that to make a convincing case. Suffering maims and blinds; it also inspires and opens the eyes. Plenty of highly creative people live "normal" productive lives, carrying themselves forward, chin up, day by day, valiantly managing their little, terrific, faithful struggles. And, too, there are plenty of creative people living conflicted, disturbed, isolated lives, like Ralph Shapey and, at various times, Robert Irwin. In light of the weight of evidence on both sides, it would be foolish to assume that despair and isolation, madness and meanness are *necessarily* linked to the creative process. A more reasonable interpretation is this: it's not that creativity and madness are necessarily linked, but rather that creativity and *deviance* (sometimes heroic, sometimes reckless) go hand in hand.

By definition, creativity requires an offsetting from the mainstream, something different, something unusual, something new. If you choose to pursue a creative approach to something, by definition you are no longer squarely within the lockstep of your field. People won't know what to do with you, how to describe you, how to consider your work, what to make of your ideas. Wounding you to the quick, they simply won't get it or like it.

Adhere nonetheless to this creative posture and even take it to the extremes of anger, resentment, arrogance, or disgust, and isolation follows. You'll be passed over for grants and prizes. Your work will be branded "difficult"—a death blow that functions as a self-perpetuating epithet. And if you have any sympathizers at all, even they will admit you're cracked, but at least do you the justice of mentioning, as Edith Sitwell once remarked about William Blake, that the crack is where the light shines through.

Is creativity linked to madness? The scientists are working on it, running batteries of psych tests, isolating genes, even examining pieces of Albert Einstein's formaldehyde-soaked brain, but the question hasn't yet produced any firm or useful conclusions. Perhaps it is more telling to ask: Is the creative life a hard and insecure one? The answer to this is: Often. And the supporting testimony is abundant:

"To be a genius you have to be something of a brute," MacArthur Laureate Ralph Manheim told me. Manheim is a highly respected translator of such brilliant and brutish authors as Louis-Ferdinand Céline, Peter Handke, Günter Grass, and others of similar weight and mass. As one of only two MacArthur Laureates, he is supported at a comfortable income for the rest of his life.

I knew what he meant by the remark—a reference to a certain kind of toughness and single-minded determination necessary to pursue creative work—which was good because Manheim wasn't inclined to comment further. Instead, he fell into a long, meditative silence, looking without seeing the Paris street scene out his window, uncharmed by the spring breeze. A grim smile wobbled across his face and I wondered if he was thinking back to one of his very first translation jobs, the assignment that launched his future: *Mein Kampf*, the work of a brute.

"I think you're always alone," the poet Doug Crase told me. "Even if you're with people, or married, or living with some-one, or surrounded by people."

"I think you always feel peripheral to this institution," said educator, author, and sociologist Sara Lawrence Lightfoot, speaking about Harvard, where she is a fully tenured professor, only the second black woman to reach such an exalted status in the university's three-hundred-and-fifty-year history. To see her—sitting tall, thick hair coiled back from a serene brow, clear dark skin set off by brightly colored wraps and baubles, a beauty from a long line of handsome, strong-willed women— is to recognize a commanding presence. To hear her talk— articulate, logical, measured—is to know at once that she has much to offer. Yet, notwithstanding her unimpeachable ac-complishments and her cultivated manner, she chooses the word "peripheral."

These experiences and feelings are all variations of the same tale, ranging from the gray shades of doubt to the black chronicles of despair. Shapey, Irwin, Manheim, Crase, Lightfoot— how are we to interpret the collective sentiment? Do we assume that to be creative we are condemned to a life eked out of the hard-bitten territory of alienation and desperation? Must we prepare outselves for the possibility that our work will be cast in the dubious critical light of an ambiguous legacy?

There are no sure answers to these questions, as each man's life spins on the axis of his own idiosyncratic bundle of talents and experiences, triumphs and petty failures. There are as yet no firm conclusions as to the relationship between the creative process and psychic disorder, but there is one small serviceable observation that we can draw from the testimony of these creators: if you're interested in pursuing creative work and in having it recognized and even rewarded, you had better cultivate an ability for self-renewal, an ability to be resilient.

BUILDING RESILIENCY

▪ 1 ▪

WHEN PETER SELLARS WAS at Harvard, his early success
in the experimental theater led to his being the first freshman
allowed to direct a production on the Loeb Drama Center's
main stage. For this momentous debut he worked up a new
reading of Edith Sitwell's verse set to the music of William
Walton in a production entitled *Façade*. He set the action in
the lobby of a gone-to-wrack Edwardian hotel. In the background he planted three screens, onto which he projected photographs from the 1926 archives of *The London Illustrated News*.
In the foreground, actors mimed Sellars's peculiar interpretation of the poetry.

The production was perceived, to put it kindly, as an im-
pudent, poorly knit exercise in tedium. Roughly forty percent
of his audience walked out every night and Sellars was driven
from the Loeb theater complex altogether and banished to the
basement of Adams House, a dark and moldy residence hall.

Slings and arrows; the hue and cry. The creative act, no
mater how brilliant or beautiful, no matter how elucidating or
fluorescent, is not always understood—let alone appreciated.
Which confirms what we already know: as with love, with
creativity there is no accounting for taste.

Many of us, when confronted with a blow to the ego of the
sort Sellars experienced—and especially at the impressionable
age of a college freshman, when we are still trying on various
ideas about what life might be about—would have retreated

to debate the wisdom of a shift in fields. The young maverick, on the contrary, immediately went to work on staging *Antony and Cleopatra* in the depths of Adams House. He claims it was a natural choice: he could use the dormitory swimming pool for the River Nile.

The MacArthur Fellows are not quitters. Even in the face of insult. Or when confronted with defeat. Or when up against humiliation, despondency, hostility, boredom, or indifference. They find a way to make adjustments, to keep at it, to stay buoyant, to believe in themselves. There is a sense of the carpenter about them, of making things work and of turning mistakes to good account. There is a smoothness of attitude and a sense of endurance, and of continuity. Smiling at each fresh indignity, they find in themselves the seeds for survival and for leadership.

Thus we come to the matter of resiliency—the opening premise being that the more you have of it, the better off you are. Fortunately, it can be built up in a number of ways.

▪ **2** ▪

"How do you build your resiliency?"

The question was put to writer Brad Leithauser. He answered without hesitation, gesturing to the various piles of paper strewn about his office: "When I can't bear to look at my poetry, I turn to my novel in progress. When the novel makes me ill, I draft the book review I promised someone. If the book review eludes me, I may sketch out an essay that I've been thinking of writing. There is always something on my desk that I can turn to, always something to work on."

Leithauser has a plan: there are eight books he would like to publish in the 1990s and the chances are very good that he will accomplish that. He had a similar plan of five books for the 1980s and, give or take a couple of months, he succeeded. Apart from the sheer drive this sort of thinking exhibits, having a lot of specific projects in varying stages of development is what allows Leithauser to keep going when his spirit lags behind his purpose.

It's the same for conservationist and businessman Patrick Noonan. When a deal to save a parkland he's been struggling with falls apart, he turns immediately to the half-dozen "other balls I have in the air." He and his organization manage several hundred deals a year. That number would be only a fraction as high if he deflected energy and concentration to tally a daily score of despair.

One of many keys to building your recuperative powers, then, is to arrange your affairs in such a way that you always have a variety of things to turn to. Not only does it help to ease the disappointment of criticism or failure, but there is an added benefit: the tendency of one project to inform another, the surprising connections that surface from one thing to the next. It is not uncommon, for example, for something in one of Leithauser's essays to provide a clue to a voice he is struggling with in a poem. Similarly, a clever negotiating technique that works for Noonan in one deal might be decisive in the next deal, or, better yet, might serve as the catalyst for refining an antiquated policy that governs all his transactions.

■ **3** ■

"How did you handle the tough times?"

The question was put to poet John Ashbery, author of a dozen volumes of poems (excluding anthologies) and winner of a long paragraph of awards, grants, and appointments that includes two Guggenheims, membership in the National Academy and Institute of Arts and Sciences, a National Book Critics Circle Award, a National Book Award, a Pulitzer, and now the MacArthur.

It didn't come easily.

Here are some descriptive terms taken from several decades

of reviews: "tuneless," "undistinguished," "drip, drabble, and squirt of garbage," "calculated incoherence," "egregious disjunctiveness," "deliberately opaque," "calculated oddities," "expeditions into the meaningless," "inaccessible," "at best bewildering, at worst boring," "about as much poetic life as a refrigerated plastic flower" . . . Sticks and stones may hurt one's bones, but words, they can kill.

One of the earliest formal works of poetry Ashbery wrote was titled *Some Trees*, which he entered in the Yale Younger Poets competition in 1956. The submission was rejected before it even reached W. H. Auden, who was judging the entries that year. Through a mutual friend, though, Ashbery's work was passed directly on to Auden, who granted him the award. Naturally, Ashbery was ecstatic—the blessing from a grandmaster of the art form is not of trifling consequence to a new and aspiring poet—but still, it took eight years to sell a measly eight hundred copies of the work. Ashbery sincerely believed that he would never publish anything else again.

Ask Ashbery about building resiliency and he talks about the support of friends—and in this he is not alone. Time and again I heard the poignant accolades and the urgent testimonials of thanks owed to spouses, mentors, confidants. Time and again I heard about quality, not quantity. Rolodex friends, the excessively charming, the pretty, the decorative, the popular, the hip, and the hot—these people aren't the ones who count when it comes to building resiliency. What counts are a few sustaining words at the right time from the *true* friend—the one who knows you, the one who cares, the one whose opinion matters, the one who tells the truth and delivers it with perspective. With a true friend the bruises fade, the wounds heal, and work at last can continue.

(As it happened, I had heard that Joseph Brodsky had a particularly well-developed facility for choosing good friends, such an important—possibly the most important—skill in the world, and so I asked him: "How do you pick your friends?"

"It's a fluke very often," he replied, "but if there's some sort of logic to it, it's that you basically pick people on the basis of where there is a degree of common denominator."

"What sort of common denominator?" I pressed.

"The common denominator?" he answered. "Well, I would say a certain acquaintance with the world of ideas. And a certain—how should I put it?—some similarity of financial bracket because you can't really be friends with either very rich or very poor; it's actually easier to be friends with the rich than it is to be friends with the poor, but it turns out neither is easy. And what else would I say? Also, in my case I am afraid to report, it requires, how should I put it, a certain dignity on the face."

"How to make sense of that?" I laughed.

"It's very easy. It's not physical attraction, really. Dante postulates somewhere, I can't remember where, that in the human face, a viewer, another human should be able to discern the phrase *Homo Dei*. 'H' being the frame. 'O' for each eye you have. 'M' is the shape of the eyebrows. 'D' is the nose and profile. 'E'—I don't remember what he makes of the 'e.' And 'i' is the center eye, third eye. Well, if I see that written on a face, that suggests some possibility for—for what?"

"Communication?" I offered.

"*Ja*," he answered, and that was the end of that.)

◾ **4** ◾

"HOW DO YOU KEEP from feeling low when research fails, grants fall through, colleagues raise their eyebrows, and you conclude that you've reached a dead end?" I asked Howard Gardner.

"As Freud said," he couldn't resist, "being the firstborn Jewish boy and having a mother that loves you . . ." Had he finished the joke it would have ended, ". . . you think you can do anything."

Stated another way, confidence (not to be confused with arrogance) builds resiliency. Confidence comes from success, to be sure, but it can also come from recognizing that a lot of carefully examined failures are themselves one path to success.

Howard Gardner isn't afraid to examine his mistakes. He doesn't run from them, but instead he steps back and takes an appraising look with a cool, friendly eye, trying to isolate what went wrong and why. Studying the matter himself and garnering opinion from knowledgeable sources, he sifts the useful criticism from the idle chatter, reevaluates his position, and sets a new, realistic goal. If the problem seems insurmountable, he will leave it altogether and not return to it until after a suitable break.

"I mean, if you keep trying something and you keep failing, I think it's very foolish to keep trying to do the same thing in the same way unless you're sure that nothing else will work. I think you have to be more pragmatic. Instead of stupidly insisting and pushing in an area that hasn't proven to be useful, you ought to put it aside and look at a different problem for a while and then return to it. The mind continues to work at it even when you're not focused on it and sometimes discovers a new angle when the spotlight has been turned off. Then when you revisit the problem, you may be in a better position to reconceptualize it and perhaps solve it. I've been very pragmatic in that way and haven't let closed doors or defeats irritate me—very much."

It's a lesson he passes on to his students. When he assigns a paper, for example, he insists on a series of deadlines that, in effect, force the students to start writing before they have framed all the issues and finished the research. The result is a kind of "strobing effect" on the problem: you hit it, back off, hit it again, back off, and so on. Each time the students approach the draft they see it with a fresh eye and from the vantage point of having stewed about it subconsciously between visits. The end result is a better and more effective presentation.

■ 5 ■

"HOW DO YOU KEEP from giving in to despair when things seem too hard?"

Dr. Joan Abrahamson, a lawyer, a painter, a writer of some three hundred songs, and a catalyst for community action, thinks about it for a minute or two and gives her unvarnished, unpackaged answer.

"There's a lot to be done," she says in her clear, quiet voice, "and that is what I concentrate on and enjoy doing."

Though only in her mid-thirties, Abrahamson has accomplished a considerable amount of good for the benefit of all. One of her earliest projects, for example, grew out of her desire to rent a large, sunny studio so that she could paint her oversized abstract canvases. In time, she wandered through the open gates of an abandoned army base in San Francisco. It struck her as the perfect facility. Clearing away the obstacles, she turned it into the Fort Mason Center, a facility for community arts and learning.

Since that time she has moved on to even greater concerns, which she manages through the Jefferson Institute, a public policy organization she founded. It seeks to implement solutions to societal concerns in the areas of the future of cities, international security, international economics, health, and creativity. The projects are as varied as the concerns suggest: the establishment of KidsPlace, which reorients a city around the needs of children; the Mayor's Institute, which brings city leaders together to exchange ideas; and the Franco-American AIDS Foundation, which she developed with the help of Dr. Jonas Salk, the purpose of which was to establish a neutral third party to hold patents until the two countries agreed on rights and royalties, without stopping the work on a cure for AIDS. The Security Project, the Economic Club, the Center for the Study of Creativity—her moral imagination and physical dedication appear inexhaustible.

Still, she is human. "My resiliency comes from the *process* of the work itself," she says, "and the hope of making a difference." These are the future-oriented words of a visionary, a woman who has a sense of what is needed for tomorrow and the confidence that it can be managed. As she speaks about her plans, quietly and with assurance, a line from the Talmud comes to mind: If I am not for myself, who will be? If I am only for myself, what am I?

By focusing on process—bringing together the resources, meeting with people, learning from them, and seeing how their ideas improve her own—even if she never reaches her goal, she has succeeded. Her satisfaction comes from the doing, a fulfillment not experienced by people who focus only on winning or losing. Ignoring or undervaluing the process and lusting after victory makes it very hard to feel that your time has been well spent if you lose; focusing only on the goal makes it very hard to retrench and regroup and be resilient if you fail.

▪ 6 ▪

"YES, OF COURSE, the defeats," said Michael Lerner, director of Commonweal, a man deeply interested in health in the broadest interpretation of the word.

For Lerner, when something bad happens he treats it as an opportunity to learn, to deepen his life experience and accumulated wisdom. He greets it, at the front door, with open arms: "Here you are, pain, old friend. I've been waiting for you to come back. You haven't been to visit for a while." It seemed an awfully warm greeting for something that hurts. I pressed for clarification.

"I am deeply grateful for all the good things in my life, but at the same time I recognize that if you make your peace of mind dependent on good fortune, you're not going to be in good shape. In yoga, there is the idea of *samtosha*, which is Sanskrit for acceptance, contentment, or satisfaction, the quality of learning how to be satisfied with what you've been given.

I work very hard at that. And you know Shakespeare talks about it in one of his sonnets—a man with satisfaction has something greater than the kings. So if something difficult happens to me, I try to welcome it, accept it, work with it. I treat it as what is happening now. I don't get too excited by my victories or too disappointed by my defeats, and in that way I come closer to peace of mind and that deep inner place that creativity comes from."

Later, wandering the Commonweal property in the morning shade of the forest and breathing the chill smell of cypress mixed with salty ocean spray, I had a chance to contemplate his dense, meditated statements. He is offering here yet another sober and significant key to maintaining resiliency in the face of troubled times. What name do we give it—attitude? Too shallow. A better word for it is philosophy, a set of beliefs that help make sense of the universe in which we exist, a system for the conduct of life, the pursuit of wisdom, the search for the ultimate reality.

Lerner's resiliency comes from his inner program: he has cultivated a view about trouble, what it means, where it fits, how to greet it, how to cope if it sticks around for a long time, how to feel when it goes away, what to feel when it returns.

There is an elegance and a depth to Lerner's mind that come perhaps from having been a student of philosophy all his adult life. In school years he was involved in political philosophy, a course of study that culminated in his doctorate. Not long afterward he shifted to a long-ranging inquiry into the philosophy of health, which, in turn, led him to examine various ways of living. He reads, he practices and integrates the lessons of yoga into his daily life, and he continues to experiment with what he has learned to refine his beliefs. With such a long-standing and sophisticated interest in philosophical questions, it is not surprising that he has developed a body of understanding by which he lives his life. Those beliefs sustain him in difficult times.

It's not the path for everyone, but, inevitably, those inclined to chart the longitude and latitude of questions as large as the Meaning of Life develop an approach to handling the disappointing times. And an inner program that does not make you feel like a failure sustains the energy and commitment required for creative work.

▪ 7 ▪

"DISAPPOINTMENTS ARE fairly rare," David Stuart volunteered, a trace of relief in his voice. "It goes back to that thing we were talking about earlier, about not really having a very good idea or definition of what it is I hope to accomplish with all this Maya stuff in the first place. In a way I'm an explorer: what I discover is what I discover. If I don't have any more specific expectations than that, it's hard to be disappointed. Most of the time something is neutral if it's not great because it's all such a mystery that even my mistakes show us something. I don't sit down with a bunch of unknown glyphs thinking I'm going to solve a problem. I don't say, 'Hey, I'm going to interpret this passage, so I better look at all the sources and find out what it says.' For me it's more an accidental thing. I have fun with it. I like to play around. It's kind of a game. Any of the things that I've come up with have never been from a stated purpose in mind. It's from having been bored one afternoon and looking through a stack of things and saying, 'Hey, this looks interesting.' It's hard to be disappointed when you think like that."

▪ 8 ▪

"OF COURSE, I've had my share of problems," said Robert Shapley, the vision scientist. But like David Stuart, he enjoys what he is doing so much that it never occurs to him to dwell on the mistakes.

"There are just a lot of interesting questions. In the study of the visual system and the brain, there are just so many good questions that you never run out of them. The source of creativity is good questions. But there are so many that you have to sort of say: Well, can I solve this one? Maybe there are ten questions and you can only solve three—still, you have three good questions. It's like a garden; you can just go out and pick the flowers and there are so many good ones, if one dies, you still have so many more."

He elaborates: "I started out in my work interested in the brain and where thought and personality come from and so forth, but those interests have receded somewhat because there is so much to know just about perception. I can't think of many things more interesting. What's an eye? What's perception? That's definitely not as grand or as global or as cosmic as string theory, but it's just very interesting. How many red and green photo receptors are there in the eye? What's the ratio? It seems like a very silly, very simple question, but number one, no one knows the answer, and number two, it's not so easy to find the answer. I play with it and I think eventually I'll find a way into the problem, and when I do I'll uncover a very simple fact which will lead to an understanding of color vision, and the wiring of the retina, and why at a football game the only color that stands out in the periphery of your vision is the red scarf or red coat someone is wearing. It will be interesting to know why that is, and with so many interesting questions like that that are unsolved, why waste your time being disappointed over something you can't understand?"

■ 9 ■

"How do I handle distressing things," asks Sara Lawrence Lightfoot, "like, for example, my feeling of being peripheral to this place? . . . Well, I recognize that it's not just this institution, Harvard, but would be something I would feel, I suppose, in most institutions. And I think there is some value to that. I think that once one is committed to the maintenance and sustenance of an institution and its patterns, then one is

less likely to take off into some pioneering or creative or interesting edge. I think there is something to not fitting in—
not purposefully nonconformist but still nonconforming in so
many ways—that has really helped me in the definition of my
work, its ideas and craft.

"There's something that can't be missed about being a
woman and a black in this institution," she continues, "the
only tenured black woman, the second in its history, that has
left a huge mark on this place, and that makes me know that
I'm not in it. I'm not *of* it. I'm here but I'm not of it. I don't
mean to imply that I feel the heavy hand of discrimination or
that anyone's blocking my path or anything like that. Rather,
I'm now trying to speak about learning how to survive and
thrive in a position of noncentrality. And I think that very
early on, probably adolescent years, I learned the advantages
of not fitting in because I was never part of the majority in a
school context, say, or a community context, so I learned how
to turn that to an advantage."

▪ 10 ▪

"So, you want to know about my unhappy times," says
Les Brown of Worldwatch.

Like Lerner, Brown has a philosophy that encompasses
mechanisms for coping. But unlike Lerner's approach, which
focuses on achieving peace of mind and equal acceptance of
the bad with the good, Brown's endurance comes from the
power of self-knowledge.

"I know what works for me and what doesn't work for me
and that helps a lot when it comes to handling mistakes and
avoiding disappointments. I know how much pressure I can
take and what to do to try and keep that manageable. I know
how much interruption I can tolerate, and so I've arranged my
office conditions and working times to limit it to acceptable
levels. I know it clears my mind to work out, and so I walk
to and from work and play ball on the weekends. I know what

kind of work really provides me with joy and satisfaction. If I have to have a paper ready by a certain date, I know how much I need to have done at the end of three months and six months and eight months. I rarely miss a deadline because I know that about how I work. I know that I need to read a lot to stay current with the information flow in my field, and so I've developed ways of making sure I get that reading done. . . ."

From the most mundane level of handling his mail to the broader issues of how to derive satisfaction from his chosen activities, Brown knows what works for *him*.

"And how have you amassed so much solid information about yourself?" I asked.

The question was easy for him: "I've tested myself a lot, maybe more than most people are inclined to do, and I've paid attention to the results."

When Brown, in his usual understated manner, says he has tested himself a lot, he isn't talking about textbook examinations or the typical predictable challenges of career trackers who have their sights set on the boardroom. Brown's challenges have been more internal, more personal, and his reach has been a lot higher than the conventional measures of success. To put the climb in perspective, consider where he is today as compared to where he started.

Today it's fair to say that Brown is easily one of the most influential people in the field of world conservation. He receives some three hundred applications for every opening in his organization. He culls information from sources as diverse as the United Nations and some dusty back alley in some forgotten Asian town. Analyzing and synthesizing what he learns, he produces publications that serve as policy-making tools in Eastern and Western Bloc nations alike, as well as in the Third World. He is a much sought-after keynote speaker. Reporters, students, congressmen, legislators, Fortune 500 CEOs, and all of Ted Turner's three hundred senior editors on staff in his Cable News Network read Brown's reports.

Tread lightly, he tells them, lest we trample the earth, good planets are hard to find.

Moreover, this private-sector activity has evolved from his work in government, first as an adviser on foreign agricultural policy during the Kennedy administration, and then for three years as the administrator of the International Agricultural Development Service, which conducted food-aid projects in some forty countries. When Richard Nixon took office, Brown left government and helped to start the Overseas Development Council, a research group focusing on Third World issues. Six years and four books later, he began Worldwatch (1974) with the help of funding from the Rockefeller Brothers.

That's the Lester R. Brown of today. The Les Brown of yesterday grew up on a tomato farm near the Delaware River. There were no books in his house; neither parent graduated from elementary school. He had planned to farm for the rest of his life, but two things changed that. First, a teacher introduced him to biography, and in reading about the lives of Abe Lincoln, Kit Carson, Andrew Jackson, George Washington, Thomas Jefferson (all "friends," he says), Brown realized that a single person could accomplish a lot. The second determining factor was a trip to India in 1956, the year after his graduation from what is now Cook College, arranged by the National 4-H Club Foundation's International Farm Youth Exchange Program. He stayed in India nearly six months. The poverty was overwhelming, and it occurred to him that the world food problem was of greater importance than the fertility of his family's tomato fields.

Biography and India set him to wondering about his own limits. And so, as a young boy, he started to pay attention and stopped letting things slide, as life is apt to do if we look away for a minute. As he met challenges, he examined all the angles. He asked himself how he felt about this or that, and why he was afraid in certain situations, and how much risk he thought he could handle, and how he felt about competition, and how much could be accomplished in the space of an hour, and how a decision about this would affect something else . . . the seeds of his extraordinary capacity for integrated thinking. It takes a secure person to climb to a high vantage point and to look squarely below at his mistakes and how he very neatly rationalized them in the past. In a lesser man this inquiry might cause him to despise himself or confirm his feelings of embarrassment or inadequacy. Not so with Brown. He was interested in seeing what he was made of.

He started testing and probing, and he never stopped. The result is that he knows himself very well, and that inner knowledge is what he relies on in trying to avoid mistakes and in managing defeats. The integrated self is a powerful thing.

■ 11 ■

THE CLUES FOR BUILDING resiliency are everywhere you look: maintain a variety of projects; choose your friends wisely; embrace your errors and disappointments to see what you can learn; when a problem seems intractable, leave it, come back to it, leave it again, and again return; invest yourself in the vision, focusing not just on the goal but on the process; be accepting of the rhythms of pleasure and pain; retain a plasticity and curiosity about the potential of your field; learn to see the advantage in a hardship; develop a philosophy that allows you to accept defeat on the same terms as you would welcome a victory; make an effort to know yourself and determine what works for you. . . .

If none of these things helps to build stamina, toughen the hide, and strengthen recuperative powers, there is always one more possibility. It comes from Joseph Brodsky, a man who has seen the inside of a Soviet prison camp and who has lived in exile in the arctic reaches of his motherland, shoveling manure, chopping wood, and crushing stone. He has experienced the isolation that an uncompromising intellect suffers when cut off from the sources of nourishment—books, friends, discussion. He has felt the despair of being refused permission to reunite if only for a brief visit with his aged parents, even when they were dying.

"In terms of disappointments and negative experiences, et cetera, et cetera, et cetera, one lives long enough that one is not really shocked by the unpleasant, *ja?* The sensation is that of recogniton, not shock. There is no joy in it, so much, but to a certain perverse extent it is joyful. You know that, well, life has only so many tricks. Human options, you see, of either kind are limited by nature. And your capacity, your ability to experience something is also quite limited. That is, you can only squeeze so much joy out of a man and only so much in the way of suffering. It's like a cow, *ja?*, she has a natural limit. And you can be shocked only so many times—after that you cease to be shocked."

Sooner or later, in every interview, the question was asked: How do you get over your disappointments? Joseph Brodsky had the best if-all-else-fails answer: "I try to forget them. As quicky as possible. And then move on."

FOR THE LOVE OF IT

THERE IS A STORY that has to be told from start to finish, no interruptions, no editorials, no sideshows. It's about love, which is relevant in this way: if the creative impulse were better understood physiologically, it wouldn't come as a surprise to me to learn that it is the heart and not the mind that controls the sparks and directs the inventiveness.

"ALL RIGHT EVERYBODY, listen up."

Ellen Stewart was standing in the middle of a gloomy theater stage in a part of New York best known to people down on their luck and students subsisting on a seriously frayed shoestring. It's a joke with Ellen that she never goes above Manhattan's Fourteenth Street. Only the stage lights were switched on, and even then half of them were burned out. In the dark of the makeshift benches all around, the glow of cigarette tips burned steadily.

A group of blue-jeaned musicians, barely discernible in the deep shadows, was experimenting with the hollow sound of a conch shell against the backdrop of a snare drum and a wired keyboard. The effect was eerie and foreboding, the lost sound of Charon poling his way across the River Styx. Perfect, one said. The others grinned.

There was no response to Ellen Stewart's attempt at order,

so she finished her breakfast of Fig Newtons washed down with gut-rot coffee, peeled off her old shoes, padded out center stage in fire-engine-red socks pulled up over tight black pants and topped with a bright pink sweatshirt studded with rhinestones, and tried again.

"All right now, everybody, LISTEN UP." She clapped her hands together theatrically for emphasis. In the hollow of the room (and considering the neighborhood) it sounded an awful lot like the sharp report of a gun.

It worked. The musicians broke off abruptly. Young aspiring actors and actresses tumbled out from the dark recesses of the seats and eddied around her feet. Hello Mama, Say Mama, What-say Mama, Mornin' Mama, Yah Mama, Uh-huh Mama. She returned all their greetings with a single Hey Doll. There are so many young people in Ellen Stewart's life at any particular instant she couldn't possibly remember all their names.

"We're gonna be busy today," she announced in a husky contralto, getting right down to business. "First off, Lloyd baby, could you run to the hardware store and get me a long pole, like a broom handle or somethin'. Here, take my coin purse. The rest of you: now who can do a skateboard? I don't care if you could do it as a child, David, lemme see if you can do it *today*. Andrew? Baby, go get those skateboards from the back. At two I have a lady comin' to teach us the flamenco. And this here is Dahnise somethin'; she's writin' somethin'. Could we have some lights in here or did I forget to pay the bill? Okay, now pay attention. Genjie, gimme a beat, honey, somethin' fluid like a river. Use that string thing I got in Africa. Uh huh, oooh, yeah, pick it up a little, that's it. Now, everybody, here's what we're gonna do in that flood scene . . ."

Watching Ellen Stewart work—bangles flashing as she waves her thin arms, fine braids of wiry hair shot through with gray tossing as she moves about, a little slow-stepped now but definite in her gestures, muttering under her breath about the fat girl who could sing the voice-over if only she had the confidence to do it, screeching at the skateboarder to slow

it down, honey, and no tricks, flashing a wide, reassuring smile
to a nervous young thing named Rosa, who kept apologizing
and telling everyone that she's never acted before—I could see
at once that she loves her work.

Should we be embarrassed to talk about such things? There
are certain times and certain circumstances when the air is so
charged with cynicism or the tart sting of irony that you
wouldn't consider speaking frankly of such a base and undis-
guised emotion for fear of sounding naïve—but this isn't one
of those times. Love of work, love of humanity, love of life,
love of art, a deep, abiding love for music—it's an emotion
that doesn't embarrass Ellen Stewart. It's the axis of her creative spin, the central theme that surfaces over and over again.
If her life were ever to be staged as a play, presumably in a
Way Off Broadway theater like this one, it would unfold something like this.

ACT ONE

Ellen Stewart, born in Louisiana, came east in 1950 via
Chicago with the hope of becoming a fashion designer. As a
youngster she won a design contest, which earned her a smack
in the mouth when she went to collect her prize for having
had the audacity to enter it, but she wasn't deterred. She had
heard of a school in New York that colored girls *could* attend
and that was her plan.

The arrangement was that she would bunk with a friend
whom she was supposed to meet under the huge old clock that
used to crown Grand Central Station. The friend never
showed. Depressed, she wandered into St. Patrick's Cathedral
on Fifth Avenue, lit a candle, and prayed for a job. God hears
the clean of heart: about a half hour later, she was employed
across the street at Saks, snipping off stray threads and pushing
a broom.

For years Ellen worked at Saks Fifth Avenue, exploring the
city on her off time, which is how she met a little Rumanian

immigrant named Papa Abe Diamond in the Jewish neighborhood down on Delancey Street. He became her good friend
who supplied her with odd bits of cloth; she became his
adopted daughter, the future fashion designer.

One day, the story continues, disaster struck in a dressing
room at the store. One of the rich white ladies was in a frenzy
over some mishap with a ball gown. It was lunchtime and no
one was around to fix it. Ellen stepped in and earned a promotion to the design department in the process. The best part
of the promotion, she tells me, was that she got to take off the
blue smock all the colored girls had to wear in those days. In
itself, that was an achievement, but the real coup was that her
own dress creations, sewn up from Papa Diamond's remnant
fabrics, were finally noticed. One thing led to another and
Ellen's ball gowns were put in Saks' windows carrying price
tags of fifteen hundred dollars.

For years—seven, eleven, who can be sure, it was so long
ago, and besides, fidelity to fact is not something that much
concerns her, not on these biographical points, not if it could
assist someone in pinning down her age; if the facts shift, she
tells me, chalk it up to a memory that keeps improving—she
worked as a designer at Saks, but increasingly she felt resentment from blacks and whites alike. Eventually she got so sick
that she thought she was dying, quit, and went off to Morocco
to recuperate. There, in a vision, the late Papa Diamond appeared to her. He repeated a story he had often told her, which
ended with the moral: Get a pushcart, daughter, and push it
for other people. If you do that, it will always take you where
you want to go.

ACT TWO

Right around this time, Ellen's foster brother, a former theology student turned playwright, got involved in a miserable
production of a play that flopped, closed, and cost him all he
had. He took it very hard, and seeing his suffering, Ellen

decided on her pushcart: she would form a theater for people like him. Aspiring actors, playwrights, stagehands, set designers—everyone was welcome.

The location she found was a run-down storefront on East Ninth Street. Her smart-looking male model friends from the freelance dress business she was running came at night to help her renovate. The neighbors, being the open-minded sort, saw these gorgeous young men come and go and assumed she was operating a prostitution ring. At first they spat at her and threw garbage on her stoop. Finally, they called the police.

As luck would have it, the officer who answered the call turned out to be an old vaudevillian who quickly took in the situation and advised her on the law. He suggested that in order to get around the licensing requirements for a theater, she serve coffee and tea and treat it as a cabaret. He also pointed out that she needed a name. Since everyone was calling her Mama at the time, someone suggested La Mama, the thought being that the prefix gave the dingy hovel a touch of class.

ACT THREE

Soon Ellen was putting on a show a week on a stage the size of a table, and serving coffee from behind an old shoeshine stand. To finance these productions she freelanced as a dressmaker for fancy Fifth Avenue department stores like Bergdorf's and Bendel's. Fortunately, she was good with a needle and likes to boast a bit about being the only American at that time to be invited to Dior's salon in Paris, the only American to have not one but two gowns at Queen Elizabeth II's coronation ball.

"Baby, I was hot stuff," she says, a trace of the Deep South Gallic still in her voice, bright lights still glowing in her heavy black eyes. Her face, though tired, is far from cheerless and still has an elasticity to it that keeps it from crumbling into a caricature of itself. Her jawline is still firm, her brow still smooth, and the whole of her expression is enlivened with red,

red lipstick. It's a face that poses neither the looks nor the spirit of a woman resigned to waiting out her time in the backwash of history. Ellen will never be the kind of old person who wails the regret that life has come and gone and nothing much has happened. She will always have a fresh story to tell.

With the dress income, she kept the ramshackle theater going, paid the rent on her railroad flat, and supported all the transients who lived with her, including her business manager, Jim (a.k.a. Jimbo) Moore, who is still with her today, nearly three decades later.

Word got around and aspiring playwrights began turning up at her doorstep clutching grubby manuscripts to their chests. "Honey, I never read the scripts. Still don'," she tells me. "What do I know about *scripts*? What do I know about the *theater*? It's people, doll, *people* that count. Without them I'm nothin'. Without the love from all these people, now where would an old black woman like me be at? I just trust my beeps."

Much has been written about Ellen's mystical beeps. Translation: anyone honest, anyone kind, anyone sincere, anyone she liked, anyone from whom she got a good feeling (which was just about every bedraggled soul who intersected her path) was allowed equal time on her stage.

In those years, playwrights knew how to work, she insists. They stayed up all night sweating out a script and would come in unshaven and looking like hell the next morning. Nobody owed them anything and they knew it. They painted, they hung sets, they fixed light bulbs, they beat the sidewalks for audiences, they passed the coffee and then the hat, begging shamelessly for contributions. They did it because they cared, and that caring was the source of their inventiveness and drive. Ellen chuckles. Of course, she's been fixing, painting, sweeping, mopping up the ketchup from the blood scenes, and beating the sidewalks, too. She inspires and personifies hard work.

"Hard work, hell!" Ellen sniggers, pursing her lips together and popping a quick breath between them in a noise of disgust.

"Hard work is one thing. There's always hard work, but look here, girl—I'm talkin' about carin'."

Lanford Wilson was one of her early playwrights and used La Mama as a base of operation for years. So did the young poet/musician/actor Sam Shepard. Shepard won a Pulitzer in 1979. Wilson picked his up in 1980. They're all her babies, she tells me. They all came to her or she found them long before they burst into fame.

A foray into the formidable bank of office file cabinets crammed with press clippings. The proud Jimbo, my guide, reveals a gospel-like litany of people who have worked on her stage—Jill Clayburgh, Cass Elliott of the Mamas and the Papas, Frederic Forest, Billy Crystal, Patti Smith, Bette Midler, Nick Nolte, Andy Warhol, Danny DeVito, the then-actress-now-novelist Ann Beattie, Elizabeth McGovern, Christopher Durang, beat poet Allen Ginsberg, Andrei Serban (whom she brought over from Rumania), Tom O'Horgan of *Hair*, *Jesus Christ Superstar*, and *Lenny* fame, Harvey Fierstein of *Torch Song Trilogy*, which premiered here, composer Elizabeth Swados, and two other MacArthur Fellows, theater director Peter Sellars and actor/clown Bill Irwin . . .

In the audiences: Rudolf Nureyev, John and Yoko, Lily Tomlin, Dustin Hoffman, Tommy Tune, Warren Beatty, Meryl Streep, Anaïs Nin, Aretha Franklin, Pierre Cardin, Harold Pinter, Arthur Miller, Ezra Pound . . . and whole handfuls of bewildered, blinking people pulled in off the streets so that the actors on stage wouldn't have to play to an empty house.

ACT FOUR

But still, the high and mighty New York critics didn't pay much mind to La Mama. Off-Broadway wasn't considered art then; the real action was uptown. To solve the problem, it occurred to Ellen that she should take her troupe overseas, where simply being an American theater company would be enough to attract some attention.

The year was 1965. She took twenty-two plays, sixteen people, and two directors, and, financed by a personal bank loan, bought them all one-way passage on a ship, a hundred and eighteen dollars per person. The Parisians weren't crazy about her, but they loved her in Copenhagen and Germany. She returned the following year, this time by invitation, and the year following that she arranged a ten-city tour.

After that, there was no stopping her. She became an expert on charter flights, stopping off in five or six different places on the way to wherever she was headed. At every stop she sniffed out the musicians and the theater crowd, and if they had no facility she organized a chapter of La Mama. Theater by theater, she formed links in the now-international La Mama chain.

Back in New York, her tiny subatomic apartment filled up with an ever-changing constellation of theater people. A dance troupe from Rome, a playwright from Seoul, a bunch of actors from Japan, a musician from a kibbutz, a bunch of pygmies from Zaire who could beat some wicked drums, a group of Eskimos who worked puppets, some Native American rain dancers, the most fantastic Greeks, a pair of graceful Egyptians, a pack of breakdancers from Harlem, alpenhorn blowers from Switzerland, songwriters from Patagonia . . .

Unceasingly nurturing, unflinchingly democratic, the Reverend Mother to the whole of the muddled, wacky, human enterprise. It's tempting to call her noble, but what has such a word to do with her? There is nothing heavenly or spectral about it: hers is an earthly affection. If her arrivals were hungry, she found food. If they needed a place to sleep, her floor was swept. If they needed a stage for their work, hers was available. If they were depressed, she would prescribe a tonic: "Honey, you need to take that play to Egypt; do it in the Pyramids. You tell me when you wanna go and I'll arrange it. . . . Baby, what you need is the Congo—they got sounds there for your opera you won't believe. When you can leave . . . Doll, this play of yours about sushi. I'm thinkin' Japan."

The La Mama theater changed locations several times before landing at its present address on the Lower East Side of Manhattan. Ellen is pleased with the arrangement, which has grown to include three theater spaces, a cabaret, an art gallery, seven floors of rehearsal space, overflow workshop room, and residence space for visiting artists. Much of the funding came from foundations. (Ellen used to go groveling at foundation doors herself, but decided that a young, white, nicely dressed lady friend of hers who knew the big words and when to curtsey was more effective. "There's still a lot of discrimination out there," she assures me, and I offer no argument.) When she first acquired the space it was, lest you wonder, completely run-down, parts of the floor soaked deep with blood from a previous owner, a sausage company.

Jimbo showed me some statistics someone had tabulated at the time of La Mama's twenty-fifth anniversary (1987), an occasion that inspires things like taking stock: 1,400 shows of theater, dance, music, video, and multimedia productions in over 21 countries, which celebrated some 14,025 actors, 4,176 musicians, 19 miles of film, 690 playwrights, and 816 dancers. Nobody counted up the number of times Ellen was arrested for a building violation, the number of aliases she used to avoid accumulating a lengthy rap sheet under her real name, the number of times she was evicted, the number of pawn tickets, the number of times exhaustion and worse sent her to the hospital . . . somehow, blessedly, all that didn't seem to matter much anymore.

■ **3** ■

BACK IN THE THEATER, things were going well with Ellen's attempt to stage the flood scene. The skateboarders finally seemed to have mastered their wheels. Lloyd came up with the requested pole and he didn't even have to pay for it. The fat girl was walloping out a sonic boom of a voice-over. The musicians had worked out a mystical sound with finger cymbals and some strange clacking instrument Ellen procured in Istanbul. And Rosa, the timid young black nymph, was beaming—Ellen had assigned her the lead role, the Goddess of Nature.

"Okay, LUNCH!" Ellen barked, "and be back in time for the flamenco lady."

On the way out she overheard two girls discussing the prospect of splitting a can of Campbell's soup and dished out a few coins so they could "get somethin' fresh with it." And put on your coats, she told them, it's damn cold out.

On the street a drunk swaggered toward us as we headed to the local diner a block from the theater. He was harmless, but in another part of town one might have crossed the street to avoid him.

"*Mama, mama, mama, bella madonna, bellissima madonna.*" He whined and pointed to his mouth as if she didn't know what he wanted. Once again she dips into her coin purse.

"*Due, due, due, madonna mia,*" he pleaded.

"One, honey." She laughed. "Mama's gotta eat, too."

At the diner, people approach her booth as if she were an omnipotent and omnipresent cross between Mother Superior and the Godfather. The policeman, the waiter, the mailman, the bum—they all know her. "So what can I do for you?" she asked them all. "You wanna siddown? You wanna cup of coffee?"

Mostly they only wanted to be near her. She cut off the testimonials gently: "All right now, baby. Oh, never mind. You go on now. Mama'll see you later. Mama'll see you tomorrow then."

And when they retreated she picked up where she'd left off, talking about her latest project, a sixteenth-century convent she bought with her MacArthur prize money way up on a hill above the little Italian village of Santa Maria Regina. She's working on converting it into an international center for artists in residence. Italy seemed an appropriate choice; artists have been nourished there for centuries; besides, the castle was fallen-down enough to come at a good price.

From the recesses of her pockets she pulled out a crumpled sketch, pushed aside her eggs, and smoothed it out. She likes the drama of the imperial architecture, huge stone arches a Roman army could march through, high vaulted rooms, the flat space of a sun-warmed meadow out back that could serve as a natural amphitheater. For the last two hundred years it's been a farm, and she thinks the fruit groves and gardens, once restored, will soothe the anxious beating of the creative breast.

"You think it's a good thin' to have done with the money?" she asked, tucking into her eggs. "If you think it's a good idea, then I'll tell you it came from my havin' to care for all these people around me. Without these people what would I be? Zee-rrr-ooo, and I'm the first to know it. I don't know why some people can't recognize that. They're always talkin' about the play this or the play that, the problem this or the problem that. Nothin' is anythin' without people—and I don't have *time* to worry about problems. No, no, no, never. *Never!* If I started woryin', worry would be the story of my life, you know? I don' have time to siddown with my head hung 'round my crotch—for what?! No sir. I gotta pitch all the time to all these open mouths.

"And now you," she says, fixing me in her appraising glare, one ear cocked to listen for the beeps. "Here you are wantin' to know about cree-a-tivity. Lemme tell you somethin', baby. Carin' is where it's at. Trust me now because I know what I'm talkin' 'bout—you got a love for what you're doin' and everythin' else, all the rest of this cree-a-tivity stuff you're wonderin' 'bout, baby, it just comes."

◼   ◼   ◼

*So, when all is said and done, I think Derek Walcott was right: To question the makeup of creative genius one has to be willing to surrender to a condition of awe, to the astonishment of the soul, to bewilder*MENT, *baffle*MENT, *humili*TY, DE-*vah-stay-*TION! *Or, as Emerson neatly put it, "Let the bird sing without deciphering the song."*

In Joseph Brodsky's apartment, the light had dulled and shadows collected in the corners. It wasn't all that late in the day, but storm clouds had blown in over Greenwich Village and with them came the mean, chill, drizzling, spitting rain that promised winter, not today maybe, not tomorrow, but soon.

Brodsky had drifted off in the current of his own thoughts, yet another cigarette squeezed between thumb and forefinger, smoking its short sweetness through before he discarded it in a gesture from another time and place.

Then—there it was.

The slight flicker in his eyes, maybe? The decisiveness with which he cast this last butt aside? Whatever it was, it was over before it could be fully registered, but intentionally or not he had signaled, however fleetingly, the end of our time together. I asked my last question.

"Certainly we've covered a lot of ground here and I am grateful for your time, but tell me, is there anything I haven't asked you that you would like to address?"

It's a question I put to most everyone and usually was rewarded with the refinement of some point made earlier, or a whole new line of discussion, which in one case lasted another three hours. In Brodsky's case there was silence. And then his answer: "No, nothing more. You see it's like this: for me to try to talk about creativity would be like a cat to chase its tail."

And with that the restless Mississippi sprang from my lap and darted out an open window. I took it as my unmistakable cue to leave, experiencing on my way out into the rain that distracting, unsettling jolt a person feels when there isn't, after all, another step at the bottom.

■

THE FORTY FELLOWS

Joan Abrahamson: Lawyer, artist, songwriter, catalyst for community action

John Ashbery: Poet, Pulitzer Prize winner

Robert Axelrod: Political scientist

Joseph Brodsky: Poet, translator, essayist, Nobel Prize winner

Lester Brown: Ecologist, President and Founder of the Worldwatch Institute

Robert Coles: Psychiatrist, teacher, writer, Pulitzer Prize winner

Douglas Crase: Poet

Richard Critchfield: Journalist, former war correspondent

Shelly Errington: Cultural anthropologist, writer, teacher

Howard Gardner: Research psychologist, writer, teacher

Henry Louis Gates: Literary critic, writer, teacher

Stephen Jay Gould: Paleontologist, teacher, essayist

Ian Graham: Archaeologist, assistant curator of Maya hieroglyphics

Shirley Brice Heath: Anthropological linguist, writer, teacher

Bill Irwin: Actor, clown, writer

Robert Irwin: Visual artist

David Keightley: Sinologist, teacher, writer

Henry Kraus: Art historian, writer, independent scholar

Sylvia Law: Lawyer, teacher, writer

Brad Leithauser: Poet, novelist, essayist

Michael Lerner: Social scientist, President and Founder of Commonweal

Sara Lawrence Lightfoot: Sociologist of education, teacher, writer

ANDREW MCGUIRE: Catalyst for community action in public health and safety issues, filmmaker
SAM MALOOF: Woodworker
RALPH MANHEIM: Translator
VED MEHTA: Writer
DEBORAH MEIER: East Harlem public school teacher and principal
PATRICK NOONAN: Conservationist
ROGER PAYNE: Whale conservationist and research scientist
TINA ROSENBERG: Journalist
JOHN SAYLES: Filmmaker, novelist, playwright, short story writer
PETER SELLARS: Theater and opera director
RALPH SHAPEY: Composer, conductor, teacher
ROBERT SHAPLEY: Visual neurophysiologist
ELLEN STEWART: Theater arts
DAVID STUART: Mayan epigraphist
ALAR TOOMRE: Mathematician, astronomer, physicist, teacher
J. KIRK T. VARNEDOE: Curator, art historian, writer
DEREK WALCOTT: Poet, playwright, teacher
FREDERICK WISEMAN: Filmmaker

■

ACKNOWLEDGMENTS

Certainly my first word of thanks must go to the forty MacArthur
Fellows who participated with interest and energy in this project.
Among them, an extra word of appreciation is owed to Robert Ax-
elrod, Richard Critchfield, Howard Gardner, Shirley Brice Heath,
Henry Kraus, Andrew McGuire, and Ralph Shapey, all of whom
took extra time and attention in answering my questions.

My thanks also to Reid Boates and Pam Dorman, the two who
made it happen; Dr. Ken Hope of the MacArthur Foundation; Daniel
Starer, my able research assistant; Paul Gallagher, Jane Isay, and
Stuart Krichevsky, for their help in obtaining and preparing for
certain interviews; Karen Colvard, for the same and for her comments
on the manuscript; Laura Shekerjian, for her solid observations all
along the way; Lou and Joseph Sydnor, for their gracious hospitality
in London; and Michael Metz, for far more than can be detailed here.

In addition to the interviews themselves, the key sources I relied
on follow.

Notes

For material related to the broadbrush discussion of creativity, I
relied especially on *The Universe Within: A New Science Explores the
Human Mind*, by Morton Hunt (Simon & Schuster, 1982); *Art, Mind
& Brain: A Cognitive Approach to Creativity*, by Howard Gardner
(Basic Books, 1982); *Maps of the Mind*, by Charles Hampden-Turner
(Collier, 1982); *The Mind's Best Work*, by D. N. Perkins (Harvard
University Press, 1981); and *The Social Psychology of Creativity*, by
Teresa M. Amabile (Springer-Verlag, 1983).

ACKNOWLEDGMENTS

Other works that were helpful include *Notebooks of the Mind: Explorations in Thinking*, by Vera John-Steiner (Harper & Row, 1985); *The Act of Creation*, by Arthur Koestler (Macmillan, 1964); *New Think*, by Edward de Bono (Avon, 1971); *On Knowing: Essays for the Left Hand*, by Jerome Bruner (Harvard, 1979); *The Courage to Create*, by Rollo May (Bantam, 11th printing, 1985); *The Creative Experience*, edited by Stanley Rosner and Lawrence Abt (Dell, 1970); *The Psychology of Consciousness*, by Robert E. Ornstein (Penguin, 1972); *Conceptions of Giftedness*, edited by Robert Sternberg and Janet Davidson (Cambridge University Press, 1986); *Creativity: The Magic Synthesis*, by Silvano Arieti (Basic Books, 1976); *The Creative Process*, edited by Brewster Ghiselin (New American Library, 1952); *Intelligence Applied: Understanding and Increasing Your Intellectual Skills*, by Robert Sternberg (Harcourt Brace Jovanovich, 1986); *Genius, Creativity and Leadership*, by Dean Keith Simonton (Harvard University Press, 1984); *The Dynamics of Creation*, by Anthony Storr (Atheneum, 1972); and *Educating Able Learners*, by June Cox, Neil Daniel, and Bruce Boston (University of Texas Press, 1985).

IN THE BEGINNING

Much of the biographical material on John D. MacArthur that appears in this introduction and in Chapters 6 and 7 was drawn from a biography of him entitled *The Stockholder*, by William Hoffman (Lyle Stuart, 1969), as well as from a sizable stack of newspaper and magazine clippings spanning over thirty years. Information about the MacArthur Foundation came from their annual reports, the clipping file maintained by the Foundation Library in New York City, conversations with Dr. Kenneth Hope, Director of the MacArthur Fellows Program, a conversation with William T. Kirby, John D. MacArthur's attorney and friend, and Waldemar Nielsen's *The Golden Donors: A New Anatomy of the Great Foundations* (Dutton, 1985).

TALENT AND THE LONG HAUL

For the material on Stephen Jay Gould, I relied largely on his own works, among them *An Urchin in the Storm: Essays About Books and Ideas* (Norton, 1987), *The Flamingo's Smile: Reflections in Natural History*

ACKNOWLEDGMENTS

(Norton, 1985, 1987), *Hen's Teeth and Horse's Toes: Further Reflections in Natural History* (Norton, 1983, 1984), *The Panda's Thumb: More Reflections in Natural History* (Norton, 1980, 1982), *Ever Since Darwin: Reflections in Natural History* (Norton, 1977, 1979), and *The Mismeasure of Man* (Norton, 1981, 1983). I am also grateful to have read James Gleick's article "Stephen Jay Gould: Breaking Tradition with Darwin," published in *The New York Times*, November 1983, and John Updike's book review of *The Flamingo's Smile*, published in *The New Yorker*, December 30, 1985.

TAKING ON RISK

For material on Deborah Meier, I am particularly grateful to have read *Quality Education in the Inner City: The Story of the Central Park East Schools*, a report by David Bensman, 1987, and *Central Park East Schools*, a report by David Bensman, 1987, and for Meier's own articles, which appear in various publications.

For material on Sam Maloof, I read numerous articles but found his own art book, *Sam Maloof: Woodworker* (Kodansha, 1983), the most helpful.

STAYING LOOSE

For material on Fred Wiseman, I saw four of his films and relied on a good-sized stack of clippings, notable among them "Watching Wiseman Work," by David Eames (*The New York Times*, October 2, 1977); "The New Documentaries of Frederick Wiseman," by Stephen Mamber (*Cinema*, Vol. 6, No. 1, 1970); "Wiseman," by Richard Schickel (*Image*, November 1972); "Frederick Wiseman," by Christopher Ricks (*Grand Street*, Winter 1989); "Movies Documenting America," by David Denby (*The Atlantic*, March 1970); "A Tribute to Fred Wiseman," by Stephen Mamber (address given at the 1976 Los Angeles International Film Exposition, March 1976); and "Wiseman's MODEL and the Documentary Project: Toward a Radical Film Practice," by Dan Armstrong (*Film Quarterly*, Winter 1983/ 1984).

Other sources pertinent to this chapter include Morton Hunt's *The Universe Within: A New Science Explores the Human Mind* (Simon &

Schuster, 1982); D. N. Perkins's *The Mind's Best Work* (Harvard University Press, 1981); *Breakthroughs!*, by P. Ranganath Nayak and John Ketteringham (Rawson, 1986); and articles and promotional brochures disseminated by Synectics, Inc., including "Unlocking the Creative Mind," by Bruce Mohl, for *The Boston Globe*, January 7, 1986.

SETTING UP THE CONDITIONS

To understand something of the tastes and interests of Douglas Crase, it is necessary to turn to his work, especially to his first volume of poetry, *The Revisionist* (Little Brown, 1981).

For material on John Sayles, I turned first to his own books, among them *Pride of the Bimbos* (Scribners, 1975) and *Thinking in Pictures* (Houghton Mifflin, 1987), and then to a stack of articles about his work.

To appreciate Dr. Howard Gardner's work, I recommend his works, among them *Frames of Mind: The Theory of Multiple Intelligences* (Basic Books, 1983); *The Mind's New Science: A History of the Cognitive Revolution* (Basic Books, 1987); *Art, Mind & Brain: A Cognitive Approach to Creativity* (Basic Books, 1982); and *Artful Scribbles: The Significance of Children's Drawings* (Basic Books, 1980).

LEARNING THROUGH DOING

Of all the research I conducted on Robert Irwin, the most thorough and insightful source was the biography of him by Lawrence Weschler entitled *Seeing Is Forgetting the Name of the Thing One Sees: A Life of Contemporary Artist Robert Irwin* (University of California Press, 1982). The specific quote about Rod Serling and the "Twilight Zone" can be found on page 71 of Weschler's book. In addition to this volume, and especially as it concerns Irwin's line works, I consulted Weschler's article "Lines of Inquiry," which appeared in *Art in America*, March 1982. Apart from these materials, I also consulted Irwin's own book *Being and Circumstance: Notes Toward a Conditional Art* (Lapis, 1985), which contains, among other things, photos of seventeen of his more important public works scattered about the country. Irwin's observation that public works projects "are riddled with contradictions, risks, failures, successes, and even a kind of black humor" comes from this book, page 33. Milton Esterow's article "How Public Art Becomes a Political Hot Potato" (*Art News*, January 1986) and Claudia Hart's "Environments of Light: Ornament in Search of Architecture" (*Industrial Design*, March/April 1984) were also instructive.

In addition, I consulted: "Controlled Environment: Larry Bell, Robert Irwin, and Doug Wheeler at the Tate Gallery" by Michael Compton, *Art and Artists*, vol. 5, no. 2, p. 45 (May 1970); "3 Los Angeles Artists," by Guy Burn, *Arts Review*, vol. 22, no. 10, p. 319 (May 23, 1970); "Robert Irwin, Gene Davis, Richard Smith: The Jewish Museum Mounts a Hard-to-Assess 3-Man Show," by Emily Wasserman, *Artforum*, vol. 6, no. 9, p. 47 (May 1968); "Robert Irwin," by Robert Atkins, *Arts Magazine*, vol. 60, no. 4, p. 102 (December 1985); "Robert Irwin," by Douglas Davis, *Newsweek* December 29, 1975, p. 53; and "Knowing in Action," by Calvin Tomkins, *The New Yorker*, November 11, 1985, p. 144.

I also consulted the following catalogs: *Robert Irwin* (Jewish Museum, 1968; essay by John Coplans); *Robert Irwin* (Pasadena Art Museum, 1968; essay by John Coplans); *Robert Irwin and Kenneth Price* (Los Angeles County Museum of Art, 1966; essay by Philip Leider); *Larry Bell, Robert Irwin, Doug Wheeler* (The Tate Gallery, May 1970); *Transparency, Reflection, Light, Space: "Four Artists"* (UCLA Art Galleries, 1971; interview of Robert Irwin included); *Notes Toward a Model* (Whitney Museum of Art, 1977; Irwin's own essay included); and *Robert Irwin* (Museum of Contemporary Art, Chicago, Illinois, 1975).

Kirk Varnedoe has authored several art books and catalogs to major shows, among them *The Drawings of Rodin* (with Albert Elsen, 1971); *Gustave Caillebotte: A Retrospective Exhibition* (1976); *Modern Portraits: The Self and Others* (editor, 1976); *Graphic Works of Max Klinger* (1977); *Northern Light: Realism and Symbolism in Scandinavian Painting* (editor with a major essay, 1982); and *Vienna: 1900* (1986), which give some indication of the man, his tastes and ideas. In addition, he lectures regularly and is at work on a collection of essays, some of the conclusions of which he kindly shared.

Henry Kraus has also authored several art books: *The Living Theatre of Medieval Art* (1967); *The Hidden World of Misericords* (1975); *Gold Was the Mortar* (1979); and *The Gothic Choirstalls of Spain* (1984). He has also written on the labor movement, *The Many and the Few* (1947), and on an interracial-war housing project, *In the City Was a Garden* (1951). Again, these works provide insight into the man, his hopes and beliefs.

The Hemingway quote comes from an interview with him contained in *Writers at Work: The Paris Review Interviews*, 2nd series, edited by George Plimpton (Viking, 1963).

INVESTING YOUR WORK WITH A VISION

Lester Brown has been the subject of a number of magazine and newspaper articles, but most helpful to me was the *State of the World* series, which explains in full how and why he does what he does.

For the discussion of the psychopathology (or alleged psychopathology) of creativity, I relied on many of the sources listed in the general works section, as well as on the work of Dr. K. R. Eissler, especially his article "Remarks on an Aspect of Creativity," *American Imago*, Spring/Summer 1978.

For a general discussion on vision and the importance of mission in a complex world, I found Willis Harman's *An Incomplete Guide to the Future* (Simon & Schuster, 1976) helpful, as well as Arthur Schlesinger, Jr.'s, essay "Creativity in Statecraft" (Library of Congress, 1983).

A CHANGE OF PERSPECTIVE

For the material on dreams and visualization, I relied on numerous works, salient among them *Creative Dreaming*, by Patricia Garfield (Ballantine, 1974); *Directing the Movies of Your Mind*, by Adelaide Bry and Marjorie Bair (Harper & Row, 1978); *Creative Visualization*, by Shakti Gawain (Bantam, 1985); *Seeing with the Mind's Eye*, by Mike and Nancy Samuels (Random House & The Bookworks, 1975); and *The New Diary: How to Use a Journal for Self-Guidance and Expanded Creativity*, by Tristine Rainer (Tarcher, 1978).

For the material on metaphor, I found the discussion contained in Morton Hunt's work *The Universe Within* (Simon & Schuster, 1982) the most helpful.

For the material on the right brain/left brain controversy, I turned

ACKNOWLEDGMENTS

mostly to Marilee Zdenek's *The Right Brain Experience: An Intimate Program to Free the Powers of Your Imagination* (McGraw-Hill, 1983); Thomas Blakeslee's *The Right Brain: A New Understanding of the Unconscious Mind and Its Creative Powers* (Anchor, 1980); and Betty Edwards's books *Drawing on the Right Side of the Brain* (St. Martin's, 1979) and *Drawing on the Artist Within* (Simon & Schuster, 1986).

My clipping file on Peter Sellars is enormous, but I especially would like to note the article by Jennifer Allen, "The Many Directions of Peter Sellars," for *Esquire* (December 1984), as well as the entry in the *Current Biography* series, January 1986.

With respect to Michael Lerner, Dr. Tom Ferguson's article "Moving Toward Common Ground in the Cancer Wars: An Interview with Michael Lerner," *Medical Self-Care* (May/June 1986), was helpful, as was Daniel Goleman's piece in *The New York Times* entitled "The Mind Over the Body" (September 27, 1987). I also am especially grateful to have received an advance copy of Lerner and Rachel Naomi Remen's article "Tradecraft of the Commonweal Cancer Help Program," written for *Advances*, vol. 4, no. 3 (1987).

A SHIFT IN THE SCENERY

Richard Critchfield's works include a book on Vietnam, *The Long Charade* (Harcourt, 1968); a village trilogy, *The Golden Bowl Be Broken* (Indiana University Press, 1974), *Shahhat* (Avon, 1978), and *Villages* (Doubleday, 1981); and a social history of his extended family, *Those Days: An American Album* (Doubleday, 1986). These works, especially the village series, best capture the man. In addition, I read several of his articles for *The Economist*, *The International Herald Tribune*, *The Washington Post*, *The New York Times*, *The Christian Science Monitor*, and *The Asian Wall Street Journal*. The reviewer who characterized his narrative style as a "rambling, idiosyncratic tour de force" was Nick Eberstadt in a *New York Times Book Review* article on *Villages* (June 14, 1981).

Brad Leithauser's works of poetry, *Hundreds of Fireflies* (Knopf, 1982) and *Cats of the Temple* (Knopf, 1986), and his fiction, *Equal Distance* (Knopf, 1985) and *Hence* (Knopf, 1989), were consulted, along with his book reviews and occasional essays.

ACKNOWLEDGMENTS

SUSTAINING CONCENTRATION AND DRIVE

The sources for John Sayles and Howard Gardner are listed under the notes for Chapter 4, "Setting Up the Conditions." The four-hundred-page, single-spaced book that Howard Gardner drafted in record time has grown and shrunk through the succeeding months of revision and is due to be published by Basic Books under the title *To Open Minds: Chinese Clues to the Dilemma of American Education*.

The starting point for material on Shirley Brice Heath is her book *Ways with Words: Language, Life and Work in Communities and Classrooms* (Cambridge University Press, 1983). After that, I turned to a handful of her publications on the language and culture of different social and ethnic groups.

For Joseph Brodsky, I started with his Nobel-winning *Less Than One: Selected Essays* (Farrar, Straus and Giroux, 1986), which contains a lot of autobiographical material. It was also helpful to read the lengthy interview with him published in *The Paris Review*, Spring 1982.

Ved Mehta, the author of some seventeen books, has likewise published autobiographical material, along with his works of biography, journalism, and fiction. In particular, *Face to Face* (1957), which is an account of his childhood in India, *Walking the Indian Streets* (1960), which recounts his return to India after college, *Daddyji* (1972) about his father, *Mamaji* (1979) about his mother, *Vedi* (1982) about his early boyhood years and the orphanage where he was sent, and *The Ledge Between the Streams* (1984), which is an account of his short stay at a school in Bombay and his departure for America at age fifteen, were most helpful, as were a number of articles by and about him.

ENCOURAGING LUCK

For material on the Mayanists, there is no substitute for the series of books entitled *Corpus of Maya Hieroglyphic Inscriptions*, a projected sixty-volume set published by the Peabody Museum, Harvard University. It is here that I began to appreciate the hardships and thrills an archaeologist faces. These volumes also contain the arrestingly beautiful drawings of Ian Graham. In addition, I relied on George Stuart's (David's father's) articles for *National Geographic* and upon Virginia Morell's "The Lost Language of Cobá," in *Science*, March 1986.

My discussion of Robert Axelrod depends heavily on his own book, *The Evolution of Cooperation* (Basic Books, 1984), which is a highly readable and entertaining account of how cooperation can occur in a world of egoists.

For the material on Bill Irwin, in addition to the usual assembly of theater arts clippings, notable among them the Mel Gussow profile written for *The New Yorker* (November 11, 1985). I attended many of his performances and rehearsals, which were very revealing.

Of value in preparing for the interview with Tina Rosenberg were her articles that appeared in *Esquire*, *The Atlantic*, *The New Republic*, and *The Washington Monthly*.

Finally, on the subject of play, among other sources I turned to Edward de Bono's *New Think* (Avon, 1971). The quote is from page 110 of that book.

THE HARMONY OF INSTINCT AND JUDGMENT

Robert Coles has written scores of books and hundreds of articles. Among them, the multivolume *Children of Crisis* series (Atlantic Press, 1967–1986) was extremely helpful, as was his collection of essays *Harvard Diary* (Crossroad, 1988) and *The Call of Stories: Teaching and the Moral Imagination* (Houghton Mifflin, 1989). The quoted passage about Ruby Bridges, the black warrior child, and Coles's own assessment of his work come from the introduction to *The Moral Life of Children* (Houghton Mifflin, 1986), pages 9 and 4, respectively. I am also grateful to his assistant, Jay Woodruff, for passing along course reading lists and for alerting me to several "indispensable" volumes that Dr. Coles turns to time and again in his classes, most especially James Agee and Walker Evans's *Let Us Now Praise Famous Men* (Houghton Mifflin, 1939, revised 1969).

For the material on Derek Walcott, I read much of his poetry, including the then recently published *The Arkansas Testament* (Farrar,

Straus and Giroux, 1987) and the anthology *Collected Poems: 1948–1984* (Farrar, Straus and Giroux, 1986). I also relied upon the numerous reviews of his plays and poetry.

DESPAIR AND ISOLATION, MADNESS AND MEANNESS

For information about the mental health of famous people, I referred to Jon Karlsson's *Inheritance of Creative Intelligence: A Study of Genetics in Relation to Giftedness and Its Implications for Future Generations* (Nelson-Hall, 1978), and to Constance Holden's article "Creativity and the Troubled Mind," *Psychology Today*, April 1987.

The sources used in connection with Robert Irwin have been listed above, under the notes for Chapter 5, "Learning Through Doing."

For Ralph Shapey, the interview itself spanned a couple of days and provided ample material. In addition, I have spent many hours listening to his recordings, in particular: "Fantasy for Symphony Orchestra" (1951), "Challenge—The Family of Man" (1955), "Ontogeny" (1958), and "Rituals" (1959) among his orchestral works; "String Trio" (1965), "Partita-fantasy for Vocal, 14 Instruments, and Percussion" (1966), "Three for Six" (1979), "Discourse" (1983), and "Fantasy" (1983) among his instrumental pieces; Sonata no. 1 (1946), "Essays on Thomas Wolfe" (1948–1949), and "Birthday Piece" (1962) among his keyboard works; and "Cantata" (1951), "Praise" (1962–1971), "Songs of Ecstasy" (1967), "O Jerusalem" (1975), and "Psalm" (1984) among his vocal works. He has written hundreds of works; my aim was to hear a fair sampling.

In addition, I have relied on a fat clipping file and found the essay by John Rockwell in *All American Music: Composition in the Late Twentieth Century* (Knopf, 1983) particularly helpful.

For Sara Lawrence Lightfoot, her own books were helpful, especially the preface to *The Good High School* (Basic Books, 1983) and the initial chapters of the biography of her mother, *Balm in Gilead* (Radcliffe Biography Series, Addison-Wesley, 1988).

BUILDING RESILIENCY

This is a round-up chapter that relied on sources already mentioned.

ACKNOWLEDGMENTS

FOR THE LOVE OF IT

The clipping file on Ellen Stewart is several inches deep. Among this material, I found the article by Elizabeth Swados, "Stretching Boundaries: The Merlin of La Mama" (*The New York Times*, October 26, 1986), especially helpful. I also attended a number of rehearsals and performances at La Mama, and am grateful, too, for my conversations with her longtime manager and all-around assistant, Jim Moore.

INDEX

INDEX